F.I.R.E.

for

dummies

A Wiley Brand

F.I.R.E.

by Jackie Cummings Koski, CFP®
Financial Educator and F.I.R.E. Expert

F.I.R.E. For Dummies®

Published by: **John Wiley & Sons, Inc.,** 111 River Street, Hoboken, NJ 07030-5774, www.wiley.com

Copyright © 2024 by John Wiley & Sons, Inc., Hoboken, New Jersey

Published simultaneously in Canada

For general information on our other products and services, please contact our Customer Care Department within the U.S. at 877-762-2974, outside the U.S. at 317-572-3993, or fax 317-572-4002. For technical support, please visit https://hub.wiley.com/community/support/dummies.

Wiley publishes in a variety of print and electronic formats and by print-on-demand. Some material included with standard print versions of this book may not be included in e-books or in print-on-demand. If this book refers to media such as a CD or DVD that is not included in the version you purchased, you may download this material at http://booksupport.wiley.com. For more information about Wiley products, visit www.wiley.com.

Library of Congress Control Number is available from the publisher.

ISBN: 978-1-394-23501-8 (pbk); ISBN 978-1-394-23502-5 (ebk); ISBN 978-1-394-23503-2 (ebk)

SKY10073685_042524

Contents at a Glance

Contents at a Glance

Table of Contents

Introduction

Welcome to *F.I.R.E. For Dummies!*

F.I.R.E. (Financial Independence, Retire Early) is an aspirational goal that sparks curiosity in many. It's an approach to personal finance that helps you reach your financial goals in a compressed time frame so that you get to financial independence much sooner than you may have ever imagined. It's like personal finance on steroids. "How" you get there involves following a simple recipe that is openly talked about in the F.I.R.E. community.

The Retire Early part of F.I.R.E. is the powerful position you may want to be in, but if you love your job, you may choose not to. The important thing is that you have the flexibility to walk away on your terms at a moment's notice if you decide that's best for you.

Although F.I.R.E. and its simple principles are available to all, some people don't even know this possibility exists or discover it much later in their careers. (You don't know what you don't know.) Luckily for you, you've found *F.I.R.E. For Dummies,* which can be your guide on your path to F.I.R.E.

About This Book

I reached F.I.R.E. in my 40s and learned a ton on my journey, but I knew I still had a few knowledge gaps to fill. So, I went on to earn certified financial planner (CFP) and accredited financial counselor (AFC) credentials to help fill in the blanks. I'm an educator at heart, and I want to share a perspective rooted both in facts and experience. In this book, I shrink advanced topics down to approachable chunks that are easy to digest.

An important element of this book is explaining the mindset around F.I.R.E. People who pursue F.I.R.E. depart from the status quo to do something different than most people. When you're going against the grain in this way, it's important to have encouragement, and you'll find that emotional support peppered throughout the book.

Each person's road to F.I.R.E. is unique, but it's possible for anyone, even those who have more challenges or obstacles in their way. It's not a perfect journey for anyone, and when you read some of my non-F.I.R.E. anecdotes, you"ll know what I mean.

You can find a lot of disparate and confusing information out there, but this book guides you through all the important areas in a well-organized, easy-to-follow format in true *For Dummies* style.

Foolish Assumptions

I'm so glad you've picked up this book and trusted me to share my expertise on F.I.R.E. As I wrote this book, I had an audience in mind; here are a few assumptions I made about you:

>> You have basic financial literacy and want to learn more. Even if you are a high school student, you can grasp the concepts in this book, especially if you've had a personal finance class (required by over half of U.S. states in order to graduate).

>> You are at the early stages of your wealth-building journey and have a desire to learn how you can accelerate the process and reach financial independence and the option to retire early.

>> You're new to F.I.R.E. or want to fill the gaps of knowledge that you may have while on your journey.

>> You want to learn more about the F.I.R.E. movement and the philosophies of creating time freedom.

>> You have overcome a few obstacles or challenges in your life and want to turn your finances around.

>> You have a desire to explore the mental and emotional side of money to help you move your finances in the right direction.

>> You have basic investment and tax knowledge but want to gain a better understanding of them.

>> You want to hear from someone who has reached F.I.R.E. and has additional expertise that can help simplify the related concepts.

This book is basic enough for any to follow, and it breaks down some complex topics in a way that will have you feeling confident you can put the pieces in place to reach F.I.R.E.!

Icons Used in This Book

Throughout this book you will find useful icons to enhance your reading experience and to note specific types of information. Here's what each icon means:

This icon marks tips or best practices that can help make things a little easier for you.

This icon points out information you'll want to remember and perhaps read twice.

This icon points out more detailed or technical information that may not be essential but still helpful.

When you see this icon, watch out! It marks important information that may save you headaches or notes something to avoid.

This icon indicates that I've given an example of how you might apply the information. Examples help reinforce what you've read.

This icon draws attention to a personal story that might help reinforce what I've just explained.

Beyond the Book

In addition to the material in this book, you can also find some access-anywhere information curated just for you online at dummies.com. I've included a helpful list of F.I.R.E. calculators and resources for finding a F.I.R.E.-friendly financial planner. Just enter **F.I.R.E. For Dummies Cheat Sheet** in the search box to find the Cheat Sheet.

Where to Go from Here

This book is organized so that you don't have to read it from start to finish. You can check out the table of contents or index and go straight to the chapter that's most interesting or valuable to you according to where you are in your journey. Pick and choose or go to selected portions of the book without feeling lost.

1
Getting Started with F.I.R.E.

Find out what ignited the F.I.R.E. movement, the basics behind achieving financial independence and retiring early, and the attraction to the powerful time freedom it brings.

Know the steps to reaching your F.I.R.E. goals by understanding your "why," stacking your knowledge, and turning what you learn into action.

Explore the psychological part of your F.I.R.E. journey by acknowledging your feelings around money, examining the realities of your unique financial situation, and embracing F.I.R.E.-friendly communities to help support you on your path.

IN THIS CHAPTER

» Focusing on the F.I.R.E. philosophies

» Harnessing the power of financial independence

» Understanding the popularity of F.I.R.E. and what sparked the movement

» Flaming perspectives from the media and others

» Embracing the different flavors of F.I.

Chapter **1**

What Is F.I.R.E.?

You may have picked up this book because of the cool acronym, but you'll stay for the vision that will begin to form in your mind — the vision of freedom to do what you love. This book is a guide to help you make that freedom materialize. Your biggest obstacle, as it is for so many people, has probably been clarity and intentionality (or lack thereof) around finances.

Wait . . . I'm getting ahead of myself. I should back up and explain what F.I.R.E. stands for, in case you don't know:

» **Financial Independence** (the F.I.) is living a life you enjoy without having to rely on a paycheck to support that lifestyle. You've heard sayings like "I'm working to pay the bills." Not a glamourous thought but it's true for so many. F.I. happens in the mind as much as in the wallet because the emotions and feelings around freedom are profound and intentional.

» **Retiring Early** (the R.E.) is decoupling from the full-time workforce much sooner than society is used to (typically in your 60s or 70s) so that you can enjoy yourself more while you're younger. Instead of working 70% of your adult life and being retired 30%, why not reverse that? To be clear, the early retirement part of F.I.R.E. is optional; you do it on your terms. Don't let anyone box you into a corner or fit what *they* think *your* retirement should look like. Hint: F.I.R.E. doesn't have to mean you **never** make another dime or do anything productive. You can flex your **freedom** any way you want.

The big picture (as illustrated in Figure 1-1) of wealth building for F.I.R.E. is

>> Increasing income, savings, and investing

>> Decreasing debt, taxes, and expenses

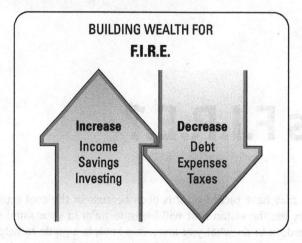

FIGURE 1-1:
Building Wealth
for F.I.R.E.

Understanding the F.I.R.E. Philosophies

There is no doctrine or fixed set of rules you need to agree to in order to be a part of the F.I.R.E. community. There are, however, some common tenets to help achieve the primary goal of buying your time back and creating freedom in your life.

Here are some of the philosophies of F.I.R.E.:

>> **Living on less than you earn:** That may mean earning a higher income, lowering your expenses, or both (see Chapters 10 and 14).

>> **Maintaining a high savings rate:** The gap you have created between your income and your expenses will give you room to save and invest more than the average. A savings rate of 50% or more is considered high, and it's the goal

you want to work toward. The more you save and invest, the faster it gets you to F.I.R.E (see Chapter 4).

>> **Keeping investing simple and low cost:** The strategy is to invest in index funds that offer a diversified basket of stocks or other investments and stay the course even when the market is down (see Chapter 12).

>> **Minimizing taxes:** Taxes are controllable, and there are many opportunities to reduce your tax liability when you understand how taxes work. This includes big areas such as tax advantaged retirement accounts and other investments with favorable tax treatment (see Chapter 15).

>> **Optimizing corners of your life that matter most:** It's impossible to optimize everything, but everyone has superpowers in certain areas. Common places in which the F.I.R.E. community optimizes are travel rewards, house hacking, and real estate investing (see Chapter 2).

>> **Being a lifelong learner and doer:** Some of the smartest people you will find when it comes to personal finance are F.I.R.E. people who are curious and act on that curiosity (see Chapter 2).

>> **Valuing community and connections:** You will find support from other like-minded people with common goals. The community has grown big enough that you can connect with others in all kinds of ways: online, in person, one on one, small groups, big groups, and so on (see Chapter 3).

>> **Enjoying the journey:** How you feel and your happiness is key even when you are hyper-focused on your goals. The psychology of F.I.R.E. is real and deserves as much mental energy as the math (see Chapter 3).

Grasping the Power of F.I.

Financial Independence (F.I.) is a powerful place to be because it opens up so many options. It's the real emphasis of the F.I.R.E. movement. In this section, I talk about time freedom and removing money as an obstacle to doing what you love.

Time freedom

Working full time at a job or doing work you don't like takes nearly one-third of your week, your month, your year. That portion of your life is controlled by your employer, and it's the price you pay when you have to exchange your time for money.

Even if you love the work that you do, it doesn't have to keep you tied to a job where someone else makes the rules. Think about how different your impact may look if you did the work you loved on your own terms. You could choose the hours, the approach, and the people you want to work with.

Realizing that there is a way to get your time back and still pay your bills is powerful. It's freeing. Many have discovered the F.I.R.E. movement after searching with keywords like "how to retire early."

REMEMBER

Heading down the path to reclaim your time doesn't mean you have to have it all figured out. You just need a reason to head in that direction, maybe something as simple as not wanting someone else to own your time. You won't have total clarity at the start of your journey, but the light gets brighter as you move closer to F.I.R.E.

Hurdling the money obstacle to do what you love

Money is often the obstacle between you and the freedom to do what you love. Removing that obstacle is essentially what you're doing by pursuing F.I.R.E.

TIP

The typical F.I.R.E. number is to accumulate a fund that's 25 times your expected annual expenses in retirement. You can achieve that target with the philosophies mentioned earlier in this chapter.

EXAMPLE

Here's an example of how to figure your F.I.R.E. number:

> You expect $60,000 to be your annual spending in early retirement.
>
> $60,000 × 25 = $1,500,000

Once you reach F.I. you have unlocked many life choices that you may not have thought you'd ever have. That freedom can lead you in all kinds of directions, including

>> Retiring early

>> Changing your career

>> Traveling

>> Spending more time with your kids or other family

I grew up in poverty, and the default reason for everything I couldn't have was money. It was the thing that always got in the way of having new clothes, eating at restaurants, or going to ride the roller coasters at Six Flags. It took a while for the idea that F.I.R.E. was possible for me to sink in, but it changed my world once I embraced it.

Who Wants F.I.R.E. and Why?

Many people would choose to spend their time in different careers and jobs if money were not a factor.

If all careers and jobs paid the same amount of money, would you change yours? Do you feel stuck in a job you don't love, or would you simply like to do the work you love on your own terms without being beholden to an employer?

F.I.R.E. is a whole community of people who reject the default construct of work and retirement. Thinking differently about the balance of labor, leisure, and life leads many people to want more freedom to define this themselves.

Most of the F.I.R.E. concepts are simple and aren't new. They are just updated versions of the advice from wise people — parents, grandparents, and other influential people — who came before you.

If you've read the book *Your Money or Your Life* by Vicki Robin and Joe Dominguez, you had an early glimpse into what financial independence and retiring early looks like. Just think about the legacy this iconic pair built and how many people they've touched since reaching F.I.R.E.

If you've never imagined having an identity that did not include your job or career, you're not alone. But there's a lot of power in creating your own identity with you as the lead character and everything else in a supporting role.

There are many different reasons people navigate toward F.I.R.E. Here are some examples:

>> One tough day at work pushes someone to the point where they've just had enough.

>> Someone has a series of reminders that they don't have the control of their time they'd like to have.

>> A person discovers a passion or project that they can't do because of commitments to work.

TIP

What's on the other side of F.I.R.E. can motivate you more than what you're moving away from. Think about your "why." Every person's why is different than the next person's. One of the great things about F.I.R.E. is that it's flexible, and there's not one precise way to do it.

ANECDOTE

My why for F.I.R.E. was to follow my big dream of creating a financially literate society. I know. I have a lot of work to do, but it's work I love, and I couldn't do it the way I want while at my full-time job. I tried, and it just became progressively more exhausting to do both.

WARNING

Don't let what the larger F.I.R.E. movement does dictate your goals. You are unique, and the only person who can design what time freedom looks like for you, is *you*.

What Ignited the F.I.R.E. Movement?

F.I.R.E. is definitely a movement, and you may be wondering what set it off. I have a theory of what gave rise to it, although other people may have other ideas.

For a long time, the workplace was set up like this:

>> Work at one place for 30 years or more

>> Build up retirement benefits via a traditional pension plan

>> Retire at 65 and collect a monthly pension for the rest of your life, which may be about 20 years if you're lucky

TIP

This scenario is what you'd call "golden handcuffs" because the promise of a big pension kept employees working with the same employer for a long time.

The shift from defined *benefit* plans (pensions) to defined *contribution* plans (401(k) and similar) started in the late 1970s and accelerated in the following decades. The financial crisis in 2008 accelerated the change. Many employers ended their pensions in favor of plans that left employees to manage their own retirement funds through workplace vehicles like a 401(k) or 403(b). (Sorry for the history lesson, but I think you know where this is going.)

As a result of employees having to manage their own retirement funds, they had less incentive to stay with one employer for 30 years. People took on the challenge of figuring out a retirement plan on their own. In walks the F.I.R.E. movement to turn things upside down.

My daughter (a teenager at the time) summed it up like this and created an illustration as shown in Figure 1-2: "So . . . you take away our pensions and make employees fend for themselves. . . . We figure it out, reach F.I.R.E., and leave work early; now you're mad at us?" As simplistic as it sounds, her summary pretty much captures the rise of the F.I.R.E. movement.

FIGURE 1-2:
F.I.R.E. summary.

Amber Koski (Book Author)

Although the COVID-19 pandemic that started in 2020 didn't ignite the movement, it definitely helped fan the flames. During the height of the shutdown, people spent a lot more time at home and limited activities of what they could do outside the home. That made many people rethink how they wanted to spend their time and reshape their futures.

Examining the Public Perception of F.I.R.E.

As aspirational as F.I.R.E. may seem to me and you, it doesn't always get a fair shake from other people. It's healthy to take a critical look at things and examine a situation from other perspectives.

In the early days, there were some stereotypes assigned to the F.I.R.E. movement. As a member of the F.I.R.E. community, I could understand where they came from, but like most stereotypes, they were overgeneralized. Here are some examples of the stereotypical perception of a person who could achieve F.I.R.E.:

» Mostly high-income people

» Mostly white men working in the tech or engineering fields

» Mostly people without kids or other extended family obligations

» Mostly people who are extremely frugal or excessive minimalists

There's a lot more I could add to this list, but I got depressed just looking at some of these because I definitely don't fit the mold, and you may not either. These descriptors in no way fully represent the F.I.R.E. community.

TIP

The source of these stereotypes was probably clickbait articles or other media content with limited scope.

ANECDOTE

I remember my first exposure to a diverse voice talking about F.I.R.E. on a major media platform. It was Jamila Souffrant, host of the podcast *Journey to Launch* (https://journeytolaunch.com/) and author of the book *Your Journey to Financial Freedom* (Hanover).

ANECDOTE

I admit that I was a skeptic when I first started exploring what F.I.R.E. was all about (back in 2014). I read some salacious headlines that got my attention, but my curious nature led me to do a lot more digging than reading a single article. I started diving into it by devouring all the F.I.R.E.-focused podcasts, blogs, and books I could find.

I recall platforms with names that focused on the more extreme parts of F.I.R.E. like frugality or minimalism. Years later I felt that focus shifted toward things like simplicity, choice, and the wealth part of F.I.R.E. from sources like these:

» The Simple Path to Wealth (https://jlcollinsnh.com/)

» Our Rich Journey (www.ourrichjourney.com)

» Afford Anything (https://affordanything.com/)

» rich & REGULAR (https://richandregular.com/)

» Wealth Twins (https://wealthtwins.com/)

» ChooseFI (www.choosefi.com)

Needless to say, there are a lot more platforms, resources, and communities where you can learn about F.I.R.E. I mention many throughout this book and offer a list of some of my favorites in Chapter 21.

Tasting the Different Flavors of FI

As I mentioned earlier in this chapter, F.I.R.E. comes with flexibility. There are many approaches to the journey, and there are now names for some of the most common F.I.R.E. lifestyles (see Table 1-1).

TABLE 1-1 **The Different Flavors of F.I.**

F.I.R.E. Flavor	Approach
Coast	Your nest egg is at a point where you don't need to make additional contributions, and it will grow enough to support your future retirement.
Lean	You're approaching F.I.R.E. on a lower income and smaller budget. Lower is relative but typically would be less than the average household income in your locale.
Fat	You're targeting a much higher number than average to live on now and in retirement. These would typically be high-income earners with bigger budgets and higher levels of spending, saving, and investing.
Barista	You have enough of a nest egg to trade in a full-time job for a part-time gig (such as a barista) that makes you happier. You still have income from the part-time job (and possibly health insurance).

Chapter **2**

Personalizing the Process of Reaching F.I.R.E.

aving the ability to retire early is a lofty goal for many, but it means retiring from a job, not life! Being able to retire early means reaching a level of financial independence — something everyone aspires to.

Some like to call F.I.R.E. a process, but I call it a journey of departing from the norm — just a little reframing that I learned in my financial psychology classes. Regardless of how you describe it, F.I.R.E. requires the planning and intentionality I talk about in this chapter. Figuring out how to optimize the steps on your journey is what will help shorten the time it takes.

In this chapter, I show you the big picture for reaching financial independence and explain how it can be compressed into a shorter period, why so many are attracted to F.I.R.E., how to stack your knowledge, and how to turn that knowledge into action.

The Big Picture, Compressed

Everyone has heard some version of what it takes to build wealth:

>> Live on less than you earn and invest the difference.

>> Don't spend everything you make.

>> Always save something.

>> Grow the gap between your spending and income.

ANECDOTE

I remember my dad uttering these "rules" time after time because he wanted his kids to do better than he had. When I was younger, I didn't exactly know what he meant, but it turns out he knew exactly what he was talking about.

These ideas are not new. My dad and earlier generations figured these out and passed the philosophies down. What is new is the path and time it takes to build wealth and reach financial independence. You can think of it like gamifying the process and knowing how to play. Fortunately, in this game, almost everyone can win without worrying about competition.

In this section, I help you reevaluate how you define "retirement age" and break down important aspects of how to build wealth to get you to your goal.

Redefining "retirement age"

You may have anchored your idea of retiring based on messaging from societal norms. Retiring early is traditionally defined in a few different ways:

>> Social Security defines early retirement before age 67.

>> Many rules around retirement accounts won't let you access them without penalty until age 59.5.

>> Many employer retirement plans won't allow benefits to start until age 55.

But F.I.R.E. puts you in control of defining retirement age for yourself, and it may be significantly younger than 55. I retired at the age of 49, but others have managed to retire far younger. So instead of taking 30 to 40 years to accumulate what you need for retirement, the time can be more like 10 to 20 years. Just let that sit for a moment . . . you are slashing the time to retirement by half — creating the life you want much sooner than you may have ever imagined.

Having the resources to retire is a function of what you earn, how much of that is spent, and investing the difference. This can also be expressed as your "savings rate," which is simply the percentage of your income that you are saving and investing. The higher your savings rate, the less time acquiring wealth will take. It doesn't have to take 30 or 40 years of work to reach a point of financial independence to have the option to retire early. What if you could cut that time in half? Wouldn't that be worth the effort?

Living on less than you earn

ANECDOTE

When I was finishing college and barely able to make ends meet, I thought living on less than I earned was nearly impossible. I always had more money going out than was coming in. I knew that working a job that paid close to minimum wage to cover my tuition and other expenses would never get me ahead. Fortunately, I finally found some relief once I finished college (reducing my expenses) and started making a higher salary as I started my career (increasing my income).

You have some flexibility in how to get to the state of living on less than you earn. The two primary levers are increasing your earnings and decreasing your expenses:

>> You can increase your earnings through your salary, a side hustle, or income-producing projects. Your main job may have opportunities for bonuses, promotions, stock options, or other financial benefits. Besides your main job, there are ways to bring in additional income that you create on your own as a self-employed person or entrepreneur. Many people find real estate to be a lucrative way to increase earnings. Chapter 10 talks more about growing your income, including a few creative ways you may not have thought of before.

>> You can decrease your expenses by spending money on what you value and cutting what you don't. No deprivation is required here; it's important to set up your spending in a way that you will stick with, and feeling deprived all the time is no way to encourage longevity. If an expense gives you joy and fills you with energy, that's probably not what you want to cut out because it's something that matters to you. I would say that smart spending matters just as much as cutting spending, and shining a light on your expenses helps you get more confident and intentional about where your money is going. You may be able to decrease expenses through one or two big hits such as housing or vehicle costs or many smaller hits like canceling streaming TV subscriptions you forgot you were still paying for or shopping around for car insurance to get a lower rate.

Some of us are better with one of these levers than the other, but you'll see the greatest impact if you can do both at the same time. This "live on less than you earn" concept is partly achieved through simply using your favorite budgeting or cash flow management tools to help with tracking because it's hard to measure what you don't track. You can use an app on your phone, create a spreadsheet, or write it out with pen and paper. If you want to dive more into these areas, check out the book *Budgeting For Dummies* by Athena Valentine Lent (Wiley).

Investing the difference

The difference in your income and expenses is the most powerful opportunity to grow your wealth. The bigger the gap, the more you have to

>> Save and invest

>> Spend

Most people feel like you have to choose one or there other, but the reality is that you can do both. In a lot of financial dilemmas two definitive options are pitted against one another. It rarely has to be absolute, and in a world of multitasking, most of us can handle doing more than one thing at a time.

Most people choose to increase their lifestyle as their income increases, and they find themselves on the "hedonic treadmill."

Hedonic treadmill is the tendency for people to quickly return to a base level of happiness despite experiencing major positive or negative events.

If you want to be in the optimal position for F.I.R.E., saving and investing more as your gap increases gives you the power to get there. Savings alone is not enough, but this is often a catch-all word that includes investing. In reality, you can't save your way to wealth if your money is just sitting in a bank account. It is unlikely to outpace inflation (around 2% according to the Federal Reserve: www.federal reserve.gov/faqs/economy_14400.htm). You have to invest money to truly see it grow, and one of the most common ways the F.I.R.E. community does it is through the stock market. You can take a very simple approach that revolves around one or more index funds that is

>> Passive

>> Low cost

>> Broad market

The easiest example is the S&P 500 index fund that simply mimics its benchmark.

The S&P 500 includes the 500 largest and most widely held U.S. companies.

TIP

Former CEO of Berkshire Hathaway, Warren Buffet, is considered one of the world's greatest investors. He was a genius at handpicking great companies to invest in. However, even he was a big believer in the idea that most people are better off investing in a simple index fund. In fact, in 2008, Buffet threw out a challenge to hedge funds (funds that actively pick stocks in an effort to outperform the market). He bet $1,000,000 that an S&P 500 index fund would perform better than hedge funds over a ten-year period (2008 to 2017). The outcome didn't surprise many people: The S&P 500 index fund beat the hedge funds.

The other wildly popular index fund that the F.I.R.E. community is enamored with is a total stock market fund. VTSAX (Vanguard Total Stock Market Index Fund) is the most admired. Its slogan of "VTSAX and Chill" is very cute and expresses the sentiment that investing can be an easy and hands-off endeavor. Of course, Vanguard is not the only mutual fund company that offers a total stock market mutual fund. All the other major brokers (Fidelity, Schwab, T. Rowe Price, and so on) have something comparable.

A total stock market index fund includes all 3,500-plus publicly traded U.S. companies (not just the 500 largest like the S&P 500).

TECHNICAL
STUFF

The S&P 500 or the total stock market index fund basically allows your risk to be spread across a lot of stocks versus investing in a single stock or trying to handpick individual stocks. You don't need to watch what these funds are doing every day; index funds are built around the premise that over the long term (20, 30, 40 years), the stock market is likely to go up. Stocks can be volatile in the short term with frequent ups and downs, but this movement usually averages out over time to result in gains over the long term.

Another way to invest the difference between your income and expenses is to contribute to your employer's retirement plan like a 401(k), 403(b), or TSP (Thrift Savings Plan). The bonus of these types of accounts is that they usually come with an employer match and tax advantages. You choose what funds you are investing in, make automatic contributions every pay period, and watch your money grow over the long run. If you're a self-employed person or investing in other accounts beyond your employer, the result is similar; you just have to put in a little more effort, and there's no company match.

I know, I've made investing sound pretty easy, and it absolutely can be. It can be as complex or as simple as you want, but research has shown that complexity doesn't equal better performance.

REMEMBER

The Attraction to F.I.R.E.

I'll admit, one of my initial attractions to F.I.R.E. was the hot acronym.

I had become very savvy with my personal finances, but financial independence? Retiring early? No way. Those things were not even in my scope of awareness. I was a skeptic.

I was drawn to the idea of cutting out early from my job and focusing more on the things I loved, on my terms. Imagining how F.I.R.E. would change your life fulfills deep desires around work and happiness, including things like

>> Escaping a toxic job you don't like

>> Freedom with your time before you're too old to enjoy it

>> Controlling your life choices without depending on a job

But for many of us, it seems impossible at first.

Many people dream of achieving these things without needing to work 40-plus hours a week until they're 60-plus. You have to pay your bills and need money to live, and what F.I.R.E. does is remove money as an obstacle to following your dreams or doing whatever it is you value.

Pensions as a reward for working a long time at one place started disappearing in the 1990s. The decline accelerated to the point that today, you'd be very lucky to find an employer (besides the government and a few very large companies) that offers a pension. The elimination of that perk diluted the attraction of giving a single employer your best years. Many of the benefits that came along with a pension (such as retiree health insurance) became less and less common, too.

The significance of this history is that the security that kept so many people tied down for decades to one employer is nearly gone, and I think that opened the door for people to consider how to plan for retirement on their own rather than depending on an employer to do it for them. Some people view this lack of professional guidance as a negative. After all, what individual employee is equipped to manage their retirement as well as highly trained institutional pension fund managers? Almost none. But people who viewed that as a positive would probably be a part the F.I.R.E. community.

The psychological aspect of F.I.R.E.

The facts and figures of retirement planning (your savings rate, the difference between your income and expenses, and so on) are important, but the most powerful part of F.I.R.E. is psychological. The feelings and emotional aspects of retiring early are motivators that go beyond what you track in your spreadsheets and apps. Some of those emotions come from how you grew up or were socialized around money and finances. Those experiences influence us and how we look at life and happiness.

For example, if a person grew up with a dad who worked hard every day and died only two years after he retired, that history plays into their thoughts about retirement. If a person's mother was stuck in a job that she hated going to every day because she needed to pay the bills, that person's thoughts about working are shaped by that experience. If a person hates their job because they feel they aren't doing meaningful work, those feelings factor into their life choices.

Take a pause and invite yourself to deeply consider F.I.R.E. Allow yourself to take a look at your reasons for your interest from a mental standpoint and let them sink in. Do something to clear your mind and imagine your dreams: meditate, do breathing exercises, take a hike or a walk. The idea is to step away from the hard numbers and see the bigger picture of what you want your life to look like. Let your F.I.R.E. plans support that dream. Your plans to pursue F.I.R.E. should be an addition to your quality of life, not a subtraction. The following reasons were some of my motivators:

>> Having more time with my adult daughter

>> Becoming more involved as a financial literacy advocate

>> Mentoring others who may have struggled in a similar way as I did growing up

The escape from the toxic job

Think about a day when you were fed up with work. Perhaps it was during a Monday morning team meeting that started with a condescending tone, the useless metrics that just caused you to be placed on a performance plan, or the constant warnings that you'd have to return to in-office work when you're doing just fine working from home.

Everyone has something that makes them unhappy about working. A 2021 Pew Research Center survey (https://pewrsr.ch/3hVWMfr) identified the top reasons Americans quit their jobs in 2021:

>> Low pay

>> Lack of opportunities for advancement

>> Feeling disrespected at work

Resignation rates in 2021 were high, giving rise to new phrases like *great resignation*, *great reshuffle*, and *quiet quitting*. (See the glossary for definitions of these terms.) I'd say that a good remedy for these issues is what I call "planning your great escape."

It's unfortunate, but you are not alone if you have a job that you don't love or even perceive as being toxic. In fact, it is one of the big reasons people tell me they're seeking F.I.R.E. They have a negative work environment, unfulfilling work, a horrible boss, or something similar pushing them away. This is enough to make you want to leave and do something different.

When you're in this position, you can choose to do one of three things (or a combination):

>> Stay and tough it out at your current job

>> Leave your job

>> Start planning for F.I.R.E. so you can quit your traditional job for good

It's this last option that leads many people discover the F.I.R.E. movement by searching online for something like "How do I retire early?" The results are many blogs, articles, podcasts, and YouTube channels dedicated to the topic, which help people realize they're not the only ones seeking to cut out early from their day job and trading their time for money.

Financial independence from a job

There are people that say they love their job and don't want to "retire early"; they just want the financial independence part of F.I.R.E. For example, hating my job was not my primary motivation to retire early. I stuck with the same employer for 21 years and never felt compelled enough to leave (although the thought creeped into my mind a few times). I enjoyed the work I did (*most* of the time), and I was very thankful for the perceived security of a regular job that included

>> Great benefits

>> A steady paycheck

>> Career growth

One of the big things I loved about my job was that I made some great friends with coworkers I will always value.

ANECDOTE

I was also interested in building the financial independence that would give me that breathing room I so longed for. My simplistic way of thinking about it was that if my employer suddenly eliminated my position or downsized my department, I didn't want to be thrown into financial insecurity when I knew a paycheck wasn't coming. I remember how awful it felt when I was laid off previously (in my 20s), which caused fear and uncertainty that I never wanted to feel again.

It's important to recognize the difference between a job and the work that you do. You can leave your job but continue your work. Here's what I mean:

>> A job is at a community hospital, but the work is nursing people back to health.

>> A job is at a public school, but the work is educating children.

>> A job is at a big cybersecurity company, but the work is keeping people safe online.

A job situation can change in an instant with a new boss, a reorganization, or changes with your employer — all things out of your control. You take control back when you have planned your F.I.R.E. exit and shift your thinking about your job.

A negative situation isn't the only reason that you may decide to retire early. You may be trying to get to something more compelling on the other side, such as doing meaningful work outside the confines of a job. Your work may become even more impactful once you're able to do it on your own terms. Choosing who you work with, how many hours you want to devote to the work, and the areas you focus on is now up to you. So, by all means, escape the toxic job but continue doing what you love.

Freedom with your time

ANECDOTE

When I left my job in 2019, I had a mental white board where I visualized a plan for my time. At the center was the thing I knew I'd be doing for the rest of my life, which was financial literacy. Everything else I did would somehow revolve around that.

I planned years prior to figure out what this freedom with my time — time freedom — would look like for me. I think that my mission of creating a financially literate society helped motivate me even more to work toward F.I.R.E.

TIP

You may not know what that thing is for you, but you're more likely to find it when your mind is clearer and not cluttered with someone else's dream.

The newfound time freedom that comes with F.I.R.E. will get you thinking about a bucket list of sorts. Some people may ask what you will do all day if you don't have a job. This is something most people never get a chance to explore because they think they'll be working most of their lives.

For most of my career, I had never really thought about how I'd spend my time if I didn't have to work because I was taught to

>> Find a good job with good benefits

>> Work there for a really long time

>> Then retire with a pension or 401(k)

Most people confine themselves to this process, and companies offer financial incentives like benefits, matching 401(k) contributions, stock options, and more to keep exceptional employees. But that doesn't mean you *have* to buy into the idea. In fact, this mindset is referred to as the golden handcuffs — financially, this process looks tempting and provides security, but it locks you in to someone else's dream.

Control of your life choices

There's a certain level of satisfaction you get from controlling your own destiny. During your working life, you often have to turn over some control to an employer, and they make a lot of choices for you (at least while you're at work). They set the mission, the priorities, and even the hours you work. Can you just change this norm? The idea of F.I.R.E. says you can, and that is a big part of the allure.

The life choices I'm talking about are a part of your planning. This is your opportunity to think about how things would look if you ruled the world (at least your world). Here are some big questions to get your juices flowing:

>> What is your life's work?

>> What's your passion?

>> What do you love getting up in the morning to do?

You may have asked yourself these questions before, but they become a lot more fun to ponder when you're working toward financial independence. You can move your life in the direction that gives you the most satisfaction instead of falling in line with the way your boss or manager wants it. You don't even need to have it all figured out, and it doesn't matter if those goals are big or small.

TIP

Your main goal may not be to retire formally, but creating the space to experiment can be eye-opening. Your F.I.R.E. journey will be one of self-discovery.

Your why of F.I.R.E.

If you haven't picked up on it already, there are many reasons why people seek F.I.R.E. It may seem like F.I.R.E. is a way to run from situations you don't like: a toxic workplace, not doing work that's meaningful to you, not having control of your time.

But what's your *why* for the other side of F.I.R.E.? Finding what lights you up and gets you excited will give you extra fuel on your path to F.I.R.E.

WARNING

Many people have trouble with defining their *why*, so you're not alone if you're not sure. It doesn't have to be a grand plan — just things that bring you happiness. It could be getting more sleep. It could be more traveling (like many in the F.I.R.E. community love to do). It could be work that you're doing on the side but would love to do more once you reach financial independence or retire.

You may not have ever been in a position to imagine what you'd want to do if money was not an obstacle. Many are conditioned from a young age to think of work in terms of money. I'm not saying that you can't make money from doing the thing you love, but knowing that you would do it regardless of the money makes a difference.

WARNING

It is not unusual for the *why* to take a little time to reveal itself to you, and it isn't necessary to precisely define it as you might for an assignment at work. It's likely to be an extension of something you're already doing but may not have thought you'd ever have the luxury to spend more time on because your job always got in the way.

ANECDOTE

One of my first meaningful post-F.I.R.E. endeavors was something you may not think is a big deal, but it was huge for me. I decided to go back to school to get my master's degree. There was this amazing financial therapy program at Kansas State University that I was drawn to. I started looking at this about a year before retiring from my corporate job and knew that I did not want to go to school while I was working. For me, the effort of holding down a job while going to school just wasn't worth it. Though I didn't hate my job, it was demanding enough that I knew it would be hard for me to do both successfully. My main reason for going back to school was not to make more money. It was basically a do-over of my academics from way back when I was an undergrad (more than 20 years earlier).

I worked full time while I was in college to pay my way through. I also had a part-time job, which meant I was working more than 40 hours a week, and the pay was barely above minimum wage. I got a little money in grants and scholarships, but it was not enough. As I did this, I still maintained my status as a full-time student (taking three or four classes) each semester. Something had to give, and it was my grades. I almost flunked out. The minimum GPA to graduate was a 2.5, and I scraped by with a 2.6. This hurt my pride a lot because I knew I was capable of much better. (I had been an A and B student in high school and took advanced classes.)

Even after more than two decades had passed, my pitiful grades as an undergrad still bothered me. When I started planning for F.I.R.E., I wanted a do-over. I would finally get the chance to go to school, focus on my studies, and not have to work while doing it. The big hurdle before I even started was getting into the program. I was supposed to have at least a 3.0 GPA from undergrad work to be accepted. Since I didn't have that, they placed me under academic probation to start (a humiliating moment). I was required to maintain a 3.0 GPA before I could get off probation.

I got a 4.0 GPA in my first three classes to meet their challenge, and the school let me off probation. Since I didn't have the time constraints of a job, I went full force and crushed it by maintaining a 4.0 GPA throughout the entire program. I graduated with academic honors. Wow, that felt incredible! I got my do-over and fulfilled one big *why* after F.I.R.E.

TIP

You have something similar that is just as meaningful to you (no matter how big or small). What you choose to do doesn't have to be a grand gesture, but whatever it is, you're in control. Life's just more fun when you choose to engage in things you love and enjoy.

The Continuum of Learning and Stacking Your Knowledge

Compound growth doesn't apply only to investing money. It also is very powerful when it comes to compounding your knowledge. Once you learn one small thing, you can build on that and keep it growing. Acquiring the skills on the path to F.I.R.E. works the same.

WARNING

Learning is a continuous process. The more you learn, the more you want to know. Some of the F.I.R.E. concepts can get deep, but you'll understand them if you keep trying. Don't get lost on things that you may feel are over your head in the beginning.

Remember that basics matter because they're what you build the foundation on. When it comes to personal finance, complexities and simplicity often yield similar outcomes. This is especially true when it comes to investing, which I talk more about in Chapter 12.

Maintaining endless curiosity

True learning is rooted in curiosity, and it's what fuels your knowledge-building process. One of the first questions I get asked is "What is F.I.R.E.?" It's easy to share what the acronym stands for, but the meaning behind it is really what gets you thinking and wondering. Do you remember when you were a kid and asked what seemed to be an endless string of questions because all the answers led to yet another question? A conversation may have sounded something like this:

Q: What are you doing

A: Working

Q: Why?

A: So I can make money

Q: Why?

A: So I can pay the bills

Q: Why?

Well, you get the idea.

This is what will happen as you explore your curiosities around F.I.R.E. You live in a moment in time where you can go deep (I mean really deep) on any topic your heart desires and get instant answers. Granted, you may not understand everything you read, watch, or listen to, but you're getting the building blocks to put it all together.

At first, I overcomplicated some things that I didn't have to, or perhaps I was just very confused about the world of personal finance. Most of the concepts are quite simple once you have a baseline. Just keep feeding your curiosity.

Leaning into your learning style

Just as important as what you want to learn is how you want to learn. Reading a book is not the only method of gaining knowledge. Think for a moment about how you best digest information and gain understanding. You may realize that reading isn't your favorite or only way to learn about F.I.R.E. or any other topic.

There are three primary learning styles:

>> **Auditory:** Listening

>> **Visual:** Watching

>> **Kinesthetic:** Physical movement and activities

You may have a combination of these learning styles with one being more dominant than the others. My dominant learning style is auditory because I love to listen to podcasts when I am hiking (this also caters to my multitasking nature). When a blog post or article is mentioned that sparks my interest, I go back and read it.

If a picture is worth a thousand words, then videos and a clever infographic may be priceless for building your knowledge if you're a visual learner. As a kinesthetic learner you may enjoy community events, group activities, or even building an ultimate F.I.R.E. spreadsheet to track your numbers.

If one type of medium does not resonate with you or promote your understanding of a certain topic, be sure to try a different one. Tapping into your best learning style will help you grow your body of knowledge more quickly and make the process feel a little easier.

Pursuing financial literacy, education, and independence

Don't laugh, but I didn't learn what net worth was until I was in my 30s. I'm a little embarrassed to say that, but I was never taught this at home or in school. It's a simple concept, and I would have easily grasped it as soon as I learned to do addition and subtraction if someone had taken the time to explain it.

Net Worth = What You Own (Assets) – What You Owe (Liabilities)

REMEMBER Not having basic financial literacy slowed down my learning around personal finance, and you may have felt the same way at some point. As a financial literacy advocate, I wish that every high school offered personal finance to at least provide the basics.

I've been keeping score in the U.S. As of 2023, only 25 of the 50 states have passed a law requiring personal finance as a stand-alone course. This is up from only six states in 2019 (see Figure 2-1). We can do better and one day soon I hope to not only see this required in U.S. schools but around the world.

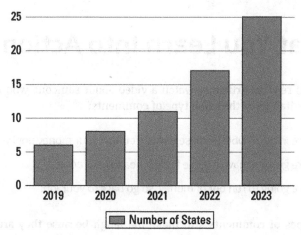

GROWTH IN STATES REQUIRING A PERSONAL FINANCE COURSE TO GRADUATE HIGH SCHOOL

Number of States

FIGURE 2-1:
The growth of financial literacy courses in schools.

You may have learned a little financial literacy in school or at home, but many of the big lessons come from mistakes you've made, so embrace those mistakes. I made many (and I'm still making them), and there is almost nothing that can't be fixed. You may not have an immediate, full understanding of all the F.I.R.E. concepts or strategies that you hear about, but your financial literacy will give you a baseline.

Basic financial literacy gives rise to more impactful learning and education, and leads to the next phase of stacking your knowledge. A personal finance topic that may have sounded completely foreign to you before may finally be coming into focus.

When I'm asked what is the best place to start learning, I say start with what you're most curious about. You will feel more motivated to figure out things that spark your interest and less likely to lose steam. That could include what is going on in your life at the moment.

ANECDOTE

I learned more about estate planning by helping my aunt after her husband passed away. It was a sensitive time for her, but she was forever grateful for my help. I was grateful to her for helping me build my knowledge in this area and getting first-hand education about things like probate, beneficiaries, and titling of assets.

With the seedling of financial literacy and the watering of financial education, you create a strong foundation to reach your ultimate goal of financial independence and beyond. You get to put that knowledge to work and plan what the financial future looks for you. Think about everything that you learn and how to fit it together to reach your goals. You don't need to know everything all at once; it's a process. You'll feel the difference as you stack what you learn each day, each month, and each year.

Turning What You Learn Into Action

When you read an article or watch a video about someone who reached F.I.R.E., you'll inevitably see the same type of comments:

>> You're in big trouble because you can't touch your money until you're 59.5.

>> You're going to have trouble finding health insurance.

>> You're going to run out of money, so go back to your job.

These types of comments still make me laugh because they are assuming that F.I.R.E. people have not thought through concerns like these or done anything about them. Articles and videos are very limited in scope and don't provide much information for the average person to go on unless they go digging on their own.

TIP

One of the early things I learned is that F.I.R.E. people are doers! They don't just educate themselves on some of the areas that commenters mention, but they figure out the best way to do it, make a plan, and execute it.

Let's just dissect one of the comments from above "You're in big trouble because you can't touch your money until you're 59.5." This is probably one of the most discussed topics in the community and was once perceived as a huge hurdle. Well, Table 2-1 lists some easy ways (more are discussed in Chapter 17) to solve this problem, and I used most of them in my own path to F.I.R.E.

TABLE 2-1   **Accessing Funds When You Retire Early**

Source of Funds	Age Restrictions	Penalty to Take Out before 59.5
Contribution portion of Roth	None	None
Brokerage account or non-retirement account	None	None
Health Savings Accounts	None	None if for health or medical expenses
Stock options or other accumulated equity compensation	None	None

When you learn something new, it's really just theory until you either talk to someone who has done it or try it yourself. That's when you really understand it. Earlier in this chapter, I talk about the big picture, and those issues are key, but don't overlook the impact the small actions can have. The compounding of every little action adds up.

Here are just a few examples:

>> Locating a forgotten retirement account from an old employer

>> Switching from a bank account that charges you a monthly fee to one with no fee and a new account opening bonus

>> Lowering your cost for internet service just by asking your provider to do so or by switching to another service

Identifying your superpowers and challenges

What's your superpower? Don't be shy; everyone has at least one. These are the things you are really strong at or certain advantages you have that may help you get ahead on your F.I.R.E. journey. For instance, you may

>> Work in a high-paying field

>> Live in an area with a low cost of living

>> Be a savvy real estate investor

On the opposite end are adversities or challenges. I see challenges as weaknesses that you are working on improving. Human nature seems to make you focus most on the negatives, and I have fallen prey to that myself. It's important to acknowledge both strengths and weaknesses. Types of weakness that may exist are

>> High expenses

>> A lot of credit card debt

>> Financial support for extended family

As tough as these challenges sound, they can all belong to the same person who has the set of superpowers in the previous list.

TIP

It's not always possible to eliminate challenges because you may be born with some of them and they may not be possible to change. Working to overcome the challenges that you can improve will help lighten your load. The key is to control what you can control.

The dichotomy of superpowers and challenges exist for us all. It's a balancing act both financially and psychologically (more about this in Chapter 3) but the goal is to have a strategy to maximize your strengths and minimize your weaknesses. The combination will help ease your path to F.I.R.E.

ANECDOTE

There's a big psychological side to dealing with weakness (more about that in Chapter 3). Table 2-2 shows just a few of my superpowers and weaknesses/challenges on my journey to F.I.R.E.

TABLE 2-2

A Few of My Superpowers and Weaknesses/Challenges

Superpowers	Weaknesses/Challenges
Living in an area with a low cost of living	Growing up in poverty
Generous employer match in my retirement account	Getting divorced
A high savings rate (about 40%)	Becoming a single mom

TIP

Reaching financial independence is a superpower in itself. It gives you options and more control over your life. The ability to walk away from a job, retire early, or start a different career are all on the table. The vast majority of people do not have options like this and perhaps don't even realize it's possible. I'm hoping to change some of that with this book.

Finding your strategy

Name your adventure. That is what you're doing when finding the strategy for reaching financial independence and creating the option to retire early. The superpowers and challenges you identify in the preceding section can help shape your strategy. The key is to maximize your superpowers and minimize your challenges.

The only strategies for reaching F.I.R.E. that matter are the ones that will work for you. The strategies you use depend a lot on where you are today because that is your starting point. If you hate your job, your first step may be to change jobs and do what you love. If you are self-employed, your strategy may be to amp up your gigs. If you are in the military, that may present the opportunity to utilize some of the benefits to your advantage.

EXAMPLE

If you are in a low-paying job, your strategy may include going back to school, getting some additional training, or taking up a trade or skill to get a better paying job or make more at the one you have.

Parts 3 and 4 of this book discuss the areas to increase and decrease to build wealth for F.I.R.E. You'll be able to better determine where you are and what strategies will work best for you.

Executing on the goals you set

As I say earlier in this section, F.I.R.E. people are doers, and so are you. After you identify the strategies that suit you and you set your goals on how to get there, it's time to take actions and execute. You don't have to do it all at once, and even the smallest steps add up.

Your goals will be included in your strategy. Tracking can help you execute actions to get to the goals, and that was what kept me on task. (Yes, I created a spreadsheet to make some projections.) A list of goals is important whether you use an app or a spreadsheet you customize yourself.

Seeing a visual reminder of long-term goals is a common characteristic of those who reach financial independence. Their thinking is focused on years and decades ahead, but that doesn't have to mean sacrificing or depriving themselves of everything they love and enjoy today.

ANECDOTE

In my case, I was working in corporate America and was with the same company for nearly 15 years when I began my journey to financial independence and started contemplating early retirement. My goals were centered around my job and maximizing some of the great financial benefits I had. Part of that included mapping out what I was going to contribute to my accounts and projecting the growth of my overall net worth. It was very empowering to see the growth and how close I got to my estimates each year.

IN THIS CHAPTER

» Examining the feelings and mindset behind F.I.R.E.

» Acknowledging the good and the bad about F.I.R.E.

» Removing the taboo of talking about money

» Finding F.I.R.E.-friendly communities

» Catching up after a late start

Chapter **3**

Understanding the Mindset and Psychology behind F.I.R.E.

One of my favorite quotes is by poet Maya Angelou:

I've learned that people will forget what you said,

people will forget what you did,

but people will never forget how you made them feel.

The spirit of her words hit on what I think is one of the most important parts of the journey to F.I.R.E.: how you feel along the way. I have long believed that there is a very strong connection between emotions and money. It's cool to talk about Roth conversions, house hacking, and savings rates, but the mindset you have about your money will trump all.

When you start understanding the math behind reaching financial independence or retiring early, the process all begins to make sense quickly. However, even with step-by-step instructions from a podcast or book, some people still struggle. Why is that? Usually, it has something to do with how they think about money and personal finance. That thinking is shaped by experiences, environment, and exposure going as far back as childhood, and that programming is hard to ignore.

The psychological aspects of F.I.R.E. haven't always been talked about, but I've noticed the topic being discussed more openly now. In this chapter, I help you get your mind around the psychology of F.I.R.E. regardless of where you start and what your finances look like. Your mindset is what will launch you on your journey.

ANECDOTE

I was so interested in this area that I started a financial therapy master's program that focused on the intersection of money and psychology. A few years ago, I didn't even know such a thing existed! It was a fascinating program, and the heart of it was exploring the things in your life that influence how you think and feel about money. Facts and figures alone don't add up to success and happiness.

Examining Who Can Reach F.I.R.E.

Whether just anyone can reach F.I.R.E. is often debated both within and outside of the F.I.R.E. community. It's a valid question, especially when you see articles that say, "I reached millionaire status and retired by age 30, and you can too." If you're 35 with a $0 net worth, you're probably not feeling confident this goal is achievable, and you may even think it's impossible for you.

I don't think everyone can reach F.I.R.E., but I do think heading down the path toward financial independence is for everyone. If you're currently barely making ends meet or overcoming adversities, it may feel impossible (it sure felt that way for me), and I think it's important to acknowledge that this pursuit is much harder for some people than others. Using your own measuring stick (discussed later in this chapter) based on your situation is much better than trying to use someone else's standards

Regardless of whether you eventually make it to F.I.R.E., one huge step you can take is to embrace the fact that it is possible to make progress no matter where you may be starting. Change is hard, especially if you're trying to reverse limiting beliefs. If you haven't been exposed to wealth-building behaviors your whole life, you're in the position of having to seek out information for yourself. It really takes a mindset shift, and that is what this chapter is all about.

TIP

The main takeaway is that anyone can get on the path or start working toward financial independence. Just imagining a better financial situation than what you currently have is one of the first steps.

More than math

If you got through high school, then the basic math behind F.I.R.E. (discussed in Chapter 2) is simple. But the mental side of this journey has power as well. It's hard to do one without the other. Understanding the numbers is just one part of the process, though.

The math can't stand alone when you are talking about life changes. When you begin to understand the numbers, you have to determine whether there are certain internal or external issues preventing you from making those numbers work. Mental blocks can be impediments to making the right moves and taking action.

TIP

Allow yourself the time to process the emotional side of making life changes to reach F.I.R.E.

Barrier busters

Some people have a lot more to overcome on their path to F.I.R.E. than others. They may need to break away from everything they learned about money growing up.

After being in a bad environment, you have two choices:

>> Repeat the cycle.

>> Do just the opposite.

The latter choice is the harder of the two because you're breaking away from what was the norm for you. Overcoming barriers is challenging, but it's necessary to move toward your financial goals.

Understanding how money works is a foreign concept for many because they may have never been taught at home or in school. For most, discussing money matters is still a taboo topic. If you can get over any hang-ups you have about talking about money, the door to learning opens, and you can embrace changes with your finances.

It's not an easy task to break barriers. Sometimes, the situation that leads you to busting through the barriers is thrust upon you, but those ignitors can prove to be very powerful motivators. Here are some examples:

>> Being the first in your family to graduate from college

>> A major health scare

>> A toxic boss or work environment

>> A divorce

>> The early loss of a loved one

TIP

Although these experiences aren't all positive on their own, they can shake you up to a point where you long to make a major positive shift.

ANECDOTE

My divorce was my big wake-up call regarding my finances. I realized that my ex-husband had $100,000 more in his retirement account than I had in mine. We had been married for more than ten years and earned similar salaries. The divorce was hard enough both financially and emotionally, but I couldn't shake the fact that there was such a huge disparity in our retirement accounts. That was enough for me to realize I needed to get my finances together for both me and my daughter. This was a really difficult time, but it resulted in a huge shift that I don't know if I would have made otherwise.

Progress while pursuing F.I.R.E.

You can't manage what you don't measure. I heard this all the time when I was working but, in that context, it was annoying because it seemed to always be measuring levels of activity rather than accomplishments. The two were rarely correlated.

Now that I see it as tracking progress on the path to F.I.R.E., the saying is more meaningful. Progress is probably one of the greatest motivators on your path. It's a great feeling to look back and see that you have moved a little closer to your goals. It can give you the mental fuel to keep going and see your progress.

TIP

No progress is too small as long as it's going in the right direction.

Here's just a few examples of ways to track progress:

>> **Moving from a 10% savings rate to 15%:** This is a relatively small change that may not seem like it's going to change the world, but you've just slashed your time to reaching F.I.R.E. with that one little thing.

>> **Switching from high-fee active funds to low-fee passive funds in your retirement account:** You'll retain more of your growth that can be compounded.

>> **Paying off high-interest credit card debt that's been hanging around forever:** You'll lighten your load going forward, and you can redirect those dollars you were using to pay off the credit cards to saving and investing.

>> **Shopping around for your internet service and cutting the costs by $40/month:** You've freed up additional dollars in your budget.

REMEMBER

Examples like these may not add up to much individually, but each demonstrates persistence and commitment to moving in the right direction. When all these little moves are stacked on top of each other, it strengthens the impact.

A plan without a downside

Even if you are hesitant or still a little anxious about this whole F.I.R.E. approach, think about this: If you decided to go down the F.I.R.E. path but later change your mind and decide you don't need to reach financial independence as quickly as you thought, you haven't lost anything. You can relax your focus on your finances or slow down your pace.

REMEMBER

The big deal here is that you've done something that's going to help your finances. Regardless of what your end goal is and when you'll reach it, you're going to be learning and opening your eyes to things that will benefit you. Even if you don't want to pursue F.I.R.E., you'll move yourself further along to whatever your goals are, and you have the experience of trying.

Acknowledging Adversities and Advantages

In the early days of the F.I.R.E movement, it was criticized for being for a bunch of white guys who were high-income engineers without kids — at least that is what the media seemed to focus on when they profiled people like Mr. Money Mustache and Mad Fientist. Do those types of people exist? Sure they do, but it's inaccurate to conclude that only that type of person could reach F.I.R.E.

Some privilege can certainly be a boost that perhaps some take for granted. For example, you may feel more confident about your chances of success with F.I.R.E. if you

>> Know you can always go live at home or you can ask your parents for money if things don't work out

>> Grew up middle or upper class

>> Have parents or other family members who started saving and investing on your behalf

>> Get financial support from family while in college so you don't have huge student loans

Just knowing that you have a safety net puts you in a position of strength that not everyone gets to enjoy.

While on my F.I.R.E. journey, I had to acknowledge that I was not in the same position as some other people because I was on my own (financially and otherwise at 18). I did, however, want to give my daughter more of a head start than I had. Since my starting place was so different from some of the stories I was hearing from others, I had to become very good at making adjustments based on my situation, and you can do that, too.

WARNING

I don't want you to get discouraged on your journey when you feel you don't fit the mold of what you mostly see represented in the F.I.R.E. community, in the media, or elsewhere. Keep in mind that there can still be valuable nuggets that you can apply to your own life, even if all of it won't work for you exactly as described.

REMEMBER

F.I.R.E. is an aspirational goal that may be a bit harder to imagine if you come from humble beginnings. The process may be harder and will probably take even longer. It may get frustrating when you see that you don't have some things that other people were given. Just remember that you are running your own race.

Later in this chapter, I talk about superpowers and focusing more deeply on the things that you're good at.

Mindset over math

When I talk about the steps to build wealth or reach F.I.R.E., I can break it down to an easy formula, which is illustrated in Figure 3-1.

Increase these things:

>> Savings

>> Investing

>> Income

Decrease these things:

>> Debt

>> Taxes

>> Expenses

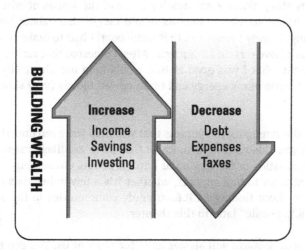

FIGURE 3-1:
The mechanics of
building wealth.

Before you start making increases and decreases, your first step is addressing your mindset. That part can prohibit everything else from flowing, so it's the initial piece to work on. It took me nearly two years to get my head around what F.I.R.E. really meant and that it was possible for me. Before that, there was no moving forward.

TIP

Some of us may be able to work on the mindset part ourselves, but it may also help to get support from friends, community, family, or maybe even a professional.

It often helps to look at the big picture. Step back and think about what lights you up and gets you excited (for some people, that's not a job). When you've identified that, you know what you're working toward. Your next step is coming up with a realistic time frame and determining the adjustments you're willing to make to achieve your goals.

Remember you have an amazing vision that you want to bring to life.

Obstacles in your journey

My journey came with lots of obstacles. At one point, I even felt that I was very unlikely to succeed in money and finances and would never reach F.I.R.E. That is what most of the statistics were telling me, anyway. I guess it's human nature to focus too much on the negative, and I still fall prey to that sometimes. A few of my obstacles were growing up poor, divorce, and becoming a single mom. I had a long list of adversities, and I think it was important for me to acknowledge that was part of my story. When I was hearing some of the stories of other F.I.R.E. people with six-figure salaries or parents who'd taught them about money when they were young, I knew I wasn't in that same boat. I had to make peace with the fact that I didn't have certain advantages. After I digested that reality, I thought more deeply about what I was good at that would help me financially and that was a much better use of my energy and brain power. Slowly (very slowly); it started to work.

Consider the strengths you possess that will help you overcome the obstacles that could get you sidetracked. Also, know that there are likely many other people in the same situation or facing similar hurdles as you. Connecting with others is one of the best ways to find support, whether it's a few individuals or a community. Read more about finding F.I.R.E.-friendly communities in the section "Finding Your F.I.R.E. People" later in this chapter.

Some type of obstacle will always exist for most of us. You can rarely change or anticipate all of them, but they don't have the power to destroy your well-laid-out plans to reach financial independence or retire early. View them as challenges and experiences you can learn and grow from.

Superpowers you can lean on

Put on your cape and take a moment to embrace your superpowers. Everyone has them — things that they excel at and are better at than most. It could be that you are a great negotiator, so you have saved thousands on things you've bought and have a higher salary because of it. Or it could be your digital marketing skills that provide for a lucrative side hustle.

It's human nature to think more about what we're not good at. I want you to fight that instinct. I want you to pause, open your mind, and think about the things that you're great at — no matter how small. Go ahead and explore, even make a brag list. That list will grow as you think deeply about superpowers that are not only valuable to you but to others as well.

I became very good at saving and investing and even enjoyed it. I didn't have to spend much time on budgeting because of my interest. I did a backward budget where I saved and invested my income first and then lived off what was left. I was always very conscientious about what I spent, but I didn't have to spend a lot of time each month working on my budget.

Some of your superpowers may come naturally or be something you've taken for granted. Maybe you live in a low-cost-of-living area, which has saved you thousands in housing costs that you can use in other areas in your life. Maybe you were able to get through college debt free and aren't saddled with student loans like many others.

This exercise gives you some space in your mind for positivity. The hope is that you'll realize some of your many strengths that impact your journey and will help you breathe a little easier.

Your measuring stick

Your idea of success is going to look very different than that of your friend, your neighbor, and any other person pursuing F.I.R.E. No two are the same. There is no true comparison between yourself and someone else because you will never truly know their full situation — just the highlight reels.

Seeing things through your unique lens is the only way to effectively measure your

>> Progress

>> Milestones

>> Success

Other people may have a different set of advantages and obstacles that will determine their approach. You need to make sure that you're using your own measuring stick for setting your goals and path to F.I.R.E. rather than using the measuring stick anyone else uses.

ANECDOTE

I had to look closely at some of the examples I was seeing from others. Even though I learned a ton from people telling their stories, a lot of the early tales I heard were from young (thirty-something), high-income people who didn't have kids. Things were very different for me in many ways. I paid attention to the information, but I had to make adjustments based on my situation. That's when I started seeing meaningful progress.

It can get frustrating if it feels like every story you hear is from people crushing it and far ahead of you. You're exposed to only a snippet of what their lives are like, but you are an expert on your own life and journey. There can be valuable nuggets from the stories of others, so just take away what is helpful to you and leave the rest.

Normalizing Conversations about Money

It didn't dawn on me just how taboo the topic of money is for most people until I started talking about my own finances. I openly shared things like my income, my expenses, my investments, even the details on my paycheck, and the responses I got were amazing. Most people think I'm crazy to be so free with the information. However, one group of people absolutely loves talking about money with me, and that's the F.I.R.E. community.

It's been energizing to have a group of people engaging in these conversations with me. And you know what? We learn a ton! Whether it was from confirmation of what I was doing or just honest and constructive feedback, it was valuable to me. So even though most people shy away from talking about money, the F.I.R.E. community is one group that invites money conversations every day.

ANECDOTE

In my family, it was not okay to talk about money except to say there was not enough. We didn't talk about things like my dad's paycheck and our bills. I've broken that cycle with my daughter; we talked about money all the time in our home. As a result, she is much more comfortable talking about money than most people.

There are many reasons why most people don't like to talk about money and why it's so taboo. Here are two:

>> There's often some shame and guilt around money.

>> Some people don't want to come across as bragging or comparing themselves to others.

If people can get past those concerns and start talking more about money topics, people might become a little wiser about their finances. You don't necessarily need to talk with strangers about how much you make, but things like how your credit score works or the different uses for a health savings account are harmless topics.

Here are a few tips on easing into a conversation about money topics:

>> Reference something that you saw in the news or read in an article, like housing prices being at historical highs. This could inspire a discussion about mortgage rates, cost of living in different areas, or property taxes that may help you or someone in the group.

>> Share a mistake that you made and ask others what they would have done or if they have any suggestions of how to tackle it the next time — for example, paying too much for a prescription medication that was not covered by your insurance or paying a monthly fee on a checking account.

>> Offer to help if you know a friend or a family member is having trouble with something such as negotiating their salary or understanding their company benefits.

As you start having these small conversations, they add up and compound your knowledge. The more you're willing to engage in discussions about money and encourage others without coming across as nosey or trying to compare yourself, the more you normalize these conversations.

Social media seems to be a place where a lot of people are willing to talk about money openly and even share updates about debt payoffs and net worth. When you get together with people, those topics shouldn't be off-limits. F.I.R.E. people do it, and I'd like to see the rest of the world normalize these conversations, too. Here are a few example to help normalize money conversations:

>> Talk to your kids when they get their first paycheck and explain how things like FICA and the other taxes work.

>> If it's a bad year for the stock market and your friends are talking about how much their 401(k) has gone down, mention that they should also look at the longer-term performance (such as three-year and five-year returns).

>> Help show your parents or grandparents how to add or change a beneficiary to a retirement or bank account.

Another area that can certainly help is teaching kids about money in school. In the U.S., there's a big push by many states to require high school students to have completed a personal finance course before graduating. As of 2023, nearly half of the 50 states have passed laws requiring it. I think that's a great way to create a foundation of talking about money from a young age.

Finding Your F.I.R.E. People

F.I.R.E. is better with friends, but what if you don't have any who want to share this journey with you? That would not be unusual. I didn't have any friends in real life who were remotely interested in personal finance when I first started on my journey.

Luckily the movement has grown, and there are plenty of places to find like-minded people, both online and in person. Just about every online platform has some type of F.I.R.E. community, forum, or group so that you can connect with others. Beyond online connections, there are now many in-person events and gatherings that can provide even more support.

Community is a huge component of F.I.R.E., and I have found that most people are extremely generous with their time and knowledge. I'm a teacher at heart, and I try to share my knowledge readily. If you keep looking, you will eventually find the right people or groups who feed your growth and are assets along your path to F.I.R.E. In the following sections, I suggest some groups and communities that will help get you started.

F.I.R.E.-friendly online communities

Online communities are a big part of your support system while on your journey to F.I.R.E. Online communities became important during the pandemic when we were all staying home with limited in-person interactions. The friendships that begin online may (and often do) lead to real-life connections. I've met so many of my fellow money nerds this way, and you can, too. In this section, I share some that are worth checking out.

ChooseFI

ChooseFI (www.choosefi.com) is probably one of the first and largest F.I.R.E. communities online. Its podcast has been around for over five years and has a huge listener base. The hosts have interviewed just about every well-known F.I.R.E. luminary and F.I.R.E.-friendly expert out there. The podcast covers some advanced topics that will make you feel like you're in a master's level classroom but also breaks down the basics in many episodes that are listed in the Podcast Essential Listening Guide (www.choosefi.com/listen).

ChooseFI has a Facebook group that has grown to more than 100,000 members with lots of activity. There are conversations about every F.I.R.E.-related topic you can imagine. The group is worldwide and has members from the United States, Canada, Mexico, United Kingdom, Australia, and many other countries.

Catching up to FI

This site at https://catchinguptofi.com is a newer (2023) online community that focuses on an underserved group of late starters. They have a podcast that has quickly grown. They also have an active Facebook group filled with mostly Gen Xers but also lots of millennials who feel like they've gotten a late start on their F.I.R.E. journey.

This platform serves a niche community that has not been shown a lot of love because most of the media real estate seemed to be focused on either millennials or baby boomers. Gen Xers fall right in the middle, and this platform is filling the gap.

Mr. Money Mustache Forums

This forum (https://forum.mrmoneymustache.com) has been around for a long time and is an extension of the popular Mr. Money Mustache blog. Mr. Money Mustache is a rockstar in the F.I.R.E. community, and there are some diehard MMM followers. Unfortunately, the forum does not use any of the major social media platforms. Group members aren't just U.S. based and include many from other countries like Australia, Canada, and the U.K. Mr. Money Mustache himself has lived in Toronto, Canada.

Bogleheads

Bogleheads (www.bogleheads.org/forum) is a well-known forum that honors Vanguard founder, John C. Bogle. The discussion on the forums mostly focuses on low-cost index investing, but there is also discussion on many other related topics. Even though this forum preceded the third-party social media platforms and they host their own on the Bogleheads site, you can also find this community on other media platforms (podcast, YouTube, and so on).

TECHNICAL STUFF

According to the Bogleheads Wiki, there are more than 120,000 registered members, and the site receives an average of nearly 2,000 posts each day.

Niche communities that focus on just about everything else

There are many other niche communities all across social media platforms, such as Facebook and Reddit. Their niches are based on demographics such as

>> Gender

>> Generation

>> Ethnicity

>> Location

>> Stage of F.I.R.E. journey

>> Special interests, such as real estate or travel hacking

To find these niche communities, just start with your favorite social media platform and do a search for the type of F.I.R.E. group you're looking for.

F.I.R.E.-friendly in-person events and meetings

Online groups are great, and were especially valuable during the pandemic, but we're emerging from the virtual world. There are lots of in-person events that anyone seeking F.I.R.E. may enjoy. These aren't big companies or organizations, so you might not see them advertised or promoted heavily or at all. They are smaller events or group gatherings.

ChooseFI local meetups

This meetup was born out of the *ChooseFI* podcast. There are groups in almost every city in the U.S. and in many other countries including Canada and the U.K. They are organized locally, and each has its own flavor. Some of them have formal meetings each month with guests, and others are more social or casual gatherings.

The local ChooseFI group in my area does case studies that are very popular. Basically, someone in the group serves as the subject, and the rest of the group crowd-sources feedback. It's lots of fun to get to know others in your local area who are also part of the F.I.R.E. community.

Visit www.choosefi.com/community/find-your-local-group to find a meetup close to where you live

CampFI

CampFI meetups (`https://campfi.org/`) all around the U.S. are organized by the founder, Stephen Baughier. The accommodations vary by location, but the general description is a money camp for adults. It has an outdoorsy vibe with activities designed to bring together attendees to support them on the path to F.I.R.E. Attendees are at different places on their journey, including people who are enjoying their post-F.I.R.E. life.

All the camps have speakers, who tend to be some well-known F.I.R.E. voices. There have even been podcast episodes recorded at some of them.

The events are listed at `campfi.org`. My very first in-person F.I.R.E. event was at CampFI in Virginia. I walked away feeling so connected, and I made friends who I still remain very close to.

Camp Mustache

These camping experiences are smaller (less than 100 people) and usually sell out very quickly. They are held at a YMCA-type campsite where the attendees do a lot of outdoorsy stuff. They're held across the U.S. and in Toronto, Canada. I attended camps in Ohio and Toronto and loved them both!

The camps don't have anything to do with Mr. Money Mustache except that the organizers and attendees are followers of his famous F.I.R.E. blog. They are independently organized, and the speakers are not big, headlined content creators, but I think that adds to the intimacy of the event.

EconoMe Conference

This conference (`https://economeconference.com/`) with the funny name is dubbed as "a party about money." That's an appropriate description because it happens on the campus of the University of Cincinnati and has a cool vibe. (I may be a little biased here because I live in the area and spoke at the first event in 2020.)

The founder of this event is a diehard F.I.R.E. advocate, Diania Merriam. She financed the conference with her own funds, and I don't think she broke even the first year, but she stuck with it. It has grown since then (to about 500 people), and it's held at the same location each year.

Bogleheads Conference

This is an homage to Vanguard founder, John C. Bogle. He is considered the father of index funds, with the most famous among the F.I.R.E. community being VTSAX

(Vanguard Total Stock Market Index Fund). The Bogleheads Conference (https://boglecenter.net/conferences/) has grown over the years from just over 100 attendees in 2008 to about 500 attendees in 2023. The focus isn't exclusive to F.I.R.E. but on smart and simple investing. That is what attracts some F.I.R.E. people to the event.

The conference's speaker lineup in 2023 included a session on financial independence by the host of the *ChooseFI* podcast, Brad Barrett and Sean Mullaney (The FI Tax Guy), who are two favorites in the F.I.R.E. community (and are referenced in this book). Some of the other popular speakers were

- » Clark Howard (*The Clark Howard Show* podcast)
- » Christine Benz (Morningstar)
- » Jonathan Clements (HumbleDollar, https://humbledollar.com/)
- » Dr. Jim Dahle (White Coat Investor, www.whitecoatinvestor.com/)
- » Dr. Jordan Grumet (*Earn & Invest* podcast and author of *Taking Stock*)

ANECDOTE Attending this gathering was on my bucket list, so I decided to nerd out and attended the 2023 conference in Maryland. I had a great time and got to spend time with several of my F.I.R.E. and Boglehead friends. It was like killing two birds with one stone to be able to attend an informative event with super-smart people I look up to and admire. If you get a chance to go, it's quite an experience, and you will walk away feeling like you learned a ton.

Bogleheads also has chapters around the country that typically meet once a month to discuss the Vanguard-style of low cost index investing. Bogleheads are famous for the three-fund portfolio. However, the groups do discuss many other topics related to investing and personal finance. The age of participants in these groups tend to be a bit older than the typical F.I.R.E. crowd.

Catching Up When You Feel You're a Late Starter

The group that gets big media attention when it comes to F.I.R.E. are the millennials (people born between the early 1980s and the mid-1990s). Baby boomers (people born between the mid-1940s and mid-1960s) are considered traditional retirees. The demographic in-between these two groups are Gen Xers (mostly 40- and 50-year-olds), and that's where you find the people who feel behind on their journey to financial independence. Some even think that there is no way they'll be able to retire early. Though this is a very large demographic, many of them also feel overlooked. Even if you are younger than this age group (say in your 30s), you may still feel like you're lagging in your effort to retire early if you're not where you want to be on your journey. It's not only about age; it's also a state of mind and how you feel about your own situation.

In this section, I discuss using your own measuring stick, why late may still be earlier than you think, and the advantages you may have to help catch up.

Using your own measuring stick

REMEMBER

You've heard this before but I'll say it again for the people in the back: It's never too late to start!

If you feel like you got a late start, and you're too close to retirement to get the full benefit of things like compound growth, you have plenty of other tools to counterbalance that (discussed later in this chapter and in Chapter 18). Your priorities and time horizon may be a little different, but the goal of financial independence and retiring early is still within reach. This chapter is dedicated to you.

Arriving late to F.I.R.E. but still earlier than most

ANECDOTE

I was a late starter, traveling along my F.I.R.E. journey in my forties so that I could retire right before my 50th birthday. When some were reaching F.I.R.E. in their 30s, I was just waking up to my finances at 38. I just had to make adjustments according to where I was when I started. It's incredible how fast things progress when you really focus on a goal. By the time I was 47, I had reached my F.I. number of 25 times my expenses. Just a couple of years later, I retired from corporate America.

If you're a late starter, the worst that can happen is that you will improve your finances as you enter retirement, whether it's early, on time, or a little bit later than you wanted. To help give you some perspective, Table 3-1 shows the "normal" retirement ages for the U.S. and a few other countries:

The general magic numbers for the time it takes from starting to pursue F.I.R.E. to reaching the goal is right around 10 to 15 years. That of course is going to vary depending on things like your income, expenses, investments, and savings rate. You may be encouraged to know that it doesn't have to take the standard 30 to 40 years.

TABLE 3-1

Normal Retirement Ages as of 2020

Country	Normal Retirement Age
United States	67
Canada	65
Mexico	65
United Kingdom	66

Source: Organisation for Economic Cooperation and Development (OECD) (https://www.oecd-ilibrary.org/sites/304a7302-en/index.html?itemId=/content/component/304a7302-en)

Just having financial independence on your mind and trying to catch up probably puts you ahead of a large chunk of the population. In fact, here's a mind-blowing statistic from the most recent (2022) Federal Reserve Survey of Consumer Finances about retirement savings:

> The average retirement accounts balance for people age 45 to 54 is $115,000.

As mentioned earlier in this chapter, I consider myself a late starter. When I was 38, I just started waking up after my divorce. I honestly think that knowing I needed to catch up helped me run a little faster. It took me roughly 10 years to reach F.I.R.E. In my younger years, I had about a 10% savings rate because that is what I heard all the experts recommend. It was at least a starting point, and I'm glad I had saved something.

When I was entering my forties and feeling behind, I realized a 10% savings rate was clearly not enough. I doubled down on my savings rate and then quadrupled it to about 40%.

I felt behind for years, but I made enough meaningful changes to retire by 49, way before I ever imagined. Looking at the situation through a F.I.R.E. lens may make it seem like that's not very early, but compared to much of the rest of the population, it is quite early.

REMEMBER

If you assume you need 10 to 15 years to reach F.I.R.E., even if you are just starting to wake up about your finances at 50, you can still retire earlier than the normal age.

Using advantages to speed up your journey

If you're a Gen Xer in your 40s or 50s, I know you can probably think of a list of reasons your late start will make things tougher for you. I'll concede that you may have a point, but you have some advantages that you may not be aware of. Try a little reframing and look at the list of things that can be a boost for you:

>> **40s and 50s are peak earning years for most people:** At this age you are likely to be further along in your career with a much higher income than when you first started working. This higher income gives you more room to increase your savings rate, pay off debts, and engage in other wealth-building activities.

>> **You're beyond the bottleneck:** In the earlier years, there's typically a lot of competing priorities coming at you at the same time, and it creates sort of a bottleneck. Having kids, paying for day care, and being responsible for mortgage debt, student loan debt, and car loans all seem to happen around the same time. These obligations coupled with the lower salary for someone just starting their career is tough. But by the time you hit your 40s and 50s, these expenses may lessen, and this can free up more of your income.

>> **Rule of 55:** This is an IRS provision for certain employer-sponsored retirement accounts like 401(k)s and 403(b)s that allows you to make distributions after you separate from the employer and avoid the 10% penalty. This is different from IRAs and other retirement accounts where you must be 59.5 to make withdrawals without penalty.

>> **Being closer to Social Security age:** Your estimates (at www.ssa.gov/) are more accurate as you get closer to retirement age. You're also more likely to have accumulated the 35 years of earnings that Social Security uses to calculate your benefit amount. Really early retirees may not have that many years of work, and it translates to a slightly lower benefit.

There aren't many platforms specifically serving late starters, but I'm glad to see that's starting to change. This book talks a lot about how important community is, and that includes people that feel they are behind.

TIP

One of those communities is appropriately titled Catching up to FI (https://catchinguptofi.com/), which I talk about in the F.I.R.E-friendly online communities" section earlier in this chapter. They have a great podcast and private Facebook group. The conversation and topics all surround mindset, money, and life for late starters of any age on the journey to financial independence.

REMEMBER

Mindset and community remain a key part of getting and staying motivated on your journey. You may feel that you are late to F.I.R.E., but you have decades of life experiences that work to your advantage. You have a long career, connections, and relationships all working in your favor as you design your post-F.I.R.E. life.

2

Organizing Your Finances for F.I.R.E.

Discover that the most important numbers on your F.I.R.E. journey are your savings rate, F.I.R.E. number, and net worth.

Gain insight into the impact of taxes and credit on all the other aspects of your finances and how to make them work to your advantage.

Know how to find important financial information that will help you get a clear picture of where you're starting.

Understand the basics of planning your estate and simple steps to avoid the unfriendly process of probate.

Get clarity on the different financial professionals and modern compensation models that are compatible with DIYers and F.I.R.E. plans and figure out how to find the right fit for what you're looking for.

Embrace celebrating big and small milestones along your F.I.R.E. journey that will help you remain focused and feed your momentum.

Chapter 4

Knowing and Tracking Your Numbers

You may start this chapter feeling like you have no idea what your numbers should be for F.I.R.E., but you'll exit with your eyes wide open. As you get started on your F.I.R.E. journey, you probably have the same question as many others: "What should I do first?" You'll get many different answers, like

» Slash your expenses.

» Create a budget.

» Get a side hustle.

» Pay off all your debt.

None of those are bad suggestions, but the conflicting answers will probably confuse you even more.

The best first step is assessing where you are currently. Many people (including me) feel lost at first, and getting a true picture of where you're at and having the desire to improve is empowering.

You may have to take a deep breath if things don't look as rosy as you'd hope, but the real win is that you know your starting point. This will help you see the areas that require the most attention. If you have a lot of high-interest debt, reducing it may be the priority. If you have a lower income, figuring out how to generate more income may be the place to start. If you haven't started saving in a retirement account, that may need to be your initial focus.

REMEMBER

When you start taking action on your path to F.I.R.E., you can do more than one thing at the same time. For example, you can invest *and* pay off your debt; it's just a matter of how much you allocate to each. As you pay off the debt, you start putting more toward investing.

In this chapter, I walk you through the important numbers to know and track as you begin your F.I.R.E. journey, including

>> Earnings

>> Expenses

>> Debt

>> Savings rate

>> F.I.R.E. number

>> Net worth

Your Total Earnings

You aren't just what you earn, but your earnings start your wealth-building cycle. It includes more than what you get from a job. You may also have earnings from a side hustle, investments in a brokerage account, real estate investments, or royalties. All these sources add up to your total earnings.

Your total earnings are an important component to building the nest egg you need to achieve F.I.R.E., and you want to make sure to use this total number when calculating your savings rate (discussed later in this chapter).

When you're considering your earnings, there are a couple of different areas you want to be clear on regarding income: gross versus net and earned versus unearned.

Gross versus net

How much money do you make? When asked that question, you probably answer with the amount of your annual salary. That income amount is the *gross* amount, but that is not what you can spend, save, or invest. The amount you take home is your *net* amount. There is a big distinction between gross and net income, and you should know and track both.

Your gross income refers to the total amount of money you earn before any deductions are taken out, such as

- » Insurance
- » Income taxes
- » Social Security and Medicare taxes
- » Retirement contributions
- » HSA or FSA contributions

Your net income is what's left after these deductions have been taken out. It's your take-home pay.

Earned versus unearned income

You might think the term "unearned income" is kind of an oxymoron or that it's contradictory. Isn't all income earned in some way? It is, but types of income are viewed in different ways, especially when it comes to how they are taxed (more on the tax part in Chapter 15).

Here are the primary differences you should know. Earned income is money from working, like

- » Wages and salaries reported on a W-2 from a job
- » Self-employment
- » Certain small businesses income

REMEMBER

To make contributions to retirement accounts like IRAs and 401(k)s, you must have earned income like those in the preceding list.

Unearned income is money you receive without actively working in exchange for it. It comes from passive sources like income from investments, such as

- » Dividends or earnings from stocks or other investments
- » Interest or account bonuses from bank accounts
- » Rental income

>> Unemployment benefits

>> Royalties

>> Social Security

Your Total Expenses

The concept that expenses equal income is a wealth-prohibiting formula. To build wealth, you want to make sure that your expenses are *less* than your income. The bigger the gap, the more you have to save and invest.

When it comes to reaching your F.I.R.E. goals, managing your expenses plays a key role. You have more control over some expenses than others, so the following sections take a look at the difference between fixed expenses and flexible expenses.

Fixed

Fixed expenses are your basic bills that need to be paid every month. They are predictable and ideal for an automatic bill-pay program.

Typical fixed expenses are your

>> Rent or mortgage

>> Cellphone service

>> Insurance premiums

>> Car loan payments

>> Internet and streaming services

You may not be able to eliminate some of these expenses, but others are great candidates for reduction. Consider regularly shopping around for things like your insurance to make sure you're getting the best rates and keeping your costs down where you can.

Variable/flexible

Your variable (or flexible) expenses are costs that can fluctuate from month to month. They are often discretionary in nature, so you have some control over how much you spend on them. Here are a few good examples:

- » Groceries

- » Alcoholic beverages

- » Entertainment

- » Dining out

- » Travel

- » Utilities (electric, gas, water)

Many people in the F.I.R.E. community use their money-saving skills to find ways to minimize their variable expenses. In my case, I found some savings in my grocery expense. I had never bothered going to Aldi or Costco (even though Aldi was right around the corner) until I heard about them in one of my F.I.R.E. groups. I didn't need to be buying in bulk at Costco, but I hit up Aldi and was shocked at how much lower some of their prices were. So now I'm hooked.

REMEMBER

It's up to you where you want to cut, but make sure you aren't making yourself miserable.

Your Total Debt

Some people tend to duck and weave around their debt and avoid thinking about it. I understand. Debt is a drag. However, it's not something you can ignore. When you organize your debt, you not only figure out what your total debt is but you can also prioritize it and possibly pay it off sooner.

From a psychological standpoint, you will feel better once you know where you stand, and that uneasy feeling in the pit of your stomach may start to go away. This is a great area to track progress because seeing the debt go down makes you feel better.

REMEMBER

Also remember that as the debt gets paid off, it has a positive impact on your net worth, which I'll talk more about later in this chapter.

Types of debt (all debt is not created equal)

Because all debt is not created equal, you will want to know the ones that can cost you the most and be an impediment along your F.I.R.E. journey.

WARNING

High-interest debt includes credit cards and short-term loans (like payday loans), and it is probably the most detrimental and costs you the most. The longer this type of debt hangs around, the more it costs you because most of what you're paying is probably going to the high interest.

Low-interest or longer-term debt like a home mortgage is much more manageable and can be compatible with your F.I.R.E. journey. I consider anything less than the rate of inflation to be low.

In the middle would be a car loan, private student loans, or other similar loans, but they are still costing you. For these, there are refinancing options (typically without a fee) that could reduce your interest or the time it takes to pay off the loan. It may make sense to pay these off as agreed if you already have a reasonable rate.

Medical debt

Medical debt is one of the biggest causes of bankruptcy in the U.S. This type of debt often arises unexpectedly and can be significant. Also, if you're dealing with a medical issue, thinking about the bills for your care is the last thing you want to have to worry about. When you're better and start to deal with the bills, there are options to set up a payment plan (typically without a fee) with the different providers or to negotiate a lower price for paying a lump sum. Be sure to check for errors because those are rampant in the medical billing industry.

Federal student loan debt

The unique type of debt that I sometimes hear bad advice about are student loans. If you have a direct federal student loan, you have more generous provisions than any other type of loan, including

>> Special provisions declared by government (COVID pause)

>> Income-driven repayment

>> PSLF (public service loan forgiveness)

>> Loan deferment or forbearance

>> Forgiveness in the case of death or disability

So these federal student loans should not be treated like other loans. Many people just go with the default repayment option, which typically is the highest monthly payment, but you have a lot of flexibility with your repayment options, so investigate what's right for you.

TIP

Use the loan simulator at https://studentaid.gov/loan-simulator/ which allows you to look at your different options.

I recommend that you aggregate all of your debts and create a nice clean checklist like the one in Table 4-1 to make sure none fall off the radar. And if you've already done this, then bravo!

TABLE 4-1   **Debt Checklist**

Type of Debt	Checked
Credit cards	
Short term loans (payday loans)	
Car loans	
Mortgages	
Student loans	
Medical debt	

One last place to locate any debts you may have missed is on your most recent credit report. The stragglers that you may have overlooked may be found there.

TIP

Free credit reports from all three credit bureaus are now available every week at www.annualcreditreport.com/index.action. These free credit reports used to be offered only once per year, but as of October 2023, the Federal Trade Commission made it permanent to offer them weekly. Be sure to grab a copy from all three bureaus because there could be missing information or mistakes on one or more.

Interest rates

When evaluating your debts, one important piece is the interest rates. This will be one of the factors that will help you determine how to prioritize the debt.

Credit card interest rates are on every statement you receive, as well as on your initial credit card agreement (that almost no one reads). Note that there are typically different interest rates for cash advances and other activities. If you don't carry a balance and pay off the balance of your credit cards in full every month, you don't have to worry about interest rates.

Other types of loans should have the rates on their monthly statements, or you can log on to your account and check. Some types of debt may have variable interest rates, so be sure you are aware if the rate is subject to change.

If you are one of the brave heroes serving our country (or plan to be) make sure you are aware of the special interest rate provisions in The Servicemembers Civil Relief Act (SCRA). According to The Military Wallet (`https://themilitary wallet.com/`) SCRA offers military members to have interest rates reduced to 6% when you join the military or activated members of the Guard or Reserves. You will have to notify your loan servicer because they won't know otherwise.

Keep in mind that this interest rate reduction only applies to debts taken out before you enter active military service.

Prioritizing debt

There's lots of discussion around the best way to prioritize paying off debt. I don't get into that debate because the bottom line is that if you've decided to pay off the debt, you're in a great place.

The two most well-known ways to pay off debt are

» Snowball method, in which you pay off the smallest debts first

» Avalanche method, in which you pay off the highest interest rates first

From a mental standpoint, it may feel better to have quick wins and pay off smaller loans. However, if you want to do it based on what's going to save you the most money in interest, the avalanche method is the better option.

Keep in mind that if you have something like a 0% promo balance transfer credit card, you want to make sure you are clear on when that offer expires. If it's closer to expiring or it's going to shoot up to a higher rate, you will want to make it a higher priority and pay it off before the lower rate expires.

Here's my best tip to managing a 0% balance transfer credit card: Use the bill-pay service from your bank or credit union to set up automatic payments and nickname it something like "0% promo" and the expiration date. It's a monthly reminder when this offer expires.

Again, if it makes you feel better to have the quick wins and pay off the smaller loans, go for it. That may be what you need to motivate you to continue with your debt payoff. No matter what, getting your debt under control is going to help lighten your load as you navigate your F.I.R.E. journey.

Paying off the debt has a positive impact on your net worth and your F.I.R.E. number.

Your Savings Rate

I don't doubt that you will very quickly get your debt down to a manageable level and start to focus on the positive side of compounding: saving and investing. Your savings rate is probably the single most important number while you're on your F.I.R.E. journey.

This key metric has a few variations, such as using gross income versus using net income. But don't focus on comparing your savings rate with others; just stay consistent with how you track yours. The first thing is to know where you're starting. Calculate your current savings rate by dividing your total savings amount by your income.

EXAMPLE

Here's an example of saving $500/month ($6,000/year) on a $50,000 gross annual salary:

$6,000 / $50,000 = .12 (12%)

You'll become highly motivated when you see that 12% savings rate slowly (or quickly) rise to 30%, 40%, or maybe even a 50% savings rate.

A viral article called "The Shockingly Simple Math Behind Early Retirement" by Mr. Money Mustache talks about how the impact of a high savings rate is shocking to most people. He simply calls out how many years to retirement is reduced based on your savings rate.

Table 4-2 shows examples of how quickly you can get to retirement based on different savings rates. I used the handy calculator at http://networthify.com/. This example assumes an annual gross income of $80,000 with a 5% annualized investment return assumption.

TABLE 4-2

Years to Retirement Based on Savings Rate

Savings Rate	Years to Retirement
10%	51.4
20%	36.7
30%	28
40%	21.6
50%	16.6

Including savings, retirement, and other investments

The term "Savings rate" includes the classic emergency savings, which is one of the first places to start saving, but that's not all it covers.

Your savings rate also includes money you're investing and not spending, such as in a workplace retirement account, like a 401(k), 403(b), and so on, traditional IRA, Roth IRA, health savings account (HSA), brokerage account, or college savings.

Expressing savings rate as a percentage of gross or net income

People use different numbers to express the savings rate. Some people use gross, and others use net income. I don't know whether it really matters, as long as you're consistent and use the same number as you track your progress. When you use your gross income, you're obviously not including taxes and other deductions.

Here's the simple formula for your savings rate using gross income:

Savings Rate = (Total Savings ÷ Total Income) × 100

For example, if you earn $80,000 annually and save $20,000, your savings rate would be 25%:

Savings Rate ($20,000 ÷ $80,000) × 100 = 25%

If you use your net income, your savings rate may end up being a bit higher (because you're starting with a lower amount). This example assumes your net income is $60,000:

Savings Rate = ($20,000 ÷ $60,000) × 100 = 33%

The next time you see someone touting a 70% savings rate, remember that they may be using their net income rather than their gross.

Including employer match in the savings rate

Your employer may match your contributions to your retirement account. If you include your employer's contribution, just make sure that it remains consistent. Also, you should only include this if you are fully vested. Some employers require you be with the organization for a certain amount of time before the matching funds actually belong to you if you leave. When you reach this milestone, you're fully vested.

I typically do not include my employer match, but it's fine if you want to. If you count the contributions, your income will increase. Here's an example:

$80,000 with a company match of 5% is an additional $4,000

EXAMPLE

Continuing with the example in the previous section using gross income, here's the difference:

» **No company match:** Savings Rate = ($20,000 – $80,000) × 100 = 25%

» **Using company match:** Savings Rate = ($24,000 ÷ $84,000) × 100 = 29%

Building the saving habit

Even if you are new to your F.I.R.E. journey and feeling like you don't have much to save, building the saving habit is still an important phase. The power of compound growth mainly comes from starting, even if it's small. If you've got only a 5% savings rate right now, don't throw up your hands just yet. No matter how little you begin with, make it automatic and stick to it. You are building a muscle that will serve you well later on.

As you improve your financial situation, make sure your savings inches up along with income increases. As you earn more, your savings rate will increase. As you pay your debt down, your savings rate will increase. Before you know it, you'll move from a 5% savings rate to 10%, then to 25%.

If you doubled your annual salary in six years and escalated your savings rate by the amounts listed in Table 4-3, you can see the impact it has.

EXAMPLE

TABLE 4-3 **Savings Rate Escalation**

Gross Income	Savings Rate	Saving Amount	Year
$40,000	5%	$2,000	First Year
$60,000	15%	$9,000	Third Year
$80,000	25%	$20,000	Fifth Year

Your Net Worth

Your net worth is one of the most important numbers to know because it paints a picture of your overall financial health. It is the value of your assets minus your liabilities:

Net Worth = Total Assets – Total Liabilities

ANECDOTE

The most powerful financial exercise I've ever done is figuring out my net worth. I was already in my 30s before I did my first one. I had all these numbers floating in my head: investment accounts, savings accounts, mortgage debt, and so on. The problem was, I never organized them or listed them all in one place and did the math. It took a few weeks to pull everything together because I didn't want to do it all at once. It turned out to be a fun exercise to find where my money was. Aggregating the debt was a little quicker task because luckily I only had two debts: my car loan and home mortgage.

I started tracking my net worth around 2012 before the cool apps came around, so I created a spreadsheet. I customized it throughout the years, and now I'm spoiled. It's hard for me to switch to an app that doesn't have all the information I'm used to seeing.

The debt section was very simple. I used these columns:

>> Type of debt

>> Amount

>> Interest rate

>> Projected payoff

You don't have to get nerdy like me, but here are the category headers I used for tracking my net worth:

>> Investment description

>> Tax treatment (Roth, traditional, other)

>> Purpose

>> Holding company

>> Tax at contribution

>> Tax at withdrawal

>> Amount

>> Date started

>> Last reviewed

>> Cost basis (the original amount you paid for an investment)

>> Growth

>> Comments

Feeling okay about starting in the red

You may be seeing red when you do your first net worth statement. When you see the number, you'll probably have one of two feelings:

>> Feeling happy because your net worth is better than you thought

>> Feeling sad because you're in the negative

Don't get bummed if you are starting with a negative net worth because you just did something great by figuring out your starting point. That's still a win. Now you know clearly where you are. From here, it's nothing but up and to the right as you pay off debt and build up your savings and investments.

If you're starting in the negative, your first big milestone may be getting to a positive net worth. Moving the needle is worth celebrating, and you will pick up speed quickly.

TIP

You can update it as often as you like. I was so excited to see my net worth growing that I started tracking it monthly. After a little bit, I scaled back to doing it quarterly. Since I retired, I've been tracking it annually.

TIP

There are some calculators and resources at the end of this chapter in the "Calculators and Tools" section that will help you very easily start and keep track of your net worth.

Assessing your assets

Assets are what you own, from your retirement account at work to your emergency fund savings account. I gave myself a high five every time I found another account to add to my assets. I figure I may not have ever remembered certain accounts if I hadn't done the exercise of listing them all in one place. So as you are doing this, consider these to be lots of little wins.

Here are some common assets to make sure you include

>> Retirement account at current employer

>> Retirement account from old employers

>> Pensions (even if they have been frozen)

>> Stock options or other vested equity compensation

>> Traditional/Roth IRA

>> Brokerage account

>> HSA account

>> College savings

>> Treasury securities

>> Bank accounts (savings/money market/CDs)

>> Real estate

>> Vehicles

REMEMBER

Assessing your assets and calculating your net worth is an essential part of understanding your overall financial health.

Limiting your liabilities

Limiting your liabilities doesn't mean you have to eliminate all your debt. For many, this is a big source of stress. Once paid off, they just sleep better at night knowing that they have rid themselves of all their debt. That is totally fine if you have the means to do so. But I don't want you to think that to reach F.I.R.E. means that you have no debt at all.

ANECDOTE

Remember, there is more than one approach to F.I.R.E. I retired from my corporate job with a mortgage because it had a very low interest rate (around 3%), and I had plans to move. After taking those two things into consideration, I decided that I did not want to pay it off. Your conclusion may be different, but the point is to do it with thought and intentionality.

TIP

I consider a low interest rate to be less than the rate of inflation (typically 4% or lower).

ANECDOTE

In 2009, I planned to purchase a car with cash. I still checked out interest rates for car loans, and I was able to get a 1.99% rate for a five-year loan, which is almost unheard of. I took the loan and didn't touch the invested funds that I had planned to use to pay cash for the car.

High-interest debt, such as credit cards, is another story. This is something you want to make a high priority to pay off because rates can be 25% or more.

So just be sure to evaluate whatever liabilities you have and then be proactive about deciding whether to keep them. If you keep it, estimate your payoff date and have a plan.

Your F.I.R.E. Number

Your F.I.R.E. number is a bit different from your net worth, and sometimes people confuse the two. The primary difference is that your F.I.R.E. number includes only investable assets that you can draw from. That means it would *not* include things like

>> A home that you live in

>> A vehicle

You would, of course, include money in your retirement accounts, brokerage accounts, and savings accounts.

Once you have this pile of money, you would simply apply the 4% rule.

REMEMBER

This is just a guide (consider it a rule of thumb) because it will vary based on factors like investment returns, changes in expenses, and unexpected life events. Some people think it should be 3.5% and others think it should be 4.5%, but the idea is that you can safely withdraw approximately 4% of your portfolio balance each year to cover expenses with a low likelihood of the money running out in retirement.

It will be essential to review and adjust your F.I.R.E. number as needed.

Obviously, if you retire early, you will have many more years than the typical 20-30-year retirement, but it's going to vary based on things like what your allocation is. Do you have mostly stocks? Do you have a lot of bonds? What other income, such as Social Security or a pension, do you have that's going to offset your expenses. And don't forget about the human capital where you could decide to work a little, or to do some passion projects that bring in money. All of these factors are going to affect how much you need to withdraw.

As you get closer to reaching F.I.R.E., these things will become clearer to you, but early on, doing the 25 times your expenses will give you the reference point you need to move forward.

Planning for 25 times your expenses (not your income)

Most financial professionals will talk about the number that you need to retire in terms of your income. Well, that might not always be representative of your spending in retirement, especially if you have a high savings rate like most F.I.R.E. people do. A more accurate way is to look at your expenses.

I think one thing that attracts a lot of people to F.I.R.E. is the simplistic things that we look at. To come up with this number, you simply multiply 25 times your expected expenses in retirement. You may also want to include taxes in your expenses.

EXAMPLE

Here's a quick example:

>> $50,000 in expenses (includes taxes)

>> Multiplied by 25

>> Equals $1,250,000

Even my 12-year-old niece can do this on the back of a napkin.

REMEMBER

This number represents your expenses in retirement, which could be slightly different than your expenses today. It may be lower or higher. If you're retiring early and you want to visit all the fabulous countries on your bucket list or take on some home improvement projects, your expenses may be more.

This is not going to be perfect math, and it will get more accurate as you move closer to F.I.R.E. Your number may change over time, but you need some type of starting or reference point.

Keep in mind that your F.I.R.E. number would also be reduced by any other type of income that you have to cover your annual spending. For instance, if you have annual passive income of $10,000, then that's $10,000 less per year you need to factor in. This is especially helpful when you get to your older years, and you possibly have things like Social Security, pension, or other types of income in retirement to offset what you need to pull from your nest egg.

Giving yourself a cushion

On this F.I.R.E. journey, I declare that precision is not required! So, what do you do instead when you can't get perfection? You simply give yourself a little more cushion — sort of a buffer for things that could go wrong.

Here are a few examples of how you might create a buffer:

>> Using 30 times your expenses instead of 25 times

>> Having income that helps offset your expenses in retirement (such as passion projects you get paid for)

>> Not including Social Security for the later retirement years (which most in the F.I.R.E. community don't include any way)

Calculators and Tools

We covered a lot of numbers, so take a long, deep breath and then slowly exhale. You're much wiser for getting to know your numbers and why they matter on your F.I.R.E. journey.

The best part is that there is no shortage of easy ways to help you figure out and track your financials. You may also want to create your own. After all, many F.I.R.E. people (including me) love their spreadsheets. The community is also very generous, so many of the spreadsheet gurus will share what they have developed.

TIP

The coolest tool is one at the Mad Fientist website (www.madfientist.com/) that he calls the *FI Laboratory*. It's a web application he developed that contains useful tools to help you on your journey to financial independence and early retirement.

Here's a list of other F.I.R.E. calculators and apps to help you organize and track your numbers:

>> FIRECalc (https://firecalc.com)

>> Playing with FIRE calculators (www.playingwithfire.co/calculators)

>> YNAB (You Need A Budget) (www.ynab.com)

>> Dinkytown (made major updates in 2023) (www.dinkytown.net/)

>> Empower (formally Personal Capital) (www.empower.com/)

More calculators and money tracking resources can be found in the Cheat Sheet online at www.dummies:com.

Chapter **5**

Understanding How Taxes and Credit Scores Work

What's that saying? *Nothing in life is guaranteed except death, taxes, and a check of your credit score.* Okay, I slid in the credit score part, but it's another thing that seems to seep into just about every part of our financial lives now.

I've found that taxes and credit are two subjects woven throughout most areas of our financial lives and deserve a chapter of their own. They both can be your best friend or your worst enemy on your path to F.I.R.E.

When deployed effectively, both can be powerful allies, but there's a sea of confusion where I don't want you to get stuck. In this chapter, I give you key terminology and fundamental understanding around the major areas of taxes and credit because both will come up often as you organize your finances for F.I.R.E.

Reviewing Tax Rates

If you've ever felt lost or intimidated when it comes to taxes, you're not alone. If you skip over the basics, it's nearly impossible to follow anything else that comes after.

But after you retire — or even if you take a short break (like a sabbatical) — from work, the tax aspect of your finances presents some unique opportunities because you will have more control over the flow of your income. So I want to step back and give you a good look at how tax rates work in these key areas:

>> Income tax (federal, state, local)

>> FICA tax (payroll tax)

>> Capital gains/losses

The annual ritual of tax returns is when all these areas can bubble up and consume your attention (whether you use a pro or DIY). Thinking about this kind of stuff only at tax time won't do much good, but if you're more aware of it all the time, you can use it as a tool for planning for F.I.R.E.

Federal and state income tax

Federal tax rates have been very friendly since 2018 because of the Tax Cuts and Jobs Act (TCJA), which lowered tax rates.

TECHNICAL STUFF

The Tax Cuts and Jobs Act (TCJA) is major tax legislation that was passed at the end of 2017 for business and personal taxes. The changes with business taxes were made permanent, but the personal tax changes are scheduled to expire at the end of 2025.

Personal tax rates range in brackets from 10 to 37 percent. The amount of income for each bracket goes up each year and depends on your filing status:

>> Single filers

>> Married filing joint returns

>> Heads of households

WARNING

These lower rates are scheduled to expire in January 2026 and will revert to previous rates of up to 39.6 percent.

It's hard to totally get away from paying federal income tax. However, depending on where you live, you may be in luck as not everyone has to pay state or local taxes. So, if you're looking to implement a little tax-focused geo-arbitrage (taking advantage of lower costs of living in an area other than where you currently live), just keep that in mind. For example, states like Florida, Tennessee, and Texas look very attractive to some F.I.R.E. people because those states don't impose a state income tax.

TIP

As of 2023, there were a total of nine states with no state income tax:

>> Alaska

>> Florida

>> Nevada

>> New Hampshire (earned income only)

>> South Dakota

>> Tennessee

>> Texas

>> Washington

>> Wyoming

TIP

Be sure to check your state or locality for the most current tax rules.

Most other states rely on state income tax to fund state budgets. There is a similar structure for local jurisdictions, but it generally will have a lesser impact than state or federal taxes.

WARNING

State or local areas without any income tax usually make up the lost revenue with other ways to raise revenue from their residents, such as higher sales tax or property tax.

Adding up the federal, state, and local income taxes can have a significant impact on your F.I.R.E. planning. Think of taxes as an expense, and plan for them with eyes wide open. Become well versed with how they work and factor them into your financial picture.

Figuring out FICA and payroll taxes

FICA (Federal Insurance Contributions Act) is a four-letter word we all hate seeing when it comes to taxes. No one wants to pay it.

TECHNICAL STUFF

FICA funds the U.S. Social Security and Medicare programs. Social Security is a social insurance program that offers income support to eligible retirees, survivors, and people with disabilities. Medicare is a health insurance program that provides coverage for eligible individuals, primarily those age 65 and older, but also certain individuals with disabilities.

If you have a job where you get a W-2, FICA is taken care of through your paycheck. You pay half the tax and your employer pays the other half. Table 5-1 shows how FICA tax breaks out.

You pay 6.2 percent of your gross earnings, and your employer pays 6.2 percent as well. Social Security has an income threshold that changes each year (for 2023, the cap was $160,200). However, there is no maximum income when it comes to Medicare.

TABLE 5-1   **FICA Tax Breakdown**

Payroll Tax	Employee Amount	Employer Amount	Total	2023 Income Cap
Social Security	6.2%	6.2%	12.4%	$160,200 (adjusted annually)
Medicare	1.45%	1.45%	2.9%	None
Total	**7.65%**	**7.65%**	**15.3%**	

If you're self-employed, you pay both the employee and employer portions, totaling 12.4 percent for Social Security and 2.9 percent for Medicare.

TECHNICAL STUFF

For high earners, there is an additional 0.9 percent Medicare tax on income above a certain threshold ($250,000 for married filing jointly, $125,000 for married filing separately, and $200,000 for all other taxpayers in 2024). This tax is only paid by employees and not matched by employers.

I know it may seem like FICA taxes go into a black hole for a long time, but later on some of that actually comes back to you in the form of

>> Social Security (as early as age 62 for retirement benefits)

>> Medicare (starting at age 65)

Many F.I.R.E. people may hope to retire earlier than their 60s. However, you'll still have a nice long life to enjoy these later-in-life benefits, so don't count them out. You are required to pay into the FICA system so why not get at least a partial return on your contributions?

It's important to note that tax rates and income thresholds may change over time due to legislative updates, so it's essential to check the most current information for accurate calculations at www.ssa.gov.

Considering the long and short of capital gains in brokerage accounts

Something that used to confuse me was long- and short-term capital gains. I thought they applied to my retirement account. I'm probably not the only one who is confused by this.

A capital gain is an investment that increased in value, and you sell it for a more than you put in.

Before you look at long-term and short-term capital gains, remember it has nothing to do with your retirement accounts, such as your traditional or Roth IRA. Those are handled completely differently.

If you have money to go into a brokerage account (which I think is a powerful account to have, by the way), there are some unique advantages and lower tax rates that you could potentially take advantage of if you hold the asset for more than 12 months. This will essentially lower the amount of money going to the IRS and increase what you get to keep in your pocket and in your investments.

Qualified dividends also receive these lower tax rates, but they do not need to be held for more than 12 months.

In the U.S., capital gains on investments held in brokerage accounts are categorized into two types: long-term capital gains and short-term capital gains.

Here's a quick example:

You purchased an index fund in your brokerage account for $3,000. Four years later, it grew to $4,500, and you sold it. That means it increased by $1,500 ($3,000 – $4,500), so $1,500 is your capital gain amount (long-term because you had it more than a year).

The distinction between long-term and short-term is significant because they determine how these gains are taxed. Table 5-2 gives an overview of each.

Assets that you hold in your brokerage account for a year or less will be taxed at whatever federal income tax bracket you are in (up to 37 percent in 2024), so there's no advantage there.

TABLE 5-2 **Capital Gains**

Type	Holding Period	Rates
Short-term	A year or less	Regular (ordinary) income tax rates
Long-term	Longer than a year	0%, 15%, 20%

However, if you hold the asset for more than a year, that puts you in the sweet spot of possibly paying 0 percent capital gain taxes. The most you would pay is 20 percent. Compare that to up to the 37 percent tax bracket for regular income types, and you can see why it's such a big deal!

The income brackets for long-term capital gains rates depend on your filing status:

>> Single

>> Married filing jointly

>> Married filing separately

>> Head of household

Table 5-3 shows an example of long-term capital gains rate for single filers. You can check the most current information and other filing statuses at www.irs.gov/taxtopics/tc409.

TABLE 5-3 **2024 Long-Term Capital Gains Rates (Single)**

Tax Rate	Income Bracket
0%	$0 to $47,025
15%	$47,026 to $518,900
20%	Over $518,900 or more

Using the example in Table 5-3, the smart F.I.R.E. strategy would be to get your taxable income less than $47,025 (single filer) and pay 0 percent in long-term capital gains for any assets you have held more than a year in your brokerage account. This may not be possible if you're still working, but after you retire, this can be a powerful way to minimize or avoid taxes.

Keep in mind that long-term capital gains are still included as part of your taxable income rather than being separate from them.

One additional nuance to long-term capital gains is that there may be an additional 3.8 percent tax called Net Investment Income Tax (NIIT) for high earners (example: single filers with a modified adjusted gross income over $200,000 or married couples filing jointly over $250,000). The number for this extra NIIT tax is not adjusted for inflation.

Tax laws change, so be sure you check for the most updated information (especially when it comes to rates). Your tax filing software or tax professional should keep up with the most current information so that you don't have to.

Winning at losing in your brokerage accounts

No one likes to lose, but if an investment didn't work out quite as well as you thought, you might as well get a little something out of the deal. You can offset a capital gain by selling another investment at a loss, which can potentially reduce your overall tax liability. That's where a little something called "capital losses" can be very beneficial.

You may also see this referred to as "tax loss harvesting."

Of course, the IRS is going to limit the amount of the capital loss you can deduct but if you can get a few coins from a bad investment, you're all the better.

Capital losses offset capital gains. If the net result is still a loss, you can take up to $3,000 to offset other income in the current year. Any unused net loss carries over to the next year to offset future capital gains.

Capital gains rules apply to any platform you have a brokerage account with, including trading apps like the following:

>> Robin Hood

>> Acorns

>> Stash

Tax laws and regulations can change, so be sure to check www.irs.gov (or your favorite tax resource) for the latest.

Getting help with understanding tax rates

Understanding the basics of how your tax rates work can help you maximize a significant chunk of your expenses that many times get overlooked. There are a lot of different tax rates and concepts around them, and you may still be scratching your head.

TIP

There are calculators that can help make it easy to estimate your taxes if you'd like to practice a little. Although www.irs.gov has some good calculators, here are a couple of platforms that are a bit more user-friendly:

>> Dinkytown.net (www.dinkytown.net)

>> Nerd Wallet (www.nerdwallet.com/h/calculators/
   financial-calculators)

Chapter 15 dives into how you can take these basics and apply them on your F.I.R.E. journey.

Capitalizing on Credit Scores

Having a high credit score (740+) can help reduce your expenses indirectly. If you have a high score, you may enjoy the benefits of your good credit and not think much about it, but for someone with a low score, there are painful reminders of the negative ramifications (being denied credit, paying higher interest rates on loans, and so on).

A higher credit score can potentially save you thousands on your F.I.R.E. journey in several different ways:

>> A higher credit score means a lower interest rate on things such as credit cards, car loans, or mortgages.

>> A higher credit score may mean lower rates for your insurance.

>> A higher credit score gives you the best shot of getting approved for rewards credit cards.

Brief basics of credit scores

Once upon a time, your credit would only be checked if you were applying for a loan or line of credit. Not anymore! Now people are poking their noses in your credit all over the place. Here are just a few reasons your credit may be checked:

>> Joining the military

>> Getting and maintaining a security clearance

>> Getting property insurance (car, home)

>> Renting a home or an apartment

>> Applying for a job (typically in financially related role)

>> Getting services like internet, cell, utility, and so on

Credit scores are one of the early topics covered in personal finance, and education about them is widely available. Your credit score is a number you want to keep track of because it can change daily. Before conducting any activity for which you know your credit will be checked, you should know where you stand.

There is no shortage of where you can easily get and monitor your score for free, including

>> Free credit score apps (like Credit Karma)

>> Credit card accounts (usually with your monthly statement)

These and many other resources also provide credit education (such as www.annualcreditreport.com or www.consumerfinance.gov).

WARNING

Be aware of places that claim to offer your credit score for free when they actually charge a fee. If you are asked to enter your credit card information or a site mentions a free trial, it's not giving you the information for free.

There are many different scoring models but most range from 350 to 850. The super achievers may want to get to that top score in the 800s, but in this case, close is good enough. Typically, you're going to get the best interest rates if your score is higher than 740. You don't get bonus points for having an 850, so your goal is to get and keep a 740 or above.

TIP

Your score fluctuates and varies (slightly) from one credit bureau to another because creditors don't report to the bureaus in the same way. Even though there can be variation, it should not be a difference of more than 20 or 30 points. If it's much more than that, be sure to thoroughly review each of your reports to figure out why the difference is more significant.

The three primary credit bureaus are

>> Equifax (www.equifax.com)

>> TransUnion (www.transunion.com)

>> Experian (www.experian.com)

The two categories that have the greatest impact on your credit score are payment history and the amount of available credit you're using, which account for 65%. There are different scoring models, but the most common weighting for each category, as shown in Figure 5-1, is

>> Payment history: 35 percent

>> Amounts owed across different types of accounts: 30 percent

>> Length of credit history: 15 percent

>> New credit: 10 percent

>> Types of credit: 10 percent

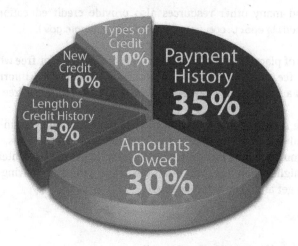

FIGURE 5-1:
Credit score
categories.

Photo credit: gemstock/Adobe Stock Photos

The wide availability of free credit scores doesn't negate the need to check the details of your credit reports because they can be marred with mistakes that can drag your score lower. You can get your free credit report from `www.annual creditreport.com` (the official site authorized by U.S. federal law).

It used to be that you could only get credit reports from each bureau once a year, but in 2023, the Federal Trade Commission (FTC) announced the permanent change to offer those reports every single week. I don't know if they'll change the URL from "annual" to "weekly," but it's a friendly nudge to you and other consumers to check your reports more frequently — for free.

What helps improve your score

Creating good habits with your credit from the beginning is much easier than fixing it after it's been hurt. Most people have made mistakes with their credit, especially when they were in the dark about their scores before they became widely available for free. The following are a few tips on things that can help, but remember that the impact on your credit score depends on your unique credit history:

>> **Make all payments on time:** The easiest way to do this is to set up auto bill pay of at least the minimum required payment. If you overlook a payment or forget about when it's due, you'll at least have the minimum payment covered and won't have a missed payment. Schedule these to be delivered at least five days before the due date to give yourself a buffer. The goal here is to keep making on-time payments 100 percent of the time.

>> **Keep your credit utilization ratio low:** This is the most impactful action to your "amounts owed" category. You want to keep your usage of revolving credit below 30 percent. Lower is better. This becomes much easier as you have more available credit.

I remember my first credit card when I was in college had only a $500 limit. My usage stayed very close to the limit. It seemed impossible to get to a 30 percent. utilization. Now that I have a lot more available credit, I can easily keep the utilization at 10 percent or lower.

>> **Maintain a mix of credit accounts:** A mix of credit types, including credit cards, auto loan, student loans, and mortgages, can have a positive impact on your credit score. This only accounts for 10 percent of your credit score, so don't feel like you need to get new loans or credit cards just to improve your mix.

>> **Review and monitor your credit reports and scores:** Use the free resources I mention at the beginning of this section to keep track of your score. Set up alerts so that you're notified of changes with your score. Now that www.annualcreditreport.com offers free reports every week, you can review your reports regularly. If you are applying for a large loan such as a mortgage or home equity loan, be sure to check your report from all three bureaus.

>> **Be careful about closing credit card accounts:** Keeping older credit accounts open can have a positive effect on your credit. The exception here may be if there is an annual fee or if that open line of credit is too tempting for you. Just make sure that you assess how that closure will impact the other factors of your credit (utilization and length of credit history).

What hurts your score

Not all activities carry the same weight, so isolating exactly what is hurting your score is critical. Identifying the negative influences will give you a clearer path to the areas you need to work on. The most likely suspects that can bring down your score include the following:

>> **Missed or late payments:** Remember that payment history is the single biggest factor in your credit score (35 percent). Even one late payment can cause your score to drop. While a 98 percent is an awesome grade in school, when it comes to your credit score payment history, that is not a great number to have. The longer the payment is missed, the greater the impact.

>> **High credit utilization rate:** Once you get above 30 percent of your available credit (also called credit utilization ratio), you have what's considered a high balance, and it will start to hurt your score. If this is temporary and you are planning to pay it off, your credit score will bounce back once you do. An example is a 0 percent interest balance transfer credit card offer. Maybe you decide to get a new roof and instead of paying cash, you get a 0 percent interest balance transfer card for 18 months.

>> **Closing credit accounts:** The act of closing credit card accounts alone may not hurt your score, but it will impact the following areas:

- It can shorten your length of credit history if it's an older card.

- It will reduce your available credit and cause your credit utilization to go up.

>> **Defaulting on loans or credit cards:** If you default on a loan, like an auto loan, personal loan, or mortgage, it can severely damage your credit. This will take time to recover, and you should work with the creditor to resolve the issue.

>> **Collection accounts:** When an account goes into collections due to non-payment, it can be reported on your credit report and have a negative impact. These accounts can include utility bills and cellphone services. These types of accounts typically don't report to the credit bureaus when you pay on time, but if don't pay they may report it and damage your credit.

>> **Negative public records:** Certain legal actions that are public records end up on your credit report, such as bankruptcy, judgments, tax liens, foreclosures, and repossessions. Court-ordered payments that are delinquent can also end up on your credit report.

How to fix a failing score

On your path to F.I.R.E., having a high credit score can save you lots of money along the way and accelerate your pace. But what happens when you have a less than stellar score? You fix it. This section will help you get started. Here are a few tips:

>> **Review your credit reports and scores.** You may have already checked your score and know that it is low and needs work. Knowing where you are starting when you want to heal your score is the first step and that means getting your reports from all three bureaus at www.annualcreditreport.com. You can get your current scores using the resources I mention earlier in this section.

>> **Dispute errors.** Your quickest hits are going to come from carefully reviewing your credit reports for errors, or fraudulent activity. Dispute anything that is not accurate by following the process of the credit report you are viewing. Look for things like:

- Medical debts (new rules went into effect in 2022 that limit these types of debt on your credit report)

- Old debts that are beyond the statute of limitations for your state

- Debts that don't belong to you

- Debts with incorrect amounts or late/missing payments

>> **Understand the problem areas.** Identify the factors that are negatively affecting your credit score. The biggest issues include late payments and high credit utilization ratios. There can also be a judgment, lien, or other negative public record that you may need to address. This will help you direct your efforts in the right area.

>> **Make all future payments on time.** If late or missing payments are bringing your score down, start making all your future payments on time. Use auto bill pay for the minimum amount as I mention earlier in this section. As the new payments are made on time, the old, missed payments will start to carry less weight. You can also set up reminders through you creditor to reduce the chances of a missed payment even more.

>> **Reduce credit card balances.** If a high credit utilization ratio is bringing your score down, make a plan to pay down the balance in a realistic way. If you have a lump sum to make a big dent all at once, that would be best. If not, just make consistent payments to get down to a lower ratio.

>> **Negotiate with creditors.** If you're struggling with payments, consider reaching out to your creditors to discuss lower interest rates or payment plans. Start by asking for a 0 percent interest rate and go from there. You may be surprised at what they're able to do.

>> **Become an authorized user.** This one can be tricky, especially if you are trying to make improvements on your own. If you have a spouse, trusted family member or friend with a good credit history, they can add you as an authorized user on their credit card. You will take on characteristics of the card (payment history, available credit, and so on). If it remains positive, then it can help your score. Conversely, if there is anything negative that happens with the card (missed payments, maxing out the card, and so on) you will take on those characteristics as well. The basic information from the card should show up on your credit report. Not all credit cards report authorized users so be sure to check with the credit card company.

Remember that you do not need to actually have the card in your possession to be an authorized user. Also, each credit card company may handle authorized users differently.

>> **Get some credit education.** The more you know, the more you grow. As you work on improving your credit, you'll be educating yourself in the process. You can find extensive credit score resources at www.consumerfinance.gov/ or use your preferred platform for learning (podcast, YouTube, blogs) to find a trusted credit educator who resonates with you.

>> **Track your progress:** Regularly check your credit scores and reports so that you can track your progress. Have an ideal credit score you want to reach or the number of points you want to increase your score. Some apps will allow you to set up alerts to get notified whenever your credit score changes.

>> **Celebrate wins:** Your hard work deserves to be celebrated, so as you hit milestones along the way be sure to give yourself credit!

WARNING

Be aware that credit repair and debt management scams are common, so be cautious of anyone promising fast fixes requiring upfront fees. If you are considering professional help, start with a nonprofit organization called the National Foundation for Credit Counseling (www.nfcc.org/).

Keeping your credit score in great shape strengthens your financial health and will help fuel your F.I.R.E. journey. Even if you don't have the best credit today, you can fix that using the tips in this chapter. Remember how tightly credit is woven into the other areas of your financial life.

Chapter **6**

Getting Your Hands on Documents and Account Information

E ver heard of the KonMari Method of organizing? It's a method created by organizing expert Marie Kondo with an approach that not just tidies up by getting rid of things but keeps the things that spark joy. You may not have her skills, but you can use a similar method to inventory and organize your financial life, sparking a little F.I.R.E. joy of your own.

In the early stages of your F.I.R.E. journey, gathering financial account information is an exercise that will give you greater clarity and insight into your situation, and you may even discover some funds you didn't know you had. If you're already on top of things, this may become a short checklist for you, but it's common to forget about something until you try to put things in order, so perhaps the list will jog your memory about an account or document you've forgotten or lost track of.

In this chapter, I guide you through how to track down important information and pull together documents from old retirement accounts, tax returns, and insurance coverages. You'll also learn how to locate loan information, how your major assets are titled, how to get information about your Social Security earnings, and how to handle rights and royalties.

Old Retirement Accounts

The most common accounts people forget about are retirement accounts from a former employer, such as a 401(k), 403(b), or pension (even if it was frozen). When you leave a job, you may have money that was contributed by your employer or that you contributed, even if you were auto-enrolled into the retirement plan without realizing that contributions were being deducted from your paycheck. Either way, gathering the information for these accounts ensures that you aren't leaving money behind that rightfully belongs to you. This section gives you tips on finding and securing money you may have left behind.

Accounts from previous employers

Do you consolidate and manage your various retirement accounts from old employers? Many people don't and end up leaving them behind.

TECHNICAL STUFF

Research shows that the average person changes jobs 12 times in their working lifetime. That could mean a dozen different accounts scattered around.

You may not even recall that you left funds behind when you separated from some of your past employers, especially if you were there for a short time. Also, more employers are starting to automatically enroll new workers into their retirement plan within a few months of employment, so the fact that you have an account might escape your notice.

Retirement funds left behind by former employees can stay with the plan for decades before the company tries to find the rightful owner or turns the funds over to the state. I'd rather you find those accounts yourself and factor that money into your F.I.R.E. plan.

TIP

If you have no idea where to locate your old retirement accounts from a former employer, I can suggest some ways to help you with your treasure hunting:

>> Check for old statements in your e-mail or other files.

>> Contact the benefits department of your old employer.

>> Contact the plan sponsor of an old retirement account (using an old statement or other records).

>> Reach out to former coworkers or colleagues who may have information about the pension plan or the process they followed to access their benefits.

>> Search the National Registry of Unclaimed Retirement Benefits (www.unclaimedretirementbenefits.com), which can assist you in locating missing retirement accounts.

>> Search your state's unclaimed property division or www.missingmoney.com (a database that aggregates information from participating state unclaimed property programs).

>> Go to the Pension Benefit Guaranty Corporation (PBGC) directory (www.pbgc.gov) to search for unclaimed pensions.

Pensions

TECHNICAL STUFF

Most traditional pensions are considered "defined benefit plans," which means that the payout at retirement is predetermined and based on a specific formula (age and/or years of service).

You may have a "frozen" pension, but don't let that term confuse you. "Frozen" doesn't mean gone. It typically means new contributions have been stopped, but the balance continues growing at the rates stated in the plan documents. The money is still yours if it is vested (meeting all the terms as defined by the plan documents).

ANECDOTE

The pension with my former employer was frozen about eight years before I retired. Although I could not make any new contributions, my account still grew by a minimum of 4% per year. This type of guaranteed investment is unlike any of the other retirement accounts I have, so I appreciate the diversification that it adds.

Traditional pensions have mostly disappeared (or been frozen) in the U.S. except in government organizations and some unions. Even if you don't fulfill the number of years of employment to get the full pension, you may qualify to receive a portion.

It used to be that employers continued to hold the pension for you when you left the company but that is starting to change. Now there are two primary pension options:

>> **Lump sum:** Taking the full cash value amount, typically rolling it over to an IRA

>> **Monthly payments:** Taking a guaranteed monthly payment amount, paid to you for the rest of your life

It is more administrative work for the pension plan to have tons of small accounts of former employees. The plan or employer often makes efforts to reach out and remind you that you have the option to take a lump sum. If the account must remain with the employer, employees can easily forget about them as time goes by. If you have a pension that has to remain with your employer, do your best to keep track of the pension until it's time for you to withdraw the funds.

ANECDOTE

I have a small pension with the company I retired from in 2019, and I receive an annual notice that includes my pension options. So far, I have decided to leave it there, but I have been very tempted early on to take the lump sum and roll it over to an IRA. For now, I will just keep track of it and include the lump sum in my net worth.

WARNING

If you have the option to take a lump sum, it doesn't mean you should. Yes, taking the lump sum gives you immediate control and allows you to invest the funds on your own if you roll it over to an IRA, but there is no guarantee on how the investments will perform. You could be giving up a valuable option that will pay you a guaranteed fixed monthly amount for the rest of your life without the worry of investment performance.

REMEMBER

Just remember that taking monthly payout options can be very generous depending on the plan provisions. You can run all kinds of scenarios (usually through the pension plan's online portal) based on these factors:

>> Age of retirement

>> Joint and survivor (payments continue to the beneficiary after the pension holder dies, usually for spouses) versus single life (payments stop after the death of pension holder)

>> Period Certain (payments guaranteed to be made for a specific number of years — such as five or ten — regardless of whether the individual lives for the entire period)

>> Inflation adjustment

>> Beneficiary age (some even allow nonspousal beneficiaries)

TIP

Actuarially, the options end up being about the same based on normal life expectancy. The pension options don't factor in things like gender, ethnicity, or health conditions — all things that can make a difference in average life expectancy. However, you can use these factors to make your decision about what to do with your pension and that could give you an edge.

REMEMBER

This lump sum versus monthly payout decision typically does not need to be made right away. Whatever you decide, it's best to get a copy of the plan documents and your balance at the time you leave or make sure you have access to your pension account online if the provider has a web portal (as most now do).

If you think you have a pension with old employers that you've lost track of, try locating them by using one of the options listed in the previous section.

Other forgotten accounts

Aside from retirement accounts, there are various other types of financial accounts and assets that you may forget or lose track of over time. Here are some common examples and tips on how to locate them:

>> **Bank or credit union accounts:** Contact the institution.

>> **IRA or brokerage accounts:** Contact the brokerage firm.

>> **Savings bonds:** Use the U.S. Department of the Treasury's "Treasury Hunt" search tool at www.treasurydirect.gov.

If all else fails, try searching www.missingmoney.com or the unclaimed property site for your state to locate forgotten financial assets. If there's money out there that belongs to you, go find it. These databases may even have funds left to you by a deceased family member that you didn't know about.

TIP

Also try searching for unclaimed property using any previous last names or aliases, such as maiden names before marriage.

TIP

You should also review old financial and legal documents, such as wills, trusts, and estate planning paperwork, to identify any overlooked assets or accounts. You can find more about these documents in Chapter 7.

Tax Returns

Our paychecks are siphoned off by income tax, and if you're a W-2 employee, it's conveniently done through your employer. Self-employed or small business owners pay quarterly taxes. The withholdings and quarterly taxes are only estimates. Your annual tax return is where it gets real.

Your tax return tells a lot about your financial life. You should keep a copy handy for your records, but also track the important parts that you can control. It's another valuable exercise for managing your finances for F.I.R.E., and in this section I explain what information may help you.

Reviewing what you've been paying in income taxes

There are different types of taxes that flow through your tax return, but the largest part is income tax, including

>> Federal

>> State

>> Local (city, county, province)

You may have only paid attention to the bottom line of your tax return: refund or payment due. Whether you prepare your own tax returns with software or you use a professional, make sure you know what income taxes you have been paying. This will usually be shown on the cover page of your return.

Other types of taxes you want to make note of are capital gains and losses (for investments).

Don't forget to look at tax credits and deductions that you've been taking, and more importantly, some you may have missed.

I dive into more detail about taxes in Chapter 15.

Maintaining digital copies of your return makes it much easier to store several years' taxes. I suggest using a secure folder in the cloud or on a local storage device that includes any supporting documents (schedules, worksheets, and so on).

TIP

When you're ready to estimate your taxes after F.I.R.E., you can look at your past returns to help determine how much you'll be paying in taxes. Even before then, what you're paying in income tax could be a big chunk of your expenses that you might be able to tweak.

Taking note of important info

The term "income" on your tax return can refer to several different types of taxes, and some can be more important or more controllable than others. You should know the big ones that are often referenced and could help you identify opportunities to reduce your taxes. (I talk about this a lot more in Chapter 15.)

Probably the most referenced number on your tax return is your Adjusted Gross Income (AGI), which is your total income minus certain adjustments like the following:

>> Student loan interest

>> Traditional contributions to self-employed retirement plans

>> Contributions to health savings account (if not already accounted for through payroll deduction)

>> Contributions to a traditional IRA

AGI is often used as a starting point to determine eligibility for various tax credits and deductions. AGI is a line on the first page of your tax return, and any deductions above that line can be taken even if you use the standard deduction. This is what is called an "above-the-line" deduction. Anything below the AGI line usually requires you to itemize to get the deduction.

TECHNICAL
STUFF

Here's an example of AGI calculation:

>> $90,000 gross income

>> Minus $10,000 401(k) contribution (through employer, which shows on W-2 but not on tax return)

>> Minus $6,000 traditional IRA contribution

>> Minus $4,000 HSA contribution (through employer, which shows on W-2 but not on tax return)

>> Minus $2,000 Health Insurance premium (through employer, which shows on W-2 but not on tax return)

$90,000 (gross income) − $22,000 (above-the-line deductions) = $68,000 (AGI)

REMEMBER

Traditional 401(k) and HSA contributions made through payroll deduction are reflected on your W-2, which means that you don't enter them as deductions on your tax return.

Here are a few other terms referenced when it comes to your tax return:

>> **Taxable income** is AGI further reduced by the standard or itemized deduction and also reduced by the qualified business income deduction.

>> **Marginal tax rate** is the amount of additional tax paid for every additional dollar earned as income.

>> **Effective tax rate** (also known as your average tax rate) is the overall percentage of your total income that you pay in taxes. It's calculated by dividing the total income tax you owe by your total income. This rate provides a more accurate picture of your overall tax burden compared to your marginal tax rate.

TIP

Think you missed any deductions or credits on your taxes as you reviewed your old returns? You still have a chance for a do over. If you discover errors or discrepancies in your previously filed tax returns, you can file an amended return (Form 1040-X for federal taxes) to correct mistakes or claim missed deductions or credits. There is a time limit of three years, so don't let this opportunity pass if you think you overpaid.

ANECDOTE

I've gone back to file an amended return because of an error made by the local office of one of the big tax preparation companies (before I started doing my own). The preparer used the standard deduction without asking me about other possible deductions I had. I paid a hefty property tax bill and mortgage interest that far exceeded the standard deduction that year (2005, when the standard deduction was much lower than in 2024). I was fuming about the mistake! I finally did something about it and filed an amended return. It resulted in an additional refund of $1,400, plus interest. A great win, and wow did I learn a lot about taxes that year!

Insurance Coverages

Insurance helps you mitigate risks, and it's wise to know what you have covered, what that coverage includes, and how much coverage you have. In this section, I share how to locate important information on your insurance coverages for life, property (home and car), disability, health, and umbrella insurance.

Life insurance

Since this benefit is designed to be received by someone other than yourself (after you're gone), it's probably one of the most important things to keep a good record of. You likely are well aware of the details of your life insurance policy because it's typically a very large dollar amount to be paid out to your beneficiaries.

It's not exactly a dinner table conversation, but at some point you need to let your beneficiaries know about your life insurance. At minimum, share the name of the company that issued the policy.

You should gather all policies and have them in one place. Your work policy can probably be retrieved from your employer's online portal. Other policies should be available from the insurance provider. Be sure to make note of the following details:

>> Type of policy (term, whole life, and so on)

>> The amount of the death benefit

>> Your primary and contingent beneficiaries on this account

Make sure to update your beneficiaries if you've had changes in your life since you first purchased the policy.

Insurance for your home and car

Your home and car insurance renew from year to year, which gives you a constant reminder. Even though these renew every year, you can switch providers or change your policy at any time.

You can also include an umbrella policy that extends the liability coverage on these insurances.

The purpose of umbrella insurance is to protect you and your assets from major claims and lawsuits that could exceed the limits of your home and car insurance policies.

Managing your insurance is a bit easier if you have the same provider for all types of insurance. Just keep in mind that bundling doesn't always result in a lower rate (although most insurance companies claim that it does).

Most providers have an app that makes it convenient to access your policy information and documents and file a claim. The most important parts of your policy to make note of is your

» Deductibles

» Coverages (collision, comprehensive, bodily injury, property damage)

» Coverage amounts

Be sure to shop around for car and home insurance to make sure you have competitive rates. "The longer you stay, the more you pay" is something I learned a long time ago when I realized the insurance provider I had been using for over a decade was charging me way more than the company I switched to after shopping around. Most people tend to stick with the same car and home insurance company for years (or decades). Companies love your loyalty but that may not translate to you getting the best price.

Paying insurance premiums annually or semiannually may reduce the cost vs. paying monthly.

Disability insurance

If you are working age, you are more likely to become disabled than you are to die, making the need for disability insurance just as important (if not more) as life insurance. If you are out of work, due to an accident or illness, having disability insurance can save your finances.

Disability insurance is designed to replace a portion of your income if you become disabled or ill and are unable to perform your regular job functions.

You should know the difference between own-occupation and any-occupation when it comes to disability policies:

» **Own-occupation coverage** considers you disabled if you're unable to perform the duties of *your specific* occupation.

» **Any-occupation coverage** considers you disabled only if you can't perform *any* occupation for which you are reasonably suited by education, training, or experience.

This distinction may become even more critical if you are highly paid, such as an engineer making $150,000 or a physician making $300,000 a year.

There are both short-term and long-term disability policies:

>> **Short-term disability:** Usually lasts a matter of weeks or months designed to cover a temporary illness or injury (such as a broken leg)

>> **Long-term disability:** Usually lasts a matter of months or years designed to cover longer term illnesses or injury (such as cancer)

Your employer may offer these as part of your benefits package. In that case, the terms can usually be found on the benefits portal.

If you buy disability insurance on your own, you should be able to get a copy of the policy from your provider.

The things you want to make note of when it comes to your policy are

>> The benefit amount (percentage of income)

>> Waiting period before the benefit starts (elimination period)

>> How long benefits will be paid

>> Whether it covers *own* or *any* occupation

>> Whether the benefits paid to you are tax free (see Table 6-1)

- For group policies from work the benefits payout normally will be taxed.

- For policies you buy on your own, benefits probably won't be taxed because there is typically tax on the premiums you pay.

TABLE 6-1   ## Disability Insurance Taxation Rule of Thumb

Premium Payments	Benefit Payouts
Taxed	Not taxed
Not taxed	Taxed

Health insurance and HSAs or FSAs

Health insurance and the accompanying health savings account (HSA) or flexible spending account (FSA) are annual elections that you only commit to one year at a time. Health insurance and associated accounts are taken from your income pre-tax, so they reduce your AGI (see the "Taking note of important info" section earlier in this chapter).

Health insurance

For health insurance, you typically have a card or an app with your policy's basic information, but be sure that you have the plan details to easily reference. Just knowing the health insurance company can be helpful in an emergency. Also, make sure the type of plan you're on matches your use of healthcare.

TIP

Don't be on autopilot with things that renew year to year, such as health insurance. Rather than sticking with the same plan year after year, review other offerings through your employer or other sources when shopping for health insurance.

FSA

A flexible spending account (FSA) allows employees to set aside a portion of their pre-tax earnings. It is owned and managed by the employer on your behalf, and you must spend down the funds each year (with a few exceptions). It's referred to as a "use it or lose it" account, so your balance is important to keep an eye on. You may associate this account with healthcare, but there are other types:

>> **Healthcare:** For medical expenses such as co-pays, deductibles, prescription medications (usually paired with a traditional health insurance plan)

>> **Dependent care:** For child care or care for an aging parent

>> **Commuter:** For commuting expenses, such as public transportation or parking

>> **Limited purpose:** For dental and vision

HSA

A health savings account (HSA) is different than an FSA. The distinguishing key word is *savings* (the funds can be saved and invested) versus *spending* (money is meant to be spent down each year).

TECHNICAL STUFF

Both accounts must be paired with an HSA-eligible health insurance plan or qualified high-deductible health plan (HDHP). This name can be a turn off (marketing needs to do a little work). I mean who wants a higher deductible?

Even though the deductible is higher than with a traditional health insurance plan, HSAs typically have a much lower monthly premium. The IRS annually defines the monthly minimum deductibles and maximum out-of-pocket amounts.

TIP

HSAs allow you to continue building the funds year after year (unlike FSAs). They are designed to be used for healthcare expenses, but there is no limit to reimburse yourself (you can digitally store receipts for years or decades).

HSAs are a F.I.R.E. favorite because you can invest in them and grow the account over the years versus spending them down. Many people plan to strategically use HSA funds in retirement, and since there is no age limit to use the funds (like other retirement accounts), they are ideal for the early retirement years before age 65 when Medicare kicks in. I take a deeper dive into HSAs in Chapter 17.

HSAs are definitely tax free in three ways, and possibly in a fourth way as well:

>> Funds going in

>> While the funds grow in the account

>> Funds going out (for qualified medical expenses)

>> No FICA tax (if contributions made via payroll deduction)

Not only are you allowed to roll them over to a different provider after you leave your employer but you can also have your own HSA while you're with your employer (still subject to the annual contributions limits). This is very different from your employer retirement account (such as a 401(k)), where you are stuck with the provider they offer and that's it.

REMEMBER

Even though you can open your own HSA, remember that contributions made through payroll deduction avoid FICA tax, which is an advantage to accounts through your employer.

TIP

Although you are required to be covered by an HSA-eligible plan to make *contributions to the account*, you don't have to be on an HSA-eligible plan to *use* the funds. You can use funds in your HSA for any qualified expenses, regardless of what type of health insurance plan you have.

REMEMBER

Remember that you own the HSA, not your employer. You should be able to access the account online even if you're no longer with your employer.

If you lose track of an old HSA, check with your former employer or the HSA provider. Most HSAs have monthly fees, so a dormant account could be losing you money every month.

Student Loans and Other Loans

It can be easy to lose track of your federal student loans especially since the pandemic payment pause (from 2020 through 2023). You may have multiple federal loans floating out there (if you haven't already consolidated them) because each semester's disbursement results in a separate loan.

There have been significant changes to student loans over the past few years, including changes in loan services, repayment options, and forgiveness options.

The single best place to start for federal loans is the official Department of Education student loan website: `https://studentaid.gov`. There, you can locate your

>> Loan servicer

>> Amount of loans

>> Current loan status

>> Current repayment plan

If you have private student loans you've lost track of, you can locate them by checking your credit report. The name of the financial institution should be listed, and you may contact them to get your loan information if you don't already have it.

WARNING

Private student loans are from commercial institutions and are handled very differently from government federal student loans.

Keep track of other loans as well, such as vehicle loans or mortgages. Since payments on these loans are due monthly, they may be top of mind. You can typically access these loans online, and it's a good idea to keep a copy of the terms and agreement in your digital files. You can find more about debts and loans in Chapter 13.

Title of Ownership for Major Assets

It's important to keep track of how ownership of your major assets, such as your home or car, is titled. Typically, ownership is established at the time of your purchase (when documents are signed by all owners).

Ownership could be listed in a number of different ways:

>> Single individual

>> Spouses

>> Joint/multiple owners

>> A trust

>> A business

To get a quick check of how your home is titled, you can usually check with the county property records online. Your car title is probably the same as your car registration. Alternatively, you can check with your department of motor vehicles.

Social Security Estimates

People in the F.I.R.E. community aren't big fans of Social Security, primarily because of the headlines about the Social Security Trust Fund running out and the expectation that it will be depleted by 2034. The projection is that benefits will be cut by about 23% at that point, unless something changes.

I think pessimism is a bit overblown (and I used to be one of the biggest offenders). The truth of the matter is that as long as there are workers paying into the Social Security system (via FICA taxes), there will be benefits paid. The trust fund is more of an emergency fund, so when it runs out, Americans basically don't have a reserve account (not good), but there is still income from younger workers. But I digress.

TIP

Even if you're not confident in Social Security being there in your old age, there are still reasons to keep track of the financial information being reported on your behalf, such as accuracy of your annual earnings.

Confirming Social Security earnings each year

The www.ssa.gov website is the place to confirm that the earnings reported on your behalf are accurate. It is good practice to review and keep this information to easily reference. The website has the most current information, but remember it changes annually. I suggest that you download a copy each year and save it to your digital files. Just make sure that your income from the most current year has been posted.

TIP

Monitoring your Social Security statements annually can also help you spot any unusual activity or discrepancies that may indicate identity theft — for example, if your annual earnings are reported to be significantly more than what you know your income was for the year.

If there are inaccuracies, they can be corrected by following the instructions on the website. It is much easier to make the correction the same year you discover a mistake versus years later when you are less likely to have the records available to resolve a discrepancy.

Reviewing default estimates

The default estimates assume a traditional retirement age of 62 or older. They use the 35 highest earning years and apply a formula that spits out your estimates.

You don't need to have 35 years of work but your benefit amount will be lower if you have fewer. As long as you have at least 10 working years (4 quarters per year) where you paid in Social Security, you will likely qualify for benefits.

When looking at your Social Security estimates, you probably only check for retirement projections, but there are other benefits listed as well, including

>> **Survivor benefits:** Benefits available to your spouse and dependents, when eligible, should you pass away

>> **Medicare Benefits:** Benefits if you have enough credits to qualify for Medicare at age 65

>> **Disability Benefits:** Benefits if you become disabled and meet the qualifications

Ex-spouses may also qualify for benefits based on their ex-spouse's record, if they were married for more than ten years.

Customizing your estimated income

Keep in mind that the Social Security estimates are based on your current earnings and the assumption that you'll continue earning a similar income until traditional retirement age (62 or older). This is rarely the case when you retire early, but you can adjust your estimates accordingly to get a more accurate picture. The www. ssa.gov tool allows you to enter whatever future income amount (including $0) you choose to run your benefit estimates.

Remember that as little as 10 years of working could qualify you for Social Security benefits.

Rights and Royalties

Published books, other published content, and digital content bring in royalties or similar types of income. Anything you earn from royalties may not rise to the significance of big celebrities and artists like Michael Jackson and Aretha Franklin, but you still want to keep track of what's yours.

These payouts are usually automatically transferred to your bank account monthly or quarterly. They can easily get lost or forgotten (especially if the payouts are small), so be sure to keep a digital record of the agreement and recent statements.

Other important information to investigate includes

>> How are rights and royalties handled after your death?

>> Have you designated a beneficiary to receive payments after you're gone?

>> Is there any type of royalty continuation agreement?

Documents and Account Information Checklist

The best tips to organize and store documents and account information are to

>> Maintain digital files and folders.

>> Download copies for your own record keeping, even if you have online access to certain accounts.

>> Make sure you update and have the most recent documents or account statements as you change providers, change beneficiaries, and so on.

You may have many of the documents and account information mentioned in this chapter at your fingertips already, but Table 6-2 gives you a handy checklist to reference that will help you identify what you may have missed.

TABLE 6-2

Documents and Account Information

Document/Account	Date Last Retrieved
Old retirement accounts	
Tax returns	
Insurance coverages	
Student loans and other loans	
Title of ownership for major assets	
Social Security estimates	
Rights and royalties	

Chapter **7**

Reviewing Possessions, Probate, and a Plan for Your Estate

A ccording to the New York office of Unclaimed Funds, in 2023, the state held nearly $20 billion in unclaimed funds. The largest amount still unclaimed was approximately $9.2 million for one estate. Though you might not have accumulated millions in assets just yet, developing an estate plan can help avoid lost assets after you're gone.

F.I.R.E. is powerful, but it doesn't make you invincible. At some point, you have to hand over the empire, so this little corner of the book is dedicated to second-generation F.I.R.E.

Understanding the Hate for Probate

When I told my daughter that she was the sole heir to my estate, she said it sounded fancy. Like most people, she thinks estate planning is a big word for people with big money. I thought the same thing for a long time but have since learned that it can take minutes rather than months to do estate planning. It doesn't have to involve a mountain of overwhelming tasks, nor does it all have to be done at once.

A big part of F.I.R.E. is being in control of your life choices, and that extends to your choices after life, too — in this case, I mean directing where your hard-earned money and other assets go after you're no longer around. Although you may have visions of 20-page wills and complex trusts drafted by a high-priced lawyer, F.I.R.E. people are smart DIYers, and that extends to some basic estate planning. While you may need the assistance of an attorney or other legal pro (especially in more complex situations), don't overlook the things you can do on your own (and may already be doing) that cost you nothing.

With that in mind, I have a couple of questions for you:

>> Have you ever named a beneficiary on one of your retirement accounts?

>> Have you purchased a home with you and another person listed on the title?

If you answered yes to either, then you've already started your estate planning.

Estate planning is a touchy topic and can often be a source of anxiety — from the thought of no longer being around for the people you love to deciding how to divvy up your possessions. But it's not something you want to leave until it's too late. If you're anything like me, the thought of getting it down will haunt you until you at least start. You'll breathe a little easier once you have things in order (and realize how simple some of them were).

Regardless of whether you take the steps to designate how your wealth should be distributed after you're gone, there is a default estate plan for everyone that is set by law through a pesky process called probate. And if you haven't decide where your assets should go, the court decides for you.

TECHNICAL
STUFF

Probate is a legal process that administers the distribution of your assets after you die. There are many ways to set up your estate so that it does not have to go through probate.

There's a lot of hate for probate and here are a few reasons why:

>> **It's public:** Probate is a court process that is a matter of public record. It doesn't matter how big or small the estate is.

>> **It takes time:** This will vary by location, but it can take many months for an estate to go through the court's process and close out the estate.

>> **It costs money:** Probate is not free. There are court and attorney fees that will eat into the value for the assets going to your heirs.

Ever heard of having "control from the grave"? Well, estate planning can give you a little bit of that control.

As you build your wealth, estate planning will be something you think about more often because you have more at stake (that you'd probably rather not have end up in probate). Instead, there are ways to specifically direct who and where your assets go. You might even feel a bit more motivated if you think of it as part of your legacy and transferring generational wealth. Your heirs don't have to be kids; they can be

>> Extended family

>> Friends

>> Organizations

In this chapter, I share some very simple ways to set up your estate planning that helps you avoid probate and have your wishes properly documented.

Brushing Up on Your Beneficiaries

Just for fun, I have a trivia question that is often a point of confusion:

Which takes priority?

>> Person named as a beneficiary on the account

>> Person named in your will that references the account

The first answer is correct. The designated beneficiary supersedes what is in a will. Naming a beneficiary on your assets is one of the quickest and easiest estate planning actions you can take.

A beneficiary is a person or entity who receives the death benefit of an asset such as a retirement account or life insurance policy.

It used to be that naming a beneficiary on your accounts or assets required that you fill out a form, sign it, and send it back to the company holding the account. Now you usually fill out a short web form for most accounts.

The details vary by provider, but most ask you for the following information about your beneficiary:

>> Name

>> Date of birth

>> Social Security number (or Taxpayer Identification Number for other types of entities like a nonprofit or trust)

>> Relationship to you

>> Percent of ownership (must add up to 100%)

This information helps with notifying the beneficiary after you're gone.

TIP

If the provider isn't able to contact the beneficiary after the account owner passes, the assets usually end up in the database for www.missingmoney.com/ or the department of unclaimed funds for your state.

You can name a single or multiple beneficiaries on most accounts. You should provide not only a primary beneficiary but also a contingent. The main reason is that if the primary beneficiary dies before you do and you haven't made a beneficiary update on your account, the contingent will kick in. This will help make sure it doesn't have to go through probate court.

REMEMBER

Minors (typically under the age of 18, but check with your state) cannot inherit assets directly and should not be listed as a primary or contingent beneficiary.

When a beneficiary has been named, the asset or account can transfer directly and avoid probate. Rest assured that the beneficiary you select — which can be an individual, organization, or trust — doesn't have any rights or authority over the assets while you're living. Having a beneficiary keeps the asset out of probate, and it does not have to be listed in your will.

TIP

Changing a beneficiary is just as easy as naming one, so be sure to keep your beneficiaries up to date as your life changes with things like marriage, divorce, birth or adoption of a child, death of a beneficiary.

Keep in mind that if you live in one of the nine community property states, certain estate planning rules may be different. In community property states, most assets acquired after marriage are treated as being equally owned by both spouses. Check with the state laws if you reside in one of these states:

>> Arizona

>> California

>> Idaho

>> Louisiana

>> Nevada

>> New Mexico

>> Texas

>> Washington

>> Wisconsin

Life insurance

The primary purpose of life insurance is to provide financial support for those you love after your life is over. When the policy is originally set up, one of the main requirements is naming beneficiaries to determine who gets paid the proceeds after you die.

Insurance proceeds are tax-free (see Chapter 6).

Most life insurance policies are in effect for decades (or, in the case of a whole life policy, for all the rest of your life). The chance of something changing and the need to update your beneficiaries in that long time period is very likely.

Let's say that you get a life insurance policy when you're single at age 25 and have your mom named as the beneficiary. By age 40, your life might look a lot different. Within those 15 years, you may have gotten married and had children, and your mom may have passed away. There will be other changes in your life that will warrant a change as well, so it makes sense to review the beneficiaries of your policy as these changes happen.

You may also have multiple life insurance policies — something that's often the case when you have a policy through your employer and different policies outside of work. You don't have to have the same beneficiary on each policy, but make sure you keep all policies current.

Retirement accounts (employer and individual)

Most workplace retirement accounts will prompt you to name primary and contingent beneficiaries when you open your account. If the retirement account falls under the rules of the Employee Retirement Income Security Act of 1974 (ERISA), you may be required to name your spouse as the primary beneficiary if you are married. It is possible to pass on your ERISA-covered plan to someone other than your spouse, but you will need your spouse's permission to designate a different primary beneficiary.

Most employer-sponsored plans, such as a 401(k), fall under ERISA, but government employee plans (such as the Thrift Savings Plan [TSP] and state employee pensions) don't. The inheritance treatment of workplace retirement accounts should be outlined in the employer's plan documents.

REMEMBER

For retirement accounts outside of your employer, such as a traditional or Roth IRA, you are not required to name your spouse as the beneficiary. However, remember the following:

>> Name both primary and contingent beneficiaries.

>> Don't name minors because they won't have the legal authority to take control of the account because of their age.

You may be prompted to select your beneficiaries when you open the account. If not, be sure to do it after the account has been fully set up.

The much talked about Setting Every Community Up for Retirement Enhancement (SECURE) act went into effect in 2020 and made changes to the rules around inherited IRAs. It essentially eliminated something called the "stretch IRA" which was an estate planning strategy used to extend the tax-deferred benefits of an IRA for decades by allowing it to be inherited by someone other than a spouse. According to the IRS, the beneficiary may need to withdraw the balance of the account within the 10 years following the IRA owner's death. The only exceptions are what the IRS calls "eligible designated beneficiaries," which include

>> Spouse or minor child of the deceased account holder

>> Disabled or chronically ill individual

>> Individual who is not more than 10 years younger than the IRA owner or plan participant

If your beneficiary falls in one of these categories, they are not bound to the 10-year rule.

The new 10-year rule around inherited IRAs is confusing even among financial professionals. If you are inheriting an IRA or want to learn more about the rules, the IRS does a great job of tackling the details on their website (www.irs.gov/pub590b). If you want something a little more lively, here are a couple of F.I.R.E.-friendly pros who have great content in this area:

>> Andy Panko (https://retirementplanningeducation.com/)

>> Sean Mullaney (https://fitaxguy.com/)

Health savings accounts

You've heard that health savings accounts (HSAs) have superpowers with their triple tax savings (as I discuss in Chapter 15), but you could say that the inheritance rules are their kryptonite. HSAs can be used similarly to retirement accounts, but they're in a category of their own when it comes to how they are treated after the death of the account owner.

HSAs are an asset for which you should name a primary and contingent beneficiary in the same manner you would with a retirement account. It does not matter whether the HSA is through your employer. If the beneficiary is a spouse, the HSA may continue with the surviving spouse. However, the rules for non-spouse beneficiaries inheriting HSAs are completely different. Once an HSA is inherited by a non-spouse, that third leg of the triple tax savings touted by HSAs disappears.

Non-spouse beneficiaries fall into two categories:

>> Individual beneficiary

>> Estate beneficiary

In both cases, the account stops being an HSA and it becomes taxable. You may not have an HSA that's very big right now, but if you have the funds invested or are still contributing, it may grow to a significant amount. It could easily be worth more than six figures if you have it earmarked for retirement, and that will mean a big tax bill for either your estate or the non-spouse individual inheriting it. However, if the beneficiary is a spouse, the HSA continues with its favorable tax treatment.

Now that you know how the inheritance to a non-spouse beneficiary works with HSAs, there are a few things to consider that might lessen the tax blow to those inheriting this account:

>> Naming a nonprofit that is not subject to taxes

>> Splitting the account among multiple beneficiaries

>> Naming a beneficiary who is in a low tax bracket

ANECDOTE

I have a six-figure HSA (which I discuss more in Chapter 17), and it represents a good chunk of my net worth. I was bummed when I learned about how HSAs funds are treated when inherited by someone other than a spouse. I plan to spend it down on healthcare as I get older, but I had to really think though how I wanted to set up my beneficiary designations, just in case I pass away while the balance is still significant. I ended up doing a combination of the three options because I don't have a spouse to be beneficiary.

Because of the unfavorable inheritance rules of non-spouse HSAs, you may want to plan for some type of drawdown strategy to minimize what's left while you're still living. In your older years, you are much more likely to have higher health-care costs than in your younger years.

REMEMBER

After age 65, you can use HSA funds for nonmedical expenses without a penalty (you'll still pay taxes), but you may not need to if you have qualified medical expenses.

You can spend down your HSA easily as you get older by using the funds on things like Medicare premiums and other out-of-pocket health and medical expenses. You probably won't have a shortage of medical expenses for which you can use your tax-free HSA dollars as you start to age.

Brokerage and non-retirement investment accounts

Regular brokerage accounts and non-retirement investment accounts have a special provision for beneficiaries called "step-up in basis" that essentially makes taxes disappear. Let me explain.

REMEMBER

Brokerage accounts and non-retirement investment accounts hold investments like stocks, bonds, index funds, or other securities.

Some of the big players in brokerage accounts are Fidelity, Schwab, and Vanguard. There are also some small, newer players that also have brokerage accounts (sometimes called trading apps), including Acorns, Stash, Robinhood, and Ally.

The growth on brokerage accounts is only taxed as capital gains rates on the growth (see Chapter 12). These accounts don't get the same tax advantages as retirement accounts, but they do have their own set of benefits, which include a step-up in basis for the beneficiaries. Basis is generally the price you paid for the investments in the account and is the portion that is not taxable.

A step-up in basis means that the person inheriting the funds will not have to pay taxes on the growth of the account like the owner would have if they sell the account prior to death.

The basis of funds in the account gets reset to the full amount inherited as of the date of death. It took me a while to really get my head around how this worked and why wealthy people seem to love this strategy, so let me make it easier for you with an example.

EXAMPLE

Let's say your Grandma Mary had a brokerage (non-retirement) account and the total amount she contributed was $50,000. It grew to $200,000 over 20 years. That means $150,000 is the growth of the account ($200,000 – $50,000). If Grandma Mary sold everything in the account, she would be subject to taxes on the growth of that $150,000. However, if she passed away and left the account to you, it's treated quite differently. If you inherited the assets in the account with the same $200,000, that would be your new basis (your starting point) and none of it would be considered growth that you would be taxed on. If you sold all $200,000 worth of assets in the account, your tax bill would be $0.

TIP

That is the magic of inheriting a brokerage account. This is important to consider when you are naming beneficiaries. There is a similar step-up in basis for a home, and I talk about that later in this chapter.

Naming beneficiaries on a regular brokerage account basically works the same as with retirement accounts, as described earlier in this chapter. It is referred to as transfer on death (TOD).

Unlike as with retirement or HSA accounts, you can have a joint owner on a brokerage account. Make sure you understand that a joint owner is different from a beneficiary. A beneficiary has no rights to the account while you're living, but a joint owner has full authority over the account in the same way that you do. When you pass, a joint owner inherits the other half of the asset with either a step-up on the inherited half (separate property) or the entire asset (community property).

Bank or credit union accounts

Bank and credit union accounts often get overlooked when it comes to naming beneficiaries. Many people do not even know that you can name a beneficiary for these accounts. Unlike retirement or other accounts with investments, most bank accounts don't prompt you to add a beneficiary at the time of account opening. Bank accounts include common banking or credit union products such as checking accounts, savings accounts, money market accounts, and certificates of deposit (CDs).

The naming of a beneficiary on bank or credit union accounts is referred to as payable on death (POD). These accounts avoid probate, and the funds are paid directly to the beneficiary after your death. Some institutions allow you to designate a beneficiary online, and others (perhaps those stuck in the 1990s) may make you go to a branch to fill out paperwork.

Accounts held at TreasuryDirect

TreasuryDirect (www.treasurydirect.gov) is a government website that allows you to purchase and invest in government securities like I bonds. In 2021 and 2022, I bonds were all the rage because of the record high interest rates they were paying.

TreasuryDirect uses the POD term for the beneficiary designation, and each security with the account is registered separately (so you can have different beneficiaries for each security within your account). For accounts at TreasuryDirect, the beneficiary must be a person, not an entity. The process is online, but it's not intuitive at all. The site was updated in 2023, which improved the user interface a bit, but it still seems a bit dated.

Homes

Not all states allow you to name a beneficiary on your home but over half of them do. The term used will vary by state, but most call it a beneficiary deed or transfer on death (TOD) deed. Most states require that you have the deed signed and notarized and then officially filed with the land records office in the county where your property is located. This can be a bit more nuanced based on the rules of the state or county, so be sure to carefully follow the instructions posted on the county's website or use the guidance of a legal professional.

Homes get a step-up in basis treatment for the beneficiary and can be very valuable. For example, if your mom leaves you a house that she paid $60,000 back in the '90s but is worth $350,000 at the time you inherit it, you don't have to pay any taxes on the growth if you sell it at that price. The new basis (can also be referred to as principal) of the home gets reset to the value of the home as of the date of death.

Vehicles

About 20 states allow you to name a beneficiary on cars, boats, or other motor vehicles. The beneficiary process for this may also be referred to as a transfer on death (TOD) by some states, and it's handled through your state's Bureau or Department of Motor Vehicles (the same place that you register your vehicle). There will be a form on the agency's website that you'll need to complete and sign (some states have the extra step of getting it notarized).

Rest assured that having a beneficiary on your car or home does not give that person any ownership rights or responsibility for the property while you're still living. Designating a beneficiary is an easy and low-cost way to avoid probate and have your property transfer directly to the beneficiary.

ANECDOTE

In 2022, I decided to name beneficiaries on both my home and car so that they would transfer directly to my daughter instead of listing them in my will, which would have to go through probate. I live in Ohio, and I found the process for both to be very easy. There are states that don't require a notarized signature for the beneficiary form on a car, but Ohio does (even though it was a simple one-page form). When I got to the Bureau of Motor Vehicles to have the form filed, I noticed that they offer notarization service at their location for $1. I wouldn't mind paying the $1 for the convenience, but it would be even more convenient if they didn't require the signature to be notarized in the first place.

Table 7-1 shows a list of the states that allow a beneficiary to be designated on a home or vehicle. Be sure to check your state for the latest information.

Digital assets

Social media, e-mail, cloud services, blogs, websites, and other accounts you access online are all a part of your digital footprint and possibly a source of income you don't want to get lost. You may not have thought about what happens to those when you're gone, but many of the big service providers of these digital assets have. The term typically used is Legacy Contact, and it works a lot like naming a beneficiary.

TABLE 7-1 States That Allow Beneficiaries on a Home or Vehicle

HOME	VEHICLE
Alaska	Arizona
Arizona	Arkansas
Arkansas	California
California	Colorado
Colorado	Connecticut
District of Columbia	Delaware
Hawaii	Illinois
Illinois	Indiana
Indiana	Kansas
Kansas	Maryland
Maine	Minnesota
Minnesota	Mississippi
Mississippi	Missouri
Missouri	Nebraska
Montana	New Jersey
Nebraska	Nevada
Nevada	Ohio
New Mexico	Oklahoma
North Dakota	Texas
Ohio	Vermont
Oklahoma	Virginia
Oregon	
South Dakota	
Texas	
Utah	
Virginia	
Washington	
West Virginia	
Wisconsin	
Wyoming	

A legacy contact is someone you choose to manage your digital account if you were to pass away. The legacy contact may also apply if you become incapacitated and can't manage your own affairs.

Here are just a few of the big tech players that allow you to set up a legacy contact:

>> Apple

>> Google

>> Facebook/Instagram

If the provider of your digital services does not allow you to name a beneficiary or legacy contact, the next step is to name them in your legal documents such as a will, a trust, or power of attorney (see the last section of this chapter). The account will have to go through probate, but there is a law that governs the transfers or inherited digital assets in a similar way to financial assets.

Cryptocurrency would also fall under your digital assets, but you won't find many that allow you to name a beneficiary or legacy contacts. The best you can do to ensure that the assets go to who you want is to put it in your will or trust that will go through probate.

Titling Your Assets

The way your assets are titled is another easy way to avoid probate and ensure that they transfer quickly and easily. These include financial accounts from banks and brokerages as well as homes and vehicles.

Titling with joint ownership means that all individuals listed as co-owners have control of the asset (unlike a beneficiary, which does not have control until you're gone). The joint owners can be spouses, partners, or family members.

Even if you have more than one owner, you can still name a beneficiary that would kick in after the death of the last co-owner listed. The exception here is accounts from TreasuryDirect (see the earlier section "Accounts held at TreasuryDirect"), where you can choose to have a co-owner or a beneficiary but not both. I discuss some slightly different provisions for homes and vehicles in the following sections.

Home

Your home may be one of the single biggest assets you own, so make sure it gets the treatment you want while you're here and after you're gone through proper titling.

TIP

A title declares the legal ownership of a home or other property. A deed is a written document that records a home or property's title.

There are usually two parts to having a home:

>> **Mortgage:** The loan you have on the property

>> **Deed:** Legal ownership of the property

Not every home has a mortgage, but every home does have a deed, and in most cases, the mortgage and deed are title with the same owner or owners. How these are titled matters when you perform any transactions with the home (selling, home equity, refinance, and so on). The final transaction would obviously be when you pass away.

Who do you want the home to go to? This question can be answered with how the home is titled on the deed. For instance, if you want your spouse to get the house (which is common), then being co-owners of the home with your spouse makes sense. It transfers directly and avoids probate. There are a few other ways that a home can be titled. Here are the most common home titling options:

>> **Sole ownership:** Only one individual.

>> **Joint tenancy with the right of survivorship** (often abbreviated as JTWROS): Two or more individuals owning the property together (often used with couples). Each person owns an equal portion of the home. If one person dies, the other(s) gets full ownership of the property.

>> **Tenants by entirety** (often abbreviated as TE): Only available for married couples. If one spouse dies, the surviving spouse gets full ownership of the property.

>> **Tenancy in common** (often abbreviated as TC): Multiple people owning the home together. Each person may sell their interest or pass it on to beneficiaries of their choosing after they pass away (does not have to be a spouse).

REMEMBER

Tenants by entirety (available for married couples only) is the only titling option that creditors can't go after if only one spouse owns the debt, even after death.

Setting up the ownership of your home is typically done at the time you first purchase. Once the title to your home is all squared away, just remember to update it when you have life changes such as a divorce or death of one of the owners.

Vehicles

The value of vehicles is very small compared to larger assets such as homes or retirement accounts, but from an estate planning perspective, it can be just as annoying to deal with. So, simplifying the transfer of a vehicle by how it's titled can be a huge help.

A car title is similar to the title to a home but a bit simpler. It's the document issued by the state that acts as the certificate of legal ownership. You can title a vehicle with more than one owner (often a spouse), and it's easily done when you register your car with your state's department of motor vehicles. The car would directly transfer to the co-owner after the other owner passes away. It does not go through probate.

Car titling rules vary by state, so double-check the process and guidelines for yours. Boats, RVs, motorcycles, and other motor vehicles driven on the road may also fall under this category. You can find most information online at the state or county department of motor vehicles website.

Organizing Common Estate Planning Documents

By now, you probably have started checking off all the ways to transfer your assets to avoid the often dreaded probate courts but also to help minimize what you need to put in legal documents. The most common estate planning documents are wills or trusts, but there are a few others that will help make sure your wishes are carried out.

TIP

Keep in mind that you may not need all the documents I talk about in this section, and they certainly don't need to be lengthy. The elements of clarity and simplicity go a long way.

Avoiding medical mayhem

Right now, you are probably in a position to make all your own healthcare and medical decisions, but think about that sliver of a chance that you might not be. In this section, I describe some of the most important documents needed to help you avoid medical mayhem.

Medical power of attorney

A medical power of attorney (also referred to as a healthcare proxy) designates another individual you trust to make healthcare decisions on your behalf if you are not able to. Whether it's a temporary or a terminal situation, the person you choose will, in a sense, have your life in their hands.

TIP

The person you name can be a spouse or adult child, but it doesn't have to be. Think about close friends or family members who you know will uphold your values and wishes when it comes to health and medical decisions. Medical facilities usually have these documents available, and many states have these forms online.

Advance directive

An advance directive (also referred to as a living will) lets you plan your medical treatment in advance. This is typically in regard to your final wishes such as

>> A do not resuscitate (DNR) order

>> Order of life support or life-sustaining treatment

>> Organ donation

TIP

A "living will" is often confused with a "last will" because they sound similar, but they are very different. A last will is applicable only after your death, but a living will (your medical instructions if you become seriously ill or incapacitated) goes into effect while you're alive.

The names used for these directives and other documents related to your final medical instructions vary by state. You can usually find these for free online from your state or reputable national organizations such as the American Bar Association and AARP.

Financial power of attorney

A financial power of attorney (POA) document assigns someone to act on your behalf when it comes to financial matters such as real estate or other financial transactions. A POA goes away when you die, but when it's a "durable" POA, it stays in effect even if you become mentally incompetent or incapacitated. So that *durable* in front of the name matters for more than making you sound smart. If you don't have a durable power of attorney, a court may be left to decide what happens to your assets or who oversees your assets in the event that you're still alive but unable to make decisions.

TIP

A POA is a simple document that you can find online, but some financial institutions may require you use their version, so be sure to check with yours. You can also restrict the POA to cover only a specific period or a certain situation (such as when you are out of the country and you need home purchase documents signed).

ANECDOTE

Many years ago, I served as POA for a good friend who was working in Afghanistan but needed to sell his home. We set up a POA for the time that he was going to be away to include signing off on documents required to sell his home. In a post-COVID, era there may be less of a need for situations like this.

Wills and/or trusts

Now, for any assets still left to transfer after you have covered all the options discussed throughout this chapter, you have the choice of a will or a trust. The main difference is that a will has to go through probate and a trust does not.

These two estate planning instruments are probably the ones you're most familiar with, but if your assets have already been taken care of by naming a beneficiary or titling, a will or trust doesn't have to cover as much as it would otherwise.

Will

TECHNICAL STUFF

A will (formally called a Last Will and Testament) is a legally binding document that outlines who receives your assets following your death. Its execution goes through the probate court.

If you used any of the transfer of assets I discussed earlier in this chapter, there is very little you'll need in your will. I covered some easy ways your assets could go directly to your heir and avoid probate. A will is not included in that category. A little known fact is that wills still have to go through probate to be validated, so it's public. The way to avoid the publicity of a will is to use one of the methods I discuss earlier in this chapter:

>> Naming beneficiaries on your assets

>> Titling your assets

If you have minor children or children with special needs, then guardianship is one of the top priorities of what you'd want to include in a will. If there is anyone you put before yourself, it would probably be your kids. Making sure they are cared for by the people or person you choose in the event of your death may be one of the best reasons to make a will.

A will may also include property for which you can't name a beneficiary or don't have a title to, such as

>> Furniture and other personal items in your home

>> Collectibles

>> Clothes and jewelry

>> Some digital assets that don't allow you to name a beneficiary

>> Pets

WARNING

Be sure to update your will and make changes as your life changes (marriage, divorce, moving to another state).

Trust

A trust is another way to keep your assets private after you're gone. It's similar to a will in that it directs where your assets go, but a trust avoids probate court. A trust is a legal entity created to hold and direct assets on behalf of a beneficiary.

Creating a trust is a two-step process:

1. Creating the trust.

2. Placing assets inside the trust (by simply titling assets in the name of the trust)

There are three essential players when it comes to setting up a trust:

>> **Grantor** (you): Creates the trust and puts assets in it

>> **Beneficiary:** Receives some or all of the assets in the trust

>> **Trustee:** Person or organization in charge of the trust

If you are the grantor, then you must authorize a person (trustee) to administer those assets for the benefit of the trust creator (grantor) and/or beneficiaries.

Beneficiaries of a trust are commonly people who may not be able to manage the assets on their own such as a minor child or a person with special needs.

Once you place an asset inside your trust, you no longer own it; the trust does. But don't worry; you can change your mind and move assets in and out of the trust as you wish while you're living as long as it is a "revocable" trust (the legal term used for being allowed to make changes). You've likely heard of this referred to as a Revocable Living Trust. Now you know what it means.

WARNING

Be sure that you title assets in the name of the trust because a trust means nothing if there are no assets in the trust's name.

Costs

You've probably heard about the hefty costs of getting a will or a trust prepared through an attorney or law firm. You've also probably heard that you can do them both online for free or at low cost. The truth falls somewhere in between. If you ask an attorney, most will say you should always use an attorney (because that's their business).

You can complete a will online. Companies like the following let you handle the process easily and with lower costs than using an attorney:

>> Trust & Will (https://trustandwill.com)

>> LegalZoom (www.legalzoom.com)

>> Nolo's Quicken WillMaker & Trust (www.willmaker.com)

TIP

I am a believer that something is better than nothing, and I'd rather see you with an online will than no will at all.

Just because you can DIY your will or trust doesn't mean you should. While the templated online versions may be a fit for simple situations, the need to work with legal professionals may increase as your life gets more complicated (such as blended families or unique distribution requests).

TIP

Some employers offer a group legal plan (including estate document drafting) as an employee benefit.

Legacy binders

Legacy binders or other types of informal instructions are not legal documents, but they can save the day. They're designed to hold all your important documents, information, and/or contacts in one place to keep things from falling through the cracks. You can store a legacy binder digitally on a thumb drive or in the cloud, physically, or a combination.

A binder like this can be put together for a few different reasons:

>> **In case of an emergency:** Include information about who to contact if there is an emergency, including your employer, someone to care for your pet, and so on. Make sure to include phone numbers and e-mail addresses for each person.

>> **In the case of your illness or incapacitation:** Note your longer-term preferences if you can't make decisions on your own, such as your doctors, a medical power of attorney document, financial power of attorney, how your bills should be paid, and financial institutions that hold your assets.

>> **In the case of your death:** Explain where important documents like wills or trusts are stored, who to contact, and any financial arrangements not in your will.

TIP

It may be as simple as creating your own spreadsheet or purchasing a complete fill-in-the-blank binder like those offered at www.emergencybinders.com. I purchased one of these binders a few years ago, and having a template was extremely helpful because there were pieces of information I wouldn't have thought of myself.

Accounts or assets may end up abandoned after you pass away if you haven't been accounted for somewhere in your estate plan. Even the provider that holds these accounts (including a former employer) may not be notified of your passing if your heirs don't know they exist.

TIP

After a certain amount of time (which varies by state) the assets will usually end up in the database at www.missingmoney.com or the department of unclaimed funds for your state.

TIP

Try a digital version of digging for change in your couch by checking these unclaimed funds sites to see if there's anything in your name (or a family member's name) that you may not have known about.

With a little planning and organization, you control and direct where possessions, assets, and accounts go when it's time to hand over your estate. Many of the methods covered in this chapter are simple, quick, and can cost little or nothing. The Cheat Sheet at dummies.com includes a checklist for organizing and transferring ownership of your estate.

IN THIS CHAPTER

» **Pulling back the curtain on financial professionals**

» **Finding financial professionals that get F.I.R.E.**

Chapter **8**

Using Financial Professionals

Y ou probably proceed with a healthy dose of skepticism when considering using a financial professional and rightfully so. The financial industry is a broad space, and it's hard for the average person to distinguish a financial salesperson from a trusted financial professional who leads with education and has a fiduciary duty (is required to act in your best interest). Even the word *fiduciary* gets overused and can't be the sole determinant of a good financial professional.

TIP

Qualifications and competence are important in finding the right type of professionals to work with, but I also want you to consider how they make you feel. This gets lost sometimes, but it's a key part of what you get from using a professional. You should feel free to ask questions and have open conversations. Also high on the priority list is knowing they support your

» Values

» Financial goals

» Life goals

Working with the right financial professional can provide value for you on your path to F.I.R.E., even though many who are on the path to F.I.R.E. prefer the DIY route. Truth is, it doesn't have to be all or none. You can do some things yourself and get help from a professional in other areas.

One big question is how you find a good financial professional who knows how to work with someone on the path to F.I.R.E. I want you to be well equipped when seeking out a financial professional, so in this chapter I talk about what traditional financial professionals know about F.I.R.E. (and don't know) and give you tips on what to look for.

Knowing What to Expect of Financial Professionals

When it comes to financial professionals, the terms you probably see the most are *financial advisor* and *financial planner,* so I'm focusing primarily on those. They are often used interchangeably, and neither of them are regulated titles. Almost anyone can (and does) use them, which is why looking at credentials or designations is helpful, although it's certainly not the only criteria to determine if a person is the best fit for you.

A financial planner looks at your entire financial picture and advises you on how to achieve your goals. The most well-known credential for a financial planner is the CFP certification, which stands for Certified Financial Planner. You may have seen the commercials and advertisements with the yellow and black theme colors, promoting the value of working with a CFP professional.

TECHNICAL STUFF

The CFP Board of Standards (the governing and disciplinary body for the CFP certification) has a rigorous process for issuing and maintaining the credential that takes years to achieve. However, not having it doesn't mean a professional is not a good planner. Nor does it mean that every CFP professional is a good one just because they hold the credential.

Regardless of what you call them or what credentials they hold, most financial professionals don't know much about F.I.R.E. — even including what the acronym stands for. Some have read articles with salacious headlines that imply that the movement is about living a bare-bones existence to retire early from a job you hate and never work again. The media highlights the most extreme and shocking stories because that is what will get more attention.

As a financial professional, I spend time around many others in the industry. Some of them don't think very highly of the F.I.R.E. movement; I can feel their disdain. As someone who has been immersed in the F.I.R.E. community for almost a decade, I can tell you that the feeling is often mutual.

ANECDOTE

I earned my CFP certification in 2022 after retiring early from my corporate job. I debated about joining the profession because I did not have the most positive opinion about the financial industry. I thought more about it as I was going through my master's program and a cool externship program that exposed me to many different and more modern approaches that I had not seen before. I realized it was a changing profession (thank goodness!). I liked what I was seeing with more of a focus on things like client education, client psychology, and clients at the beginning of their wealth-building journey. I had two choices:

>> I could continue to stay on the outside with a negative perception of the profession.

>> I could become an insider and be a part of the change.

I chose the latter.

In this section, I discuss the typical approach of financial planners to give you clarity on the traditional financial planning model and the more modern options that have moved beyond that old model.

Understanding the typical approach of financial planners

The focus of many traditional financial planning firms is retirement, but not for those in their 30s and 40s. Their typical clients would be those approaching the traditional retirement age of 60 or older. Conversations focus on things like pensions and annuities, investment withdrawal strategies, Social Security, Medicare, and required minimum distributions.

These are the primary areas of concern for those nearing their 60s, so it makes sense that a professional would center their practice around these topics.

Most financial advisors/planners work with traditional retirees because significant wealth is held within workplace retirement plans, such as 401(k) or 403(b) accounts. In retirement, upon termination of employment, these accounts can (finally) be rolled into an individual retirement account, managed by advisors who charge their fees solely based on the account's value. The transfer of accounts naturally leads to retirement-focused planning.

The retirement landscape has changed significantly over the past few decades, and now most of the retirement burden has shifted from employers to the individual. Think about your parents or grandparents and what their retirement planning looked like. A common scenario was

1. Get a job with good benefits.
2. Work there for 40 years.
3. Retire at 65 with a monthly pension.
4. Turn on Social Security and Medicare.
5. Live for another 10 to 20 years.

It's an easy rinse-and-repeat process that didn't take much planning. Using this recipe, the average worker probably didn't need much help from a professional. The subset that financial professionals could serve would be wealthier people with more complex situations.

REMEMBER

The profession still leans heavily toward the wealthy, and most of the training and education focuses on strategies that would be of interest to this group of potential clients.

Gaining clarity on the traditional model

Investment assets seem to be the cornerstone of financial planning, but the reality is, it's merely one component. The financial planning profession began on the backbone of investments, so that was a big part of the services they provided. Back in the day, the term *stockbroker* was often used because that is what a lot of firms primarily did. Fast forward to today, and investments can be one of the easiest and cheapest parts of a financial plan thanks to things like

>> Passive index funds

>> Low expense ratios

>> No brokerage or trading fees

>> No or low minimum amount to start with

TIP

Financial planning today should be much more comprehensive and include more than just the investing slice. Some of the other areas that are very helpful on your F.I.R.E. journey are

>> Taxes

>> Retirement

>> Estate planning

>> Cash flow planning

>> Insurance

WARNING

Having the costs of financial planning services based on investment assets doesn't seem to be in line with how things work today. But that is the legacy compensation model that was established long ago and is now deeply rooted in the industry. As you can imagine, this is starting to change as consumers become more knowledgeable about how the industry works.

Assets under management (AUM) is the most popular compensation model for financial planners and is what most people are familiar with. AUM has been somewhat of a dirty word in the F.I.R.E. community because of how much fees can eat into the earnings of your investments, not to mention that many in the F.I.R.E. community believe in passive index funds and want to manage their own assets.

The following points help to clear up what AUM is and isn't:

>> It's a set amount paid to an advisor based on the size of your investments.

>> It may be a percentage or a flat-fee amount.

>> The fee typically comes out of your investment accounts that the advisor is managing.

>> The typical fee is about 1 percent and may include a reduction in fees for bigger accounts.

>> The fee is typically billed quarterly and listed as a line item on your statement (it may be on one of the last pages).

>> A special IRS carve-out allows AUM fees to be excluded from your gross income when they are directly paid from the retirement account that is being managed (such as IRAs).

WARNING

There are clear benefits to the advisors using the AUM model because it's easy to bill clients, and it provides a stream of income for them regardless of the other work they are doing (or not doing) for the client. Having the fee taken directly out of the account makes it less likely to be questioned in the same way as if the client had to send a payment to them out of their checking account.

On the other hand, some people may prefer this type of automation and value having someone else manage their investments. I'm just a big believer in clarity and transparency. When you do your budget, each expense line item is expressed as a dollar amount and not a percentage; this should be the same for AUM fees you pay for investment management.

Table 8-1 is an example of how a 1% AUM fee translates into dollars.

TABLE 8-1   **1% AUM Fee Translated into Dollars**

Assets	Impact of 1% AUM Fee: Quarterly	Impact of 1% AUM Fee: Annual	Impact of 1% AUM Fee: Five years
$500,000	$1,250	$5,000	$25,000
$750,000	$1,875	$7,500	$37,500
$2,000.000	$5,000	$20,000	$100,000

EXAMPLE

I'm not judging whether these fees are high. I just want you to know what you are paying in real numbers. An AUM of 1 percent sounds like nothing, but $100,000 over five years may feel like a much bigger number.

I can't think of many of my F.I.R.E. friends who are fans of the AUM model. It does seem a bit dated to still be tying the cost of financial planning services to the size of your investible assets. It really doesn't make sense to people who don't even want anyone managing their investments in the first place. There are many other financial planning areas that do matter to those on the path to F.I.R.E., which I talk about later in this chapter.

WARNING

AUM planners can still call themselves "fee-only" or "fee-based" and that just adds to the confusion. These are buzzwords that you may get tripped up on. It's best to be clear and use plain language around what you're looking for. For instance, "I'd like to continue managing my own investments and don't want to move my accounts." If an advisor has an AUM model and requires you to move investments to them, they're probably not a good fit for you.

Moving beyond the traditional model

Trying to figure out how the different financial planning models work may make you feel like you're in Oz. And the wizard behind the curtain? That would be the players in the industry who aren't being transparent about their fees. I'm part of the profession, and even I get confused sometimes. It should not be that way.

You deserve clarity where your money is concerned, and there are some new fresh faces in the profession trying to help. Now there are modern compensation models that are friendly to consumers and the F.I.R.E. community.

TIP

Although pricing is not the only factor in choosing a professional to work with, the compensation model matters. So that you have a good understanding of the non-AUM models, here is a guide:

>> **Fee only:** Only charge fees for the services they offer and are only paid by you. They don't receive compensation or commissions for recommending certain investments or financial products. This is a broad term, however, that could still be structured in a way to charge you based on the size of your investments (a percentage or flat fee). So if you are looking for a firm that doesn't charge AUM, look a little closer if they are using this language.

>> **Advice only:** Provides advice and professional guidance on the major areas of financial planning including investments. They don't manage investments or require you to move your investments to them like most AUM firms do. A good example would be advising you on the investments in your retirement accounts, but the firm doesn't have to manage them. This may be attractive to DIYers who want to continue managing their own accounts but want help with other areas.

>> **Hourly:** Charges an hourly fee much like you would pay an attorney. You only pay for the advisor's time while meeting with you or working on tasks for you. As with the advice-only compensation model, advisors typically don't manage investments or require you to move your investments to their firm. This could work well if you have a project or something specific you want professional help with on a short-term basis. For instance, if you want someone to take a second look at your withdrawal strategy or investments in your retirement account. This model may also be good for DIYers.

>> **Subscription:** Charges a regular fee (typically monthly or quarterly) for ongoing planning work. Subscriptions have a defined scope of what is included in the fee, which typically would be planning services, meetings, and other types of check-ins. This model gives you access to the planner on an ongoing basis during the subscription period that falls within the parameters of your agreement.

You may see directories or databases that use these terms, and firms are finally starting to clearly display pricing information on their website.

Working with F.I.R.E.-Friendly Experts

Sometimes you can have your cake and eat it too. Early on, the F.I.R.E. community and financial planners were the antithesis of each other. Now there are people in the F.I.R.E. community who have become financial professionals (some even earning their CFP certification) to help others on the path. Since education is a big part of financial planning and achieving F.I.R.E., I think it's a powerful combo.

TIP

On top of that, you have well-respected voices of brilliant experts who provide a ton of value to the F.I.R.E. community (even if they don't have formal credentials). They share their knowledge through online communities, blogs, podcasts, videos, books, and other one-to-many platforms.

I'm talking about people like

>> JL Collins (https://jlcollinsnh.com)

>> Karsten Jeske/Big Ern (https://earlyretirementnow.com)

>> Sean Mullaney/FI Tax Guy (https://fitaxguy.com)

>> Cody Garrett (www.measuretwicemoney.com)

>> Mad Fientist (www.madfientist.com)

>> Frank Vasquez (www.riskparityradio.com)

Though the one-to-many platforms are only going to provide general information and education, don't minimize all the valuable knowledge you can gain. These will help you with a DIY approach or at least give you more insight into what you need professional help with.

TECHNICAL STUFF

The word *fiduciary* is thrown around a lot in the financial planning world, and you would think that all professionals would put your interest before their own. Not true in all cases, especially with a big financial institution that sells the products their advisors may recommend. Even when they are a fiduciary, you should still make sure they are competent in the areas you are seeking help with. F.I.R.E. people tend to lean toward independent practices that are freer to customize their services and less likely to have conflicts of interest.

TIP

Here are a couple of other low-cost financial planning resources used by many in the F.I.R.E. community and DIYers:

>> **NewRetirement** (www.newretirement.com): Self-directed financial planning software that allows you to build your own retirement plan

>> **PlanVision** (https://planvisionmn.com): Very low cost initial and ongoing investment advisory and financial planning services. Also provides customized dashboards using an in-depth professional-grade software called eMoney.

DIYing with help

The DIY approach is a core value for many in the F.I.R.E. community. You research, use online calculators, and employ slick tools to track your numbers. But DIY doesn't mean do it *all* yourself. You know your strengths, and though they may be hard to acknowledge, you know your weaknesses, too. There are things you love to do and some you don't. The most efficient way to keep your momentum is to focus on the things you love and enjoy.

Financial coaches and counselors can be a great source of guidance and motivation on your path to F.I.R.E. (especially in the beginning). These can often be people who have reached financial independence or retired early themselves or have special training in the field of financial coaching. There is no licensing or credentials required to do this type of work, but there are some available. One of the most recognized is the Accredited Financial Counselor (AFC) credential, which focuses on coaching, counseling, and education.

TIP

You may notice that there are more professionals now integrating the psychological and mental side of personal finances in their practices. This additional training comes mostly in the form of educational programs that focus on behavioral finance or financial psychology. These can be a valuable addition to what a financial professional has to offer beyond savings rates and Roth conversion strategies. You can search for these types of professionals at the Financial Therapy Association (`https://financialtherapyassociation.org`). Some of them also share their expertise on public platforms.

Getting a second look at your numbers

At the beginning of your pursuit of F.I.R.E, your finances may only require information on common topics that are widely available like

>> Eliminating debt

>> Calculating your savings rate

>> Figuring out your net worth or F.I.R.E. number

>> Determining what types of accounts to invest in

As you move further along in your journey, you may have to start thinking about some of the more advanced topics. If you have the natural curiosity I talked about in Chapter 2, you may welcome the opportunity to learn more and figure things out yourself. That is why I say F.I.R.E. people are some of the smartest people I know.

So how do you know you got it all right? As thorough as you may be with your F.I.R.E. planning, you will have blind spots. You're setting up your finances for a very long time that could be decades longer than someone retiring at a traditional age. You may want to have someone double-check things for you.

Where do you go if you want to get a second opinion? Who should look at your plans and projections to see if they are as solid as you think they are? Or where do you go to get some ideas from someone looking through a different lens? As much as I love the pros giving out free education and guidance via a public platform, your unique situation may require more customized help. In the following sections, I describe some of the qualities you should think about when you're selecting someone to support you.

ANECDOTE

I'm part of a group in my area that does case studies. We are presented with a volunteer from the group who shares their financial picture and then we give feedback and suggestions. Everyone seems to love it, and at minimum, there is a lot of learning going on. It may not rise to the occasion of what you would get with a professional, but hearing the perspective of other like-minded people has value.

Chapter 3 covers where you can find F.I.R.E.-friendly online communities (such as ChooseFI or Catching Up to FI) and local in-person meetings and events (such as CampFI and the EconoMe Conference).

Looking for clear and transparent pricing

One of the positive trends I've seen among financial planners is being more transparent with pricing. This may give you an indication of what to expect before you go any further. Their website should give you a quick understanding of

>> **How their business operates,** including the compensation model (as I talk about earlier in this chapter). You should be able to clearly tell if their model is AUM, subscription, project based, hourly, or a combination.

>> **Pricing schedule for the services** they provide (or a range or starting point). There may be variations based on size of assets complexity or estimated hours.

>> **If there are any minimum requirements** based on assets, net worth, or other criteria.

TECHNICAL STUFF

There are regulatory bodies like the SEC (Securities and Exchange Commission) and state agencies that require a certain level of public disclosure regarding pricing, but why should you have to dig into all of that on your initial search? When firms clearly share their pricing it sends a message about how they operate and that may carry some weight as you think about the type of person you'd like to trust with your financial life.

This reminds me of the trend of salary transparency for job postings. Years ago, almost no employers (unlike most government employers) posted salaries for open positions or even a range. Now that has all changed and employers know that it is a must if they want to get potential candidates to apply. You can think about the message it sends if they are not willing to post the salary for the job. It's kind of the same thing when it comes to a financial planning firm posting their pricing for potential clients.

Those on the path to F.I.R.E. typically want to run the numbers and know exactly how much a service costs (as a dollar amount) before they sign up. This is not possible with the AUM model because the investment account balances vary.

Understanding credentials and types of professionals

You can easily drown in a sea of letters that stand for credentials because the financial industry is riddled with them. They may not be meaningful to you on the surface, but they do represent the qualifications of the professional that obtained them.

TIP

You may also come across certain licenses of financial professionals, and it's important to note that those are different from credentials. *Licensing* is a legal requirement to engage in specific financial activities (such as selling investment products). So, the license to sell a product is very different from a credential designed to demonstrate the qualifications of a professional.

For some credentials, the focus is clear but for others, not so much. One of the best resources to use to decode them is the *FINRA Professional Designations* tool which lists over 200 (www.finra.org/investors/professional-designations).

TECHNICAL
STUFF

FINRA stands for the Financial Industry Regulatory Authority and is the agency that helps regulate U.S. financial firms and professionals. They don't approve or endorse any professional credentials, but they provide information on

>> The issuing organization

>> Qualifications and training requirements

>> Verification of who holds the credential

>> Complaints and disciplinary standards

TIP

FINRA also provides a tool called BrokerCheck (https://brokercheck.finra.org) to help research the background and experience of financial professionals.

To save you a little time, here is a list of some well-known credentials you may see related to financial professionals:

>> Certified Financial Planner (CFP) focuses on comprehensive financial planning.

>> Chartered Financial Consultant (ChFC) focuses on financial planning (similar to CFP).

>> Certified Public Accountant (CPA) focuses on tax and accounting.

>> Chartered Financial Analyst (CFA) focuses on investment analysis.

>> Chartered Life Underwriter (CLU) focuses on life insurance planning.

>> Enrolled Agent (EA) focuses on tax (credential issued by the IRS).

>> Chartered Financial Analyst (CFA) focuses on investment analysis.

Making a list of what help you desire from a professional

TIP

Not only are there firms that specialize in the area you are looking for, but there are also ones that focus on certain groups like the military, big tech, academia, or the medical field. Here are some services that come up quite often in the F.I.R.E. community that people may look to a professional for help:

>> Second look at overall plan

>> Retirement strategy for early retirees

>> Roth conversion strategy

>> Tax strategy

>> Estate planning

There are many other areas you may need help with, but the idea is to be intentional about the services you want. If you want to continue managing your own investments, you don't need someone whose primary business model is managing investments. Conversely, if you want help with tax strategy, look for a professional who specializes in tax planning and perhaps holds the CPA or EA credential.

If you're seeking a financial planner to work with you on your F.I.R.E. journey, here are a few tips for you as you start your search:

>> Make a list of the areas you want help with from a financial professional and make sure that matches up with what they offer.

>> Review the website for basic information (services, specialties, pricing, business model, fiduciary status).

>> Check the credentials and background of the professionals.

>> Check with others who have worked with the professional.

>> See if the professional has any public content (podcast, book, YouTube, interviews) you can check out.

>> Be sure to consider how the professional makes you feel.

Chapter 9

Celebrating Your Wins

I can't help but get excited when I hear someone discovered F.I.R.E.! I can see the burst of energy, the endless curiosity, and the big dreams on the horizon. You're probably feeling that way right about now.

I want you to keep that feeling throughout your journey and the best way to do that is to celebrate your wins along the way. The F.I.R.E. community will cheer right along with you. I see posts every day in many of the groups I'm in where people share their thrilling milestones like reaching their first $100K or sharing that they officially reached their F.I.R.E. number, and they get tons of virtual high-fives from others in the community.

There's nothing wrong with going hard and fast but burnout is real, and you need things to keep you motivated. Even if you reach your goal in ten years, your journey can seem like it's taking a long time, and I've seen some people lose steam while on their path. You need to find a way to celebrate your achievements and make your journey as enjoyable as possible.

How you celebrate may be as simple as a glass of wine to toast yourself or publicly sharing on social media for the world to see. Whatever you do, you're providing metaphorical applause to your soul and a happy nudge to keep going.

Early Achievements

I love the wins early in the journey because the beginning is when a person is the most enthusiastic about the F.I.R.E. process and all that it holds once achieved. The beginning is also when you're probably the most curious and determined to see results and gain momentum.

REMEMBER

Using your own measuring stick to evaluate your successes will bring you more joy than comparing yourself to others. The achievements that are a big deal to you may be meh for someone else, so you're the only one that can truly define what's a win.

TIP

The psychological aspect of pursuing F.I.R.E. is a real thing. (Read about it in Chapter 3.) To keep from getting discouraged, make sure you take advantage of some early and easy wins. Frankly, some days when everything seems to be going wrong you just need an easy win. In this section, I talk about some of the first milestones you're likely to reach.

Paying off debt

Some people start their F.I.R.E. journey after they've paid off significant debt, but others start on the path while they're still tackling it. Emotionally, debt can feel like a heavy load, and it can be hard to imagine life on the other side of it. Making a plan to pay off your debt in a smart, strategic way as outlined in Chapter 13 can serve as your guiding light.

Debt payoff is a journey — much like F.I.R.E. is. Making progress is huge and you pick up steam along the way.

TIP

All your debt doesn't have to be gone before you recognize the discipline, organization, and habits that you're building. Those things will serve you well through the rest of your journey, so it's good to acknowledge the good work you're doing by using those skills to make progress.

Slowly you'll start seeing a transition from debt accumulator to debt eliminator. and that's a meaningful shift. When your debt is paid off, you can reroute the funds you were using for debt payments to other wealth-building efforts.

It's worth celebrating a few smaller milestones on the way to the big goal of paying off debt. Here are some examples:

>> Pausing use of a credit card that only adds to the debt you already have. This is the point when you stop the bleeding and start to heal.

>> Paying off ultra-high interest debt. This could be the dreaded payday loan type of account or a credit card that may have had a default interest rate triggered.

>> Cleaning up old debt, such as accounts in collections or default, that has been dragging your credit score down.

>> Paying off all credit card debt. This one achievement has so many positives, such as being rated with a higher credit score, which could impact how much you're paying for things like car insurance.

>> Paying off all your debt including car, home, and student loans.

Achieving any one of these takes focus that you should be proud of. Being debt-free doesn't come naturally in a consumerist society because you get constant messages that tell you to spend and spend more. So paying off your debt means you're bucking the norm and making the shift to more positive financial moves. You win!

Getting to zero is a big deal

Getting to zero doesn't sound very impressive on the surface, but if you're coming from a negative net worth, it's a "jump for joy" moment. When you move from a negative to a positive net worth, that's getting to zero — something that will probably feel tremendous.

In the early part of your life, it's common to be in the red and have a negative net worth because of things like student loans, a car loan, a home loan, and credit card debt. So finally breaking even with your assets and liabilities is significant.

Reaching a net worth of $0 is a clear indication that you're moving to a solid foundation. Celebrating this milestone is not just about the present but also about setting yourself up for F.I.R.E.

Right about now, you should hear that voice in your head saying, "Keep going." Once you get to zero, pat yourself on the back and look forward to achieving your next financial goals.

Building an emergency fund

You've probably heard a lot about building an emergency fund. It's a foundational part of personal finance that you should not skip. The main reason is that if something goes wrong in the early stages of pursuing F.I.R.E., you don't want it to derail your plans.

Having three to six months' worth of savings is a good goal and will help you breathe easier and get you on your way to solid footing. Working to create an emergency fund also helps you start building the savings habit that is essential on your path to F.I.R.E.

REMEMBER

Remember that some early milestones can be done at the same time. You can be working on your emergency fund while you're paying off debt. Both are important, and as you reach the goal for one, you can shift more of your resources to the other.

TIP

Beef up your emergency fund a bit more if you'd like it to cover an extended period for things like an unplanned sabbatical.

Having more cushions in place only helps add to your safety net and reduces the chances of you derailing your F.I.R.E. plans. This could be an FU (forget you) or OS (oh, shoot) fund in which you have tucked away enough money to cover you if you walk away from a job or discover you have made a big mistake (we all make them) you need to fix. This FU/OS fund could be the difference between dealing with a high-stress situation and leaving your mind at ease.

Saving your first $100K

According to Malcolm Gladwell, 10,000 hours of practice is how long it takes to achieve mastery in a particular field. In a financial context, I think it takes $100,000 to build a savings habit, and that's why the $100K may seem like the hardest.

REMEMBER

Of course, $100,000 may seem like a drop in the bucket compared to your big F.I.R.E. number (see Chapter 4), but this is a marathon not a sprint. You're starting to stack some valuable skills as you navigate the early stages of your journey.

The first time you see six figures in your accounts, it will confirm that what you're doing is working. When you make it over this hump, it's going to feel much easier to build the next $100,000.

Whether it took you several months or several years to get to this milestone, your consistency and focus are to be celebrated. Go ahead, do something to savor the moment: scream, post, or share in a way you won't forget. You deserve it!

Maxing out your tax advantaged accounts

Maxing out the contributions to your tax advantaged accounts is a sure indicator that you might be well on your way to reaching F.I.R.E. These tax-advantage accounts give you dual benefits: the special tax treatment of the account itself and the growth of the investments within those accounts. The benefits are so good that the IRS limits what you can contribute to them each year (see Chapter 15). These tax-advantaged accounts include

>> 401(k) or other workplace retirement plan

>> IRA (traditional or Roth)

>> Health Savings Account (if you have access to one)

>> 457 account (if you have access to one)

TIP

To pull off maxing out your tax-advantaged accounts, you would have to have an income to support this level of savings. Being able to make these contributions is indicative of the health of other parts of your financial life including a strong income, living on less than you earn, and optimizing taxes. See Chapter 15 for more about tax-advantaged accounts and limits.

ANECDOTE

I remember when I first got to the point of maxing out all of my tax-advantaged accounts. It was empowering! It gave me my first glimpse into just how early I would probably be able to retire, and at the time I was happy with 55.

More Exciting Milestones

The milestones don't stop there, and the momentum keeps building while on your path to F.I.R.E. This section is filled with targets and goals that are also worthy of celebrating once reached.

Hitting your earnings targets

Reaching your earnings targets can give you more money to put toward achieving your other goals on your way to F.I.R.E. Increasing your salary at your day job is not the only way to do this. You can also increase your earnings from other sources like a passion project or side hustle and endeavors that generate passive income. See Chapter 10 more about growing your income.

Being lucky enough to find a job that you love in the process of pursuing your earnings targets can be extra helpful. If you're no longer running away from a job you don't like (as is the case with many people), you may have an increased willingness to continue working a bit longer, which gives you more time to reach your F.I.R.E. number (or means you can have a larger F.I.R.E. number).

Reaching your ideal savings rate

Reaching your ideal savings rate is not as hard as you think. It's a gradual process, and once you hit it, what a feeling!

Your savings rate is the number that will get you to F.I.R.E. and is a function of how much of your income you save (read more in Chapter 4).

Your savings rate may not have to be as high as you think. Being realistic and putting a time frame on when you hope to reach it will make it more achievable.

If you make $60,000, you may not find it feasible to have a 50 percent savings rate and still live a comfortable life. However, if part of your goal is to increase your earnings to $120,000, then the formula may work.

I suggest that you track your savings rate annually. You can even create a little competition with yourself by comparing your estimated savings rate year over year.

Simply tracking your savings rate makes you a winner. Even if you fall short of your goal in a given year, you should not get discouraged. You may even become extra motivated to kick it up a notch.

Reaching F.I.

This is when you have accumulated enough savings and investments to cover your living expenses and lifestyle without relying on a traditional job for income.

Getting to this point affords you flexibility to

>> Step away from your job and take a long break or sabbatical

>> Transition to other work or endeavors

>> Retire altogether (on your terms)

ANECDOTE

When I reached this point, I was not quite ready to retire and worked another two years. I did, however, use the time to plan my exit from corporate America and figure out my early retirement endeavors.

Reaching your net worth goals

When it comes to building your net worth, you may be stronger at one part of the equation than the other. Whether you're better at reducing your liabilities and debt or better at saving and investing, the number tells a lot about the health of your finances.

TIP

To come up with this number, you have to first pull together your accounts (by using an app with a net worth tracker or doing it on your own).

The first time you do this, it could take a little time depending on how many accounts you have, but pulling all your numbers together is a win in and of itself.

REMEMBER

Net worth = Assets – Liabilities

Plotting the growth of your net worth is motivating because it shows how hard work with your finances manifests over time. Regardless of where you started, there is no greater feeling than watching your net worth go up.

Milestones in your net worth should be acknowledged. You may want to give yourself some recognition when you do each of the following:

>> Doubling your net worth from where you started

>> Reaching the halfway mark to your target

>> Achieving $1,000,000 net worth (because it's such a cool number to see and everyone wants to be a millionaire!)

ANECDOTE

I was 38 before I did my first net worth statement, and it was the most powerful exercise I've ever done with my finances. I took weeks to pull everything together, but seeing all my accounts together on one page was so satisfying!

Marking milestones on the way to your F.I.R.E. number

Your F.I.R.E. number is a bit different than your net worth. Your F.I.R.E. number includes only assets that you can actually access to live on, so it doesn't include your vehicles, furniture and jewelry, and your home if you're living there.

REMEMBER

Your F.I.R.E. number is 25 times your annual expenses.

If your expected annual expense in retirement is $50,000, your F.I.R.E. number would be

EXAMPLE

$50,000 × 25 = $1,250,000

Reaching this number is probably your greatest indicator that you are financially able to retire early, but getting there doesn't happen overnight, and the work you do deserves celebrations along the way. As you get close, it's so much fun counting down the months, weeks, and days until you hit this big mark. With a number this big, it's worthwhile to acknowledge getting halfway or even a quarter of the way there.

REMEMBER

You don't have to retire as soon as you reach your number, but you now have the option to do so. This puts you in a powerful position and gives you the ultimate freedom to

>> Control your time

>> No longer depend on a paycheck

>> Do what you love on your terms

F.I.R.E. BINGO

You can put all your wins together in a little game called F.I.R.E. bingo (see the figure).

Play along and see how many milestones you've hit so far. How many will you hit five years from now? You'll notice that there are also spots for supporting your F.I.R.E. friends, and it will be even more fun if you play along with other people.

F	I	🔥	R	E
FIRST $100K SAVED	REACH IDEAL SAVINGS RATE	REFLECT ON LESSONS FROM FAILURES	FIND YOUR TRIBE	FULL EMERGENCY FUND
DEBT PAID OFF	INVESTMENT INCOME EXEEDS WORK	EMBRACE FEELINGS & EMOTIONS	$1,000,000 NET WORTH	NET WORTH DOUBLED FROM BEGINNING
$0 NET WORTH	CELEBRATE AN EARLY WIN	CELEBRATE A F.I.R.E. FRIEND	SHARE YOUR WINS	HIT YOUR F.I.R.E. #
MAX OUT TAX-ADVANTAGED ACCOUNTS	START BROKERAGE ACCOUNT	$0 NET WORTH	HALFWAY TO YOUR F.I.R.E. #	REACH NET WORTH TARGET
HIT EARNINGS TARGET	FU/OS MONEY FUND	GIVE BACK IN YOUR OWN WAY	HALFWAY TO NET WORTH TARGET	REFLECT ON LESSONS FROM WINS

3

Increasing Income, Savings, and Investing

Identify the areas you can focus on to grow your income, including earnings and benefits from a regular job, passive or semi-passive income, and even money from passion projects.

Find out why increasing your savings rate can be the greatest accelerant to your journey to F.I.R.E. and what types of accounts will have the greatest impact.

Get excited about how powerful simple investing can be on your path to F.I.R.E. using the concepts of compound growth, passive index funds, and minimizing costs and fees.

Chapter 10

Working Wonders by Growing Your Income

The F.I.R.E. philosophy says that exchanging money for your time is what you're trying to get away from, right? The daily grind, the constant hustle, the boss calling all the shots. But it's not all bad. In fact, increasing your income is the best way to supercharge your F.I.R.E. goals. Reducing your expenses is part of the equation, but that can only go so far. Your income has a heck of a lot more room to expand than your expenses have room to shrink.

Your earnings start the wealth-building cycle and set the tone for your F.I.R.E. journey. You don't have to have a high income (like some suggest), but you do have to live on less than you earn to create enough space to save and invest.

Having a lower income may be a concern, but it doesn't mean totally dismissing the idea of achieving F.I.R.E. You know the minimum amount that you need to cover your necessities like housing, food, utilities, and transportation. If it takes your entire income to cover those, there's not much room to save. If you recognize this in your personal situation, that's half the battle. You can then work on strategies to increase your income.

Your income is dynamic and typically goes up over your working lifetime. Just because you start out with a low income doesn't mean it will stay there.

REMEMBER

This chapter covers areas to optimize your income through earnings from a job or side hustle, passive and semi-passive income, and other earnings that can give an extra bump to your total income.

Maximizing Earnings and Benefits from Your Job or Side Hustle

Landing a job or a side hustle is how we are conditioned to start our adult lives and the main way to get the income flowing. They come packaged not only with direct exchange of money for your time but also with benefits and other residuals that work to your advantage when maximized. In this section, I cover W-2 jobs, 1099 employment, and variable income jobs.

The beauty and the beast of a W-2 job

A W-2 employee is someone who works for and is paid directly by an employer. The employer gives the employee a W-2 tax form that reports the employee's yearly income. You could say that the F.I.R.E. community has a love-hate relationship with W-2 jobs:

>> **The love:** It's one of the most direct routes to create an income, and it's a steady, predictable paycheck.

>> **The hate:** It's the exchange of time for money that we're trying to get away from by seeking F.I.R.E.

Having a regular job can be one of the biggest promoters or a bit of a drag on your F.I.R.E. journey. Yes, I'm talking about the difference between a high-paying job with great benefits and a lower-paying job with no benefits.

The monetary compensation of your salary and bonuses are probably the headline you look at first, but don't bury the lede, which is often your employee benefits. If you have worked a W-2 job most of your life like I did, you may take your benefits for granted, but they're an asset you can leverage along with your salary.

Overall salary ebbs and flows with the strength of the job market, but the primary determinant is your career field and location. For instance, an engineer in California (a high-paying job in a high-cost-of-living area) is going to make a lot more than a teacher in Mississippi (a lower paying job in a low-cost-of-living area).

You have opportunities to improve on the salary piece to bring more income from your W-2 job to help reach your F.I.R.E. goals. The following are a few that will have the greatest impact.

Negotiating salary

When you want to remain with a company, perhaps because you like the job, the company, the benefits, or the people, but want to take home a higher salary, there are ways to increase your earnings through

>> Promotion

>> Changing positions

>> Renegotiating salary

>> Maximizing benefits

For some people, *negotiation* implies an adversarial approach to salary increases, and not everyone is comfortable with this. However, you can reframe it as a win-win situation by thinking of it as equalizing the deal so that both you and your employer are happy. Whatever you call it, there are all kinds of online resources to research salaries by characteristics such as position, location, and years of experience. Negotiation becomes much easier when you've done a little homework to help maximize your salary potential. Try one of the following sites to help with your homework:

>> Glassdoor (www.glassdoor.com)

>> Indeed (www.indeed.com)

>> Salary.com (www.salary.com)

TIP

You may also find some good salary transparency threads on social media with people in your field openly discussing what they make.

One other great resource is a platform called Salary Transparent Street (www.salarytransparentstreet.com) that promotes pay transparency. It was created in 2022 by a young woman named Hannah Williams after she found out she was underpaid. She's like a roving reporter, who asks people three rapid-fire questions:

>> What do you do?

>> How much do you make?

>> Where do you live?

From there, the willing subjects talk a little more about their career (which is so refreshing in a world of opacity when it comes to salary).

TIP

You can find most government (federal, state and local) salaries somewhere on the agency's website. This is the ultimate transparency. Government and not-for-profit organizations typically pay lower salaries than private companies but may offer better benefits such as more generous retirement provisions and may qualify you for the Public Service Loan Forgiveness (PSLF) program.

TIP

These same resources can also be leveraged to negotiate a salary increase at your current employer. If your employer does not want you to leave, they may match a competing offer just to keep you from leaving. The cost of onboarding a new employee to replace you is likely more than what it would cost to give you a higher salary to stay.

ANECDOTE

I was one of those W-2 employees who remained with the same company for 20 years. I didn't get a gold watch, nor did I have a high salary. I know of many coworkers who left for different employers and got significant increases — some claimed they got over 50 percent more. It was so tempting to leave and do the same thing. But by that time, I had earned some generous benefits that were more favorable to longer-tenured employees, like an escalating 401(k) match and increasing vacation time. I convinced myself this was enough to stay as long as I did. But looking back, I should have changed jobs years earlier, enjoyed a much higher salary, and perhaps reached F.I.R.E. even sooner. Like most people, I have those little regrets of things I could have done differently, but the truth is, no single mistake is going to lead to financial ruin.

Switching employers

Frequently changing employers used to be a negative on your resume, but that has clearly changed. The days of retiring from the same company at which you had your first job are long gone.

Some of the biggest bumps in salaries will come when you switch employers, especially in a strong job market where employers have trouble filling open positions and are willing to entice potential employees with higher salaries. Employers may be more willing to entertain your request for a higher starting salary, but you may need to start the conversation by asking, using some of the tips mentioned earlier in this chapter. Knowing the climate of the job market can put you in a position of strength.

It's not unheard of for people to earn 50 percent more in their new job than they did at their previous job. On the other hand, staying with the same employer may get you modest raises such as 3 to 5 percent per year, which barely keeps us with inflation.

Evaluating benefits

The benefits part of the equation of a W-2 job can be a powerful partner to your salary and serve as a lightning rod for your F.I.R.E. journey. These additional non-monetary payments add value to your overall compensation.

The big three in benefits are typically

- **Health insurance:** Less comes out of your pocket to pay premiums because your employer picks up the tab for most of it (commonly 50 percent or more).

- **Retirement:** Usually employers match your contributions to a 401(k) or other employer-sponsored plan. Though pensions are very rare these days, some still exist, primarily with government agencies and public education systems.

- **Paid time off:** Usually holidays, vacation, and sick time.

These benefits can be worth thousands of dollars every year. Because this can factor into your overall compensation, see if you can get the benefits package before making a decision on your job choice. Employee benefits can be extensive and vary widely. The value of each of them will depend on how much they mean to you and your situation.

TIP

Many government agencies and large companies now have a place on their public-facing website with detailed benefits information.

REMEMBER

Some benefits are based on your tenure with the employer or may require a certain number of years for the employer contribution portion to vest (typically with retirement accounts).

To give you a reference, Table 10-1 is a list of some benefits that may be just the thing to help power your F.I.R.E. plans.

The love and hate of a 1099

As with a W-2 job, people often have a love/hate relationship with self-employment:

- **The love:** You can deduct certain expenses, and you may have more flexibility to control your work structure.

- **The hate:** It's not always steady or predictable, and you're on your own when it comes to taxes, insurance, retirement, and other benefits.

TABLE 10-1 **Common Employee Benefits**

Employee Benefit	Notes
Health insurance	Usually multiple plans to choose from (including traditional and HSA-eligible); usually subsidized by employer
Retirement plans (defined contribution like 401(k), 403(b), or TSP)	Plan that specifies contributions made by you, which you are responsible for, and which your employer is responsible for
Retirement plans (defined benefit plan like pensions)	Plan with a predetermined payout at your retirement that's based on a specific formula
457 plan	Typically, only available for state/local government or nonprofit organizations; withdraw at any age if you have separated from the employer
Employee Stock Purchase Plan (ESPP)	Mostly provided by big companies that offer discounted (commonly 15%) stock to employees — for example, Amazon, Apple, Microsoft, Walmart
Paid time off	Vacation, sick leave (some even offer unlimited time off)
Stock options and equity compensation	Given as incentives to certain employees (usually management level or in key positions)
Dental/vision insurance	Usually subsidized by the employer
Health Savings Accounts	Often subsidized by the employer
Flexible Spending Accounts	For health, dependent care, and/or transportation; often subsidized by the employer
Short-/long-term disability insurance	Usually based on tenure with employer
Life insurance	Typically, term insurance, for which a certain amount may be covered by employer and/or low-cost group rates
Education assistance	Reimbursement or assistance for college tuition or professional development
Flexible work arrangements (especially since the pandemic)	Options like remote work, flexible hours, or compressed work weeks
Parental leave	Paid time off for new parents beyond standard vacation or sick leave

TECHNICAL STUFF

Independent contractors provide services to a company (or companies) but are not direct employees of the organization. They can also be referred to as self-employed. The company issues a 1099 tax form that reflects the contractor's earnings for the year.

If you're self-employed or have a small business, it's basically all on you to manage things (which can be good and bad depending on how you look at it). You may have a higher salary than you would have with a W-2 job, but you also must take care of more expenses on your own.

TECHNICAL STUFF

As a self-employed person, the total income reported on your taxes is the net of your expenses (Income − Expenses = Net Income).

Health insurance is an expense you'll need to find on your own (similar to the need to find health insurance when you retire early).

It's a common myth that it's impossible to have health insurance if you're self-employed, but it is doable. The most common options are

>> Health Insurance Marketplace at healthcare.gov

>> Enrolling through a spouse's or partner's employer's plan (if allowed)

>> Insurance broker

>> Professional membership associations

>> Health Sharing Plans (not technically insurance but are alternative programs in which medical expenses are shared among members, and are often faith based)

You're also on your own for saving for retirement. There are many different options for self-employed and small business owners to get into tax-advantage retirement accounts with similar limits to larger employer-sponsored plans. Here are a few to consider:

>> **Solo 401(k):** For self-employed individuals to contribute both as an employer and employee, potentially allowing for higher contribution limits compared to traditional IRAs.

>> **SEP IRA** (Simplified Employee Pension): For self-employed individuals or small business owners with few or no employees. It allows for tax-deductible contributions, and the employer can contribute up to a certain percentage of their net earnings.

>> **SIMPLE IRA** (Savings Incentive Match Plan for Employees): For small businesses with 100 or fewer employees, including self-employed individuals. It requires employer contributions and offers a simplified setup compared to a 401(k).

REMEMBER

You may have the option to do a traditional or Roth IRA like everyone else if you meet the qualifications.

You can deduct certain expenses if you are self-employed or have a small business. There are many business-related expenses that you likely incur already, such as internet, mobile phone service, health insurance premiums, and professional memberships, that you may be able to deduct. Reviewing what you can deduct each year will help you maximize your self-employment income.

The IRS doesn't like lavish expenses, so be careful to stay within the most current tax code guidelines.

One of the favorites in the F.I.R.E. community for tax-related education is The FI Tax Guy (https://fitaxguy.com/), who has great content for self-employed people and small business owners.

Variable income

Things get a little tricky when you have a variable income, as when you're in the real estate, creative, or service industry or are a tipped worker. This can be a side gig or your main job, and you may get a W-2, but the work is typically contract work (1099 employment).

This can be looked at as a glass half empty or glass half full situation. To maximize this work arrangement for reaching your F.I.R.E. goals, it's critical to take advantage of the highs. Use your high-income months to shovel away as much as you can. You should be modest with what you use as your base income if this is your main job.

My earnings from my main job were partly variable commissions. It was hard at first, but I got used to living off my base salary, so when I had really good months of commissions, I knew I had more flexibility with it. I also had a few months that were big disappointments, but thankfully it didn't wreck my finances.

If you love what you do as a tipped worker (for example, musician, dancer, or bartender), focus on ways you might be able to increase your income by changing employers or adding additional clients. If you see your tipped work as a temporary situation, then use the flexibility in your schedule to prepare for your next career.

I've not seen many full-time tipped workers on the F.I.R.E. path, but I believe there is space for everyone on this journey. So does Barbara Sloan, creator of the platform Tipped Finance (www.tippedfinance.com). She was a tipped worker herself and recognized there was a void when it came to financial education for this type of work. She gives some great tips (no pun intended) for people who work on tips and are looking to get their finances together.

Capitalizing on Passive and Semi-Passive Income

With passive income, you can get creative, as many F.I.R.E. people do. Not all income has to come from the daily grind of a job or exchanging time for money. In this section, I cover earning income from the growth of investments, royalties or commissions, and real estate rentals.

Growth of investments

When it comes to investments, you first may think of your retirement accounts, but those are for later, after you reach F.I.R.E., right? The investments I'm talking about here are income before you F.I.R.E.

Money you can use now is mainly from a regular brokerage account (also referred to as a taxable brokerage account). The key is that it is not a retirement account, so there is a lot more flexibility and no age restrictions.

You decide what assets you want to hold in the account (such as a stock index fund). You could get income from the growth and/or dividends:

>> **Growth:** Profits earned when you sell an investment for a higher price than what you initially paid. This is the most straightforward way to make money from investments.

>> **Dividends:** Some investments, like stocks, pay dividends — periodic payments to shareholders from the company's profits. You do not have to sell the underlying securities to collect the dividends.

The other places you might have growth from investments is through employee stock purchase plans (ESPP), which I explain in Table 10-1 earlier in this chapter. These often give employees a discount on purchasing the company's stock (often 15 percent).

WARNING

ESPPs can be a generous benefit, but holding on to individual stocks (even from the company you work for) is a lot riskier than an index fund that may have thousands of different stocks.

If you decide to sell your company stock, that is more income for you if there is growth (which is highly likely if you received a 15 percent discount on the front end). The company will dictate any restrictions placed on the holding period for the stock. Stock options and other equity compensation from an employer work similarly but are typically only for individuals in certain positions at the company.

Although the growth and dividends from investments can provide income on the path to F.I.R.E., it is even more powerful to use as a bridge after you F.I.R.E. (read more about this in Chapter 17). Because there are no strings attached in terms of age, you can decide to use the funds in this account as early as you like without a penalty. You will also have more time for the funds to grow and compound even more (see Chapter 12).

Even though there's no penalty for using the funds, there are tax implications when selling the investments:

>> **Dividend:** Taxed as ordinary income
>> **Growth:**
   - Short-term (held 12 months or less) capital gains are taxed at your regular income rates.
   - Long-term (held more than 12 months) capital gains are taxed as long-term capital gains (0 percent, 15 percent, or 20 percent, depending on your income). I talk more about capital gains in Chapter 15.

WARNING

All investments come with risks, and there is no guarantee of growth. Always consider your risk tolerance with this and other investments.

Earning royalties or commissions from books or other content

Fast-changing technology has created a space for people to turn their knowledge, skills, and talents into money online by becoming digital content creators. Books are still a great way to generate royalties and commissions, but there are so many ways to repurpose the content or create original content to earn even more money, such as

>> Blogging

>> Podcasting

>> YouTube

>> Online courses

>> Social media

The way to earn commission or other types of income from creating content doesn't have to be advertisements (which you probably find just as annoying as I do). Other alternatives include

>> **Affiliate marketing:** Promoting products and earning a commission for sales made through your referral links

>> **Sponsorships:** Partnering with brands to create sponsored content

>> **Digital products:** Selling e-books, courses, or digital art

>> **Subscription models:** Offering premium content through subscriptions on platforms like Patreon

TIP

The list gets huge. There may not be super riches in all of these for you, but any additional income from doing something you enjoy and are good at is a win. Not everyone gets that from their main job, and what you do on the side or freelance could grow into your next major endeavor.

Being a property owner for short- or long-term real estate rentals

One of the major subsets of the F.I.R.E. community is real estate investors. When it comes to real estate for generating income, my observation is that you either love it or you hate it. Those who do it are passionate, which is half the battle.

There are several ways you can earn income from real estate:

>> Short-term rentals like Airbnb

>> Long-term rentals like annual leases of homes or apartments

>> Flipping homes (like buying a fixer-upper and selling it for more)

People who manage rentals would all probably agree that real estate isn't totally passive, regardless of the approach you take. No matter what your situation, the more you do, the better you get at managing your process, which leads to less work than you had to do on the front end. I know quite a few F.I.R.E. friends who have their process down to a science.

TIP

Not only can the additional income from real estate help accelerate your path to F.I.R.E., but it can also be a means of funding your early retirement (see Chapter 17). If you want to explore investing in real estate or property management, hands down, two of the best and biggest resources are BiggerPockets (www.biggerpockets.com) and Afford Anything (www.affordanything.com).

Reaping the Rewards of Other Income

So far in this chapter I've discussed the more common types of income, but there are other sources of income to keep in mind. They often get overlooked but can add some extra funds to offset expenses in your household. This section covers unemployment benefits, credit card bonuses and other rewards, and bonuses for opening bank and brokerage accounts.

Unemployment benefits

There are times on your path to F.I.R.E. where you will lose your job through a layoff or other unexpected separation from your employer. The years 2022 and 2023 were some of the worst in over a decade for job loss, and technology workers (a well-represented field in the F.I.R.E. community) were hit the hardest. According to the website https://layoffs.fyi, which tracks layoffs in the tech world, there were 165,000 tech employees who lost their jobs in 2022, and over 250,000 in 2023.

Being downsized or laid off might seem like a F.I.R.E. killer, but this break in working doesn't have to lead to no income or a derailment of your plans. That's where unemployment benefits come in. While it is likely not going to be enough to cover your full salary, it could provide some income during the gap from one job to another.

If you were already living on less than you earned and have an emergency fund in place, getting by on unemployment may be even more doable.

Each state has a set maximum for unemployment benefits, and it varies widely. Table 10-2 shows examples of a few states.

TABLE 10-2 **Sample Unemployment Benefits**

State	Maximum Weekly Benefit (2024)
California	$450
Colorado	$742
Florida	$275
Georgia	$365
Kansas	$540
Missouri	$320
New York	$504
Texas	$563

Source: Adapted from Saving to Invest / savingtoinvest.com/maximum-weekly-unemployment-benefits-by-state, Last accessed Mar 05, 2024.

States may change their maximum amounts, so be sure to check the latest for your state.

If you get a lump sum severance (which is typical), you can still file for unemployment; it just cannot start until you're no longer paid by your employer (so it could be a week after you received the lump sum).

When I was laid off from my job with a utility company in 1999, I didn't think I qualified for unemployment benefits because I got six weeks' worth of severance (in a lump sum). However, when I dug into it more, I was able to get unemployment, plus I got the six weeks of severance. Guess what? I was out of work for exactly six weeks before I started my next job. That next job was the last one I would have before I F.I.R.E.d (20 years later). I made more money during that time of unemployment than if I had been working. It was a miserable time, so this little bonus was welcomed.

Credit card bonuses and other rewards

The F.I.R.E. community loves travel, and the main way to offset this potentially expensive hobby is through credit card rewards. There are also very generous cash rewards and other incentives for those who don't necessarily do a lot of traveling.

These rewards aren't like income from a job, but they certainly can help cover some of your expenses, like airfare, hotel stays, or simply extra cash to spend how you want.

The art of reward credit cards is making sure you do not carry a balance on them. If you carry a balance and pay high interest rates, that negates any benefits you get from rewards or bonuses. If you pay your card off in full, every month, then the credit card rewards and incentives can be a tremendous value in the form of travel, cash back, or new account bonuses.

Having a healthy credit score is essential in making this work to your advantage. Typically, a credit score somewhere around 760 or higher will enable you to qualify for the best offers. If you're not quite there yet, check out some of the tips in Chapter 5.

Travel reward cards can be directly from an airline or from a major credit card company that partners with multiple airlines and hotels. Both typically will come with an annual fee (often waived the first year, possibly the second if you ask). However, the rewards are typically so generous that they far outweigh the annual fee.

TIP

Be sure to do the math to make sure your value from the card makes sense to continue with it.

The favorites in the F.I.R.E. community are Chase travel rewards because they typically have some of the most generous bonuses. However, most major banks offer travel rewards cards. Here are some of the big attractions for these types of cards:

>> Huge new account bonuses that include a lump sum of miles or points such as 50,000 miles when you spend $5,000 in the first three months. This $5,000 example equates to about $1,700/month and may be easy to get to when you think about all the things you may use credit cards for (without going into debt), like groceries, gas, internet, and cellphone.

>> Miles or points for each dollar you spend on the card and other incentives. Sometimes there are extra perks like free companion tickets on airlines, free nights at hotels, free upgrades on airlines or hotels, or waiving of baggage fees.

>> Many travel reward cards will not charge a foreign transaction fee when you make purchases outside the country. Most credit cards charge a 3 percent fee. So, if you travel to other countries, this "little" annoying fee can add to the cost of your trip.

TIP

There are many blogs, websites, and other platforms dedicated to the travel reward cards category and their constantly changing offers. A few sites have stood the test of time and do a great job of keeping up with the latest information:

>> Travel Miles 101 (www.travelmiles101.com)

>> Doctor of Credit (www.doctorofcredit.com)

>> The Points Guy (https://thepointsguy.com/)

Travel reward cards are a lot of fun and will help fulfill your visions of dream destinations, but you may also crave cash. Some cards offer rewards that are straight up cash back and have incentives similar to travel rewards cards, except that you earn cash instead of travel.

TIP

There are reward credit cards for just about any area of your life from grocery stores (like Kroger and Walmart) to retailers (like Apple and Best Buy). Don't overlook the bonuses and other credit card incentives in this chapter that could be a little boost to your income and make your dollars go further.

Focusing on the things that matter to you is key to enjoying your F.I.R.E. journey. You don't need to cut out those things to reduce your expenses, but you can be smarter about how you pay for them like using reward cards.

Bonuses for opening bank and brokerage accounts

The bonuses I talk about in this section will equate to a small part of your total income, but let's just consider them icing on the cake. It's worth noting that banks and brokerages want to hold your money. When you're their customer, it benefits their bottom line. For this, they want to entice you with valuable cash incentives.

The most critical part with these bonuses is to read the terms and conditions first (usually the tiny print at the bottom of the offer). They will have rules that you have to follow to collect the bonus. I would hate for you to make the effort to go after a bonus and not do everything that's required to get what you expected.

Requirements to earn the bonus will be something like

>> Initial deposit required

>> Balance needed to maintain and a duration

>> When the bonus will be paid out

TIP

Make sure the bonus incentives outweigh the other values you get from an account such as interest rates or fees.

Banks

Bonuses from banks mostly come in the way of new accounts and are widely available. They are available for checking, savings, or money market accounts.

The amounts of bonuses will vary. They're often based on the amount of your deposit or the balance you maintain but will likely range somewhere from $100 to $500 or more for opening a new account. The sum is small, but you also expend a small amount of effort — simply opening an account and reading the terms in most cases.

Some banks will make you jump through a few more hoops, like having a certain number of debit card transactions each month during the bonus period or having other services with the bank. Depending on the bonus, you may find this to be worthwhile or not worth the return on investment.

TIP

Keep in mind that you do not need to close your main checking account to open a new one if your purpose is just to get the bonus money. You can treat it as a secondary account and keep everything else that you have set up with your main account (such as bill pay, automatic drafts, and so on).

Banks offering these bonuses can be found at

>> Big national banks (like Chase and Citi)

>> Online banks (like Ally and Discover)

>> Regional banks (like PNC and US Bank)

You can go online to find a good listing of bonuses using aggregators such as

>> Nerdwallet (www.nerdwallet.com)

>> Bankrate (www.bankrate.com)

>> Hustler Money Blog (www.hustlermoneyblog.com)

Bonuses rarely outweigh high monthly fees, so always look for a no-fee account.

The money that you receive from bonuses counts as taxable income, so expect a 1099-MISC tax form for the year in which the bonus was paid. It is taxed at the same rate as your income.

Brokerages

The bonuses for brokerage accounts can be more lucrative than with bank accounts. Some are for new accounts only, but these bonuses often extend to existing accounts. There could be bonuses for the following types of accounts:

» IRAs

» IRA rollovers (from an employer-sponsored retirement account)

» Regular brokerage accounts

Nearly every big broker out there offers these bonuses, but the one I have rarely seen offers from is our beloved Vanguard. No worries though; Vanguard funds are available at other brokers. Here is a list of the most common brokers that offer bonuses:

» Ally Invest

» Chase

» Fidelity

» M1 Finance

» Merrill Edge (Bank of America)

» Schwab

One of the best strategies to take advantage of these bonuses is when you are planning to move funds in an employer retirement plan to an IRA after you have separated from service. Going from one provider to another is considered a trustee-to-trustee transfer. If you have already decided to do this, you may as well earn a little extra cash for doing it.

Be sure to consider all the factors in determining whether a rollover is right for your situation.

Just so you get a sense of how big these bonuses can be, here's an example of a type of graduated schedule for bonuses at a broker:

>> $100,000 to $199,999 deposit: $250

>> $200,000 to $499,999 deposit: $600

>> $500,000 to $999,999 deposit: $1,200

>> $1,000,000 to $1,499,999 deposit: $2,500

Bonuses for these accounts are treated as growth. So however the growth on the account is handled, it would apply to the cash incentives you receive.

EXAMPLE

For example, on a Roth account with a bonus of $600, the bonus is simply treated the same as the other growth in your Roth account. So, if you're older than 59.5 and have had the account for more than five years, the growth is tax free. This makes the bonus even sweeter.

You can do an unlimited number of trustee-to-trustee transfers directly from one brokerage to another (not transferred to you). Be sure to keep track of your accounts and the bonuses you have coming.

Here are a few other things to look out for when it comes to broker bonuses:

>> Is it for new customers only?

>> What type of accounts are allowed?

>> How long does the money have to stay in the account?

>> Do rollovers or transfers count?

Like with all the other types of bonuses, be sure to read the rules carefully because there could be some gotchas.

Chapter **11**

Moving Fast by Increasing Your Savings Rate

Racing to the finish line is not the goal of F.I.R.E., but if you want to pick up the pace, there's nothing more powerful than increasing your savings rate. It's a key metric in your journey and it's one of the most important when measuring your time to reaching F.I.R.E.

As I describe in Chapter 4, your savings rate is a function of the gap between your income and expenses. You simply divide your savings amount by your income to come up with a percentage. Here's a quick example using your gross income:

EXAMPLE

Savings: $15,000/year (contributions to savings and investing)

Gross income: $80,000/year

Savings rate: 19 percent

Savings Rate = ($15,000 / $80,000) = .19 (19 percent)

You can use net income rather than gross income if you prefer, but always use the same one to track your progress as you increase your savings rate over time.

TIP

It may not be helpful to compare your number to someone else's because they may be calculating their savings rate differently than you are.

REMEMBER

Remember that savings rate also includes investing such as

>> Workplace retirement accounts

>> Traditional or Roth Individual Retirement Accounts (IRAs)

>> Health Savings Account

>> Brokerage account

Even if you're starting small in the beginning, forming a savings habit early in your F.I.R.E. journey and pushing it up over time will have a massive impact. A high savings rate is what makes it possible to reach financial independence in 10 or 15 years versus 30 or 40 years. In this chapter, I talk about why your savings rate matters, how high your savings rate should be, and where to save.

Understanding Why Your Savings Rate Matters

If you make $200,000 per year and you spend $250,000, you will never get to financial independence because you're not saving anything. In fact, you're creating a deficit for yourself that is compounding (the bad kind) and working against you. So, a high income does not guarantee wealth or the ability to reach F.I.R.E.

REMEMBER

A high income alone is not going to give you the momentum you want if you don't rachet up the savings rate.

The amount of income that you keep, save, and invest (rather than spend) is what truly matters. Understanding the powerful correlation between a high savings rate and shortening your time to F.I.R.E. is compelling.

If you save about 10 percent and you stay at 10 percent your entire working life, you're probably okay to retire at a traditional age (in your 60s). Sliding that savings rate up a bit is where the magic happens to get you on your way to F.I.R.E.

EXAMPLE

For every additional 5 percent you're able to increase your savings rate, you shave off about three years to reaching F.I.R.E. This assumes a modest 5 percent annualized investment return and retiring with 25 times your expenses. Take a look at the example in Table 11-1.

TABLE 11-1

Why Your Savings Rate Matters

Savings Rate	Years to Retirement
30%	28
35%	24.6
40%	21.6
45%	19
50%	16.6

TIP

Try out `Netify.com`'s **early retirement calculator** at `http://tinyurl.com/2jrr85zd`.

Determining Your Savings Rate

But First, Save 10: The One Simple Money Move That Will Change Your Life (Et Alia Press, 2020) is the name of a book by Sarah-Catherine Gutierrez that basically says you've got to start saving somewhere, so it's okay if it's a modest amount like 10 percent. The point is, you're getting out of the paycheck-to-paycheck cycle and ready to pay yourself first.

When you're first starting out, there is no number too small, because at the beginning, you are in habit-forming mode. You are building a muscle that will get stronger as you focus on creating regular, consistent, and automatic savings.

ANECDOTE

My savings habit started with a two-dollar bill because I thought they were special. I got my first one when I was a junior in high school because they were (and still are) rare compared to other bills. Every time I went to the bank to cash my paycheck from my first job, I would ask for another two-dollar bill. I kept saving more and more of those two-dollar bills all through high school, then through college, and even after adulting.

I never counted exactly how many I had until my daughter asked me (I was in my 30s). When I finally counted them, I had 1,800 two-dollar bills ($3,600). All that time I had been creating the habit of saving and didn't even realize it. I was consistent, I kept increasing the amount, and I nearly made it automatic. I'm still obsessed with two-dollar bills, but instead of saving them, I give them away to high school kids as I teach them about money. Nothing like paying kids to learn!

chones/Adobe Stock Photos

TIP

Your first major milestone should be an emergency fund (if you haven't already established one). The common guideline is three to six months' worth of expenses (not income), and that's a reasonable target. But if you're headed down the F.I.R.E. path, you'll want a bit more so you can walk away even before you hit your number. This is what's called an FU fund (which I say stands for *forget you*, but you can call it what you want — you get the idea). The amount may not be enough to retire on but still enough to serve as buffer from your job to your next endeavor by allowing you to undertake something like one of the following:

» Extended time before taking another job

» A short sabbatical

» A career change

» A runway to start your own business

TIP

The elusive 50 percent or more saving rate comes from the early advocates of the F.I.R.E. movement, who were mainly high-income earners (often in tech or engineering) with very low expenses.

Fifty percent is an ambitious savings rate that will get you to F.I.R.E. at lightning speed. This is a goal for some, but remember that it depends on how soon you want to reach F.I.R.E. and you need to have a big enough gap between your income and expenses to support it.

According to the U.S. Census Bureau, the median household income in America in 2022 was about $75,000 per year. A 50 percent savings rate would be $37,500 and you'd have to live off the remaining $37,500. If you started this at age 23, you'd reach

F.I.R.E. by age 37 (assuming an 8 percent annualized investment return), as summarized here:

Income: $75,000

50 percent savings rate: $37,500

Expenses: $37,500

Assumed rate of return: 8 percent

Starting age: 23

Years to F.I.R.E.: 14

Age at time of F.I.R.E.: 37

Total amount saved at time of F.I.R.E.: $562,000

Total value of portfolio (savings and growth) at time of F.I.R.E.: $981,000

TIP

I used the calculators at www.playingwithfire.co/calculators for this example.

It's unrealistic for most people to try to get to a 50 percent savings rate right out of the gate, so if you're not there yet, you have plenty of company. If you're a higher-income earner, let's say $200,000, then maybe $100,000 to live on is possible. But if you're just starting your career in your 20s, making $60,000 a year, the idea of living off $30,000 is much less likely.

TIP

You'll hear many financial experts suggest a 10 to 15 percent savings rate. I think the point that sometimes gets missed is to continue to escalate that savings rate, right along with the rise in your income.

ANECDOTE

I never quite made it to a 50 percent savings rate. Perhaps if I calculated it based on my net income rather than gross or if I included my employer contribution, it would have been closer, but my savings rate peaked at about 40 percent. My company 401(k) match was extremely generous: if I put in 7 percent, they put in 9 percent and that gave me a lot of extra fuel.

I saved and invested even before I did a budget because that's what I was good at; that was my superpower. I was really surprised the first time I calculated my savings rate because I had no idea. I was only counting my contributions to my 401(k) because I knew exactly what percentage that was. By the time I added contributions to my Roth IRA, health savings account, investment club, and brokerage account, it was about 40 percent.

I've seen the headlines where people were saving 50 percent, 60 percent, and 70 percent, and I thought, "Oh, I will never get that high," but now I realize they may have just been calculating it slightly differently or perhaps they had a much higher income than I did. (My salary was less than $100,000.)

TIP

Once you start tracking your savings rate, it's a thrill to watch it go up even if it's by just 1 percent. What matters is that you're moving the needle and headed in the right direction. In the beginning, you may also have competing priorities if your expenses are high or you're working on paying down your debt.

The key is to make progress and increase your savings rate over time. Ten percent is a good starting place. As you develop the habit of saving, you can start increasing your rate. Before you know it, you'll be at 30 percent, 40 percent, perhaps even 50 percent along with your increase in income and your reduction in debt and expenses.

When you begin the big shift from spender to saver, you'll feel like you got a head start if you've already started some level of savings. You won't be starting from zero, and you will have saved something.

Here's an example if you started with just 10 percent in your first 10 years from age 22 to 32):

EXAMPLE

10 percent per year saving/investing

Salary: $60,000

Savings: $500/month ($6,000/year)

Growth: 8 percent return

Total after 10 years: $91,473

That $91,473 is your starting point, instead of $0!

Figuring Out Where to Save

When deciding what type of savings or investment vehicle to use, your primary considerations are the goal for the money and when you will need it. If you're saving for retirement, it can be decades before you need it, but if you're building up an emergency fund, you can need that money next month.

This section covers how to figure out where to save for short-term, medium-term and long-term goals.

Short-term savings

Short-term savings will be exactly that; they will go into a short-term savings vehicle such as

>> Checking account

>> High-yield savings account (HYSA)

>> Money market account

This will be your emergency fund money, and you may get that built up quickly. The primary goal for this account is being able to quickly access the money. It's very important to have this cushion in case something goes wrong or you happen to screw up (as we all do from time to time). You don't want to throw off all your F.I.R.E. plans, especially when you're early in the game.

TIP

Interest rates on short-term accounts will vary and typically pay more when inflation is high.

Medium-term savings

Medium-term savings are funds you will hold on to a little longer. You may be saving for specific goals such as

>> A down payment on a home

>> College funding (within a few years of needing it)

>> A down payment on a car or to pay cash in full

The time horizon in these situations is usually between three and five years. You don't want to put this money at significant risk, and it should remain accessible for the time frame you need it. With college, it depends on how close you are to needing the funds for school. If you are within three to five years, consider that medium-term savings. If you have longer, such as when you're starting to save for a new baby that won't start college for 17 years, you can consider it long-term savings.

Examples of savings vehicles for medium-term savings are

>> High-yield savings account

>> 529 college savings plan

>> I Bonds

>> Certificates of deposit (CDs)

TIP

CDs have fixed rates for a period of time versus savings or money market rates, which are variable and can change at any time.

These are all lower risk investments that may not return as much as the stock market in most years, but you have the peace of mind that this money is available when you need it. You won't have to worry about the fluctuations of the stock market. Remember the scary drop in the stock market in spring of 2020 when the pandemic first hit? How about in 2022 when the stock market was down 18 percent for the year? You don't want your medium-term savings to be affected by situations like these.

Long-term savings

Long-term saving and investing will be your biggest bucket and are primarily what you'll be relying on for early retirement. Even if your plan is not to fully retire early, you want to be in the financial position that gives you options.

Savings in this bucket should be treated like a marathon, not a sprint. This means that you can take risks for greater returns (such as with stocks) because you have time for any downturns to recover. Dollar cost averaging is also ideal here.

TECHNICAL
STUFF

Dollar cost averaging is making contributions on a regular schedule (weekly, monthly, per pay period, and so on) to your investments over time.

The most common (and highly discussed in the F.I.R.E. community) types of accounts for investing for the long term are

>> Workplace retirement, such as 401(k), 403(b), and Thrift Savings Plans

>> Roth and Traditional IRA

>> Health Savings Account (if you want to use it as a long-term vehicle)

>> Regular brokerage account

TIP

The popular VTSAX would fall into long-term savings.

By the time you really get to work with your long-term savings, you've likely built up the habit and strengthened your savings muscle. You will have reached a place where saving is automatic and starts to increase as your income increases. This puts you in a powerful position to really start to accelerate your time to F.I.R.E.

TIP

You will not need your long-term savings all at once. For example, if your F.I.R.E. number is $1.5 million and you're retiring at 45, you don't need your entire $1.5 million at the beginning of your retirement. It's going to be spread over the term of your retirement years, which may be four decades or longer.

REMEMBER

Remember that you can make contributions to more than one type of savings at a time. It may be counterintuitive, but we are a nation of multitaskers with everything else, and we can do the same with our savings.

For instance, you can still contribute up to your employer match while doing short- or medium-term savings. It's just a matter of allocating how much goes to each bucket of savings. Until you reach your ideal emergency fund, most of the savings would go to that. This won't make or break your F.I.R.E. plans, but it will keep you from missing out on the free money from an employer match and get your long-term investments growing.

REMEMBER

In Chapter 12, I talk more about getting your money to grow for these long-term investments, but remember the biggest part of growing your nest egg is making contributions. The savings part must happen first and then you can look more closely at growing your investments.

This beginning phase is accumulation mode and building the savings habit by

>> Being consistent

>> Making it automatic

>> Slowly increasing it over time

IN THIS CHAPTER

» **Demystifying the complexity of investing**

» **Understanding the power of compound growth**

» **Beginning your investing at work**

» **Investing on autopilot**

» **Simplifying the steps to investing**

» **Managing your investments**

Chapter **12**

Investing and the Undeniable Power of Compound Growth

I n the F.I.R.E. community, investing can be one of the easiest parts of getting to your F.I.R.E. number, which is contrary to how things work in much of the personal finance world. I admit that the "VTSAX and Chill" philosophy (see Chapter 19) is a bit of an oversimplification of investing, but it doesn't have to involve complex strategies or require special expertise. Simple investing can yield the same or often better results than intensive focus by the pros.

TIP

Increasing your investing as you decrease your expenses, debt, and taxes powers your drive toward F.I.R.E.

Your investments will not only grow as you make contributions to your accounts but also through compounding, which is growth on top of growth. It almost sounds like magic, but it's a simple concept that everyone can revel in.

In this chapter, I want to be your educator, cheerleader, coach, and mentor by helping you make sense of investing so that no fear or confusion stifles your ability to maximize this part of your journey.

Is Investing Too Complex?

Complexity can be the thief of progress. If you freeze up or get confused about how to even understand what you're investing in your 401(k), your default may be to say it's just too hard and give up. If you feel that way, it's not your fault. The world of investing *does* seem confusing. Everyone seems to have a no-fail, mind-blowing investment strategy that will solve all your problems, when all you really want is for your money to grow. It can get confusing.

EXAMPLE

Let me give you an example by using some investing terminology that helped me explain to my 14-year-old daughter what a mutual fund is. She asked, "What is a mutual fund?" Hmmm . . . how do I explain this complex thing to a teenager in a way she would actually understand? Here's my simple answer and the textbook or industry answer. Which one is easier to understand?

Simple Answer	Typical Industry Answer
A basket of stocks (or other investments)	An investment option where money from many people is pooled together to buy a variety of stocks, bonds, or other securities

Both are correct, but one seems much simpler to understand and remember. The daughter I mentioned repeated the simple answer to a friend of mine weeks later without me having to even prompt her. This helped me quickly realize that investing doesn't have to be hard; I just need to explain it better and keep it simple.

Unfortunately, the financial industry doesn't help much with things like simplicity and ease, but investing can be both of those.

TIP

Research has shown that complexity doesn't equal better performance in the investing world, and many of the world's greatest investors (including Warren Buffett) agree.

In the F.I.R.E. community, the person we affectionately call the "Godfather of F.I." is J.L. Collins. He captured the simplicity of investing on his website (www.jlcollinsnh.com) in his 26-part stock series. He then turned it into a book, *The Simple Path to Wealth* (JL Collins LLC). The anthem of the F.I.R.E. investment philosophy is to keep it simple.

J.L. Collins's follow-up gift to investors who loved the simple approach was *Pathfinders* (Harriman House), which collected the stories of people who followed the simple path. I love a good money story and think you will enjoy the variety of perspectives in this book and hear others share the good, the bad, and the ugly on their path to financial independence.

How Does Compound Growth Work?

You can't save your way to wealth. Letting your money sit in cash or a savings account may feel safe, but in the long run, it will get eaten up by inflation. Savings has a place for short-term use, such as your emergency fund, but the only way to get your money growing for the long term is to invest it and enjoy the power of compounding.

TIP

Compounding can work for you or against you:

>> When it comes to debt, it works against you because the interest being charged makes your balance grow.

>> When it comes to investing, it works for you because the interest and growth being earned makes your balance grow.

I want it to work for you! Less of the compounding debt and more of the compounding of investments is what gets you closer to F.I.R.E.

TECHNICAL STUFF

Compound interest is the term often used when it comes to investing, but I purposely use the term *compound growth* because we're not talking about only the interest — like for a savings account — but also the growth of the investment returns and dividends.

EXAMPLE

Here is my favorite example of compound growth to get to $1,000,000:

Invest	$50/week
Investment type	S&P 500 (or similar stock index fund)
Annual Growth Assumption	9% (compounded weekly)
Years	40
Total after 40 years	$1,000,000

$1,000,000 is the magic number that gets a lot of people's attention, especially young people just starting out. I even turned this into a card that I give to family and friends for graduations and birthdays with a crisp new $50 bill (or I send $50 via a money transfer app). I call it "You're My Millionaire," and I give them the first $50 to get started. On the back of the card is an amortization schedule that shows how the investment compounds year after year (see Figure 12-1).

Image credit: Amber Koski (VisuallyAmber.com)

Sometimes I get a little carried away and love to show how you can get to $1,000,000 in half the time, as shown here:

Invest	$18,000 at the beginning of each year (including company match)
Investment type	S&P 500 (or similar stock index fund)
Growth Assumption	9% (compounded annually)
Years	20
Total after 40 years	$1,000,000

TIP

Have a little fun and run some assumptions of your own using a compound growth calculator. Here are a few that I like:

>> Compound Interest Calculator at www.investor.gov

>> Compound Savings Calculator at www.dinkytown.net

>> Compound Interest Calculator at www.bankrate.com

Why Start at Work?

The best advice you can give to a younger coworker is to make sure they contribute to the employer's retirement plan to get the employer's matching contribution. They may think you're a little crazy because retirement is not on the mind of most 22-year-olds, but they will love you later.

ANECDOTE

For a long time, I did not think of my 401(k) plan at work as investing, and I certainly was not thinking about retirement in my 20s. The money didn't even feel like it was mine because I couldn't touch it until so far in the future. However, I did do the match my company offered (read more in the "Company match" section later in this chapter) because it was easy and I thought I should be doing something.

A workplace retirement plan is where most people start investing even if they don't realize that's what they're doing. This is how you probably started as well. Beyond the tax advantages I mention in Chapter 15, there are a few other simple reasons why investing through work is a good idea:

>> There's a short list of investment options (usually 10 to 15).

>> There's usually a company match (typically 3 to 6 percent).

>> Contributions come straight out of your paycheck, so you don't "miss" having the money because it never hits your regular bank account.

TIP

It's becoming more common for employers to automatically enroll people in this benefit, so you may be in this situation.

In the days of traditional pension plans the employer managed the plan and the investments. All employees had to do was work long enough to earn a guaranteed monthly amount after they retired. Those days are nearly gone and have been replaced primarily with retirement plans where you must manage the investments yourself. Typical investment accounts include

>> 401(k)

>> 403(b)

>> 457(b)

>> TSP (Thrift Savings Plan)

The specific rules and investment choices of each plan vary by employer, but what they have in common is that you are responsible for choosing the investments in the plan. You don't have to pick from thousands of individual stocks; typically, there is a short list of about 10 to 15 funds to choose from (more about this later in the chapter).

TIP

Canada, the United Kingdom, and many other countries besides the United States have similar employer-sponsored plans.

Your employer-sponsored retirement plan will likely be your biggest pot of money because

» You will probably start putting money into it earlier than with any other account, so the compound growth is working longer.

» The contribution limits are higher than other tax-advantaged accounts ($23,000 in 2024 and adjusted for inflation each year).

» Once you turn 50, you can contribute even more (which is perfect if you're catching up).

Company match

Employer matches bring new meaning to the term *matchmaker*. It's one of the greatest benefits an employer can make available to all their employees to encourage wealth building. Even better, it can help you reach F.I.R.E. sooner.

The typical employer match is 3 to 6 percent of your pay, and some do even more. Don't underestimate the boost this match can give your account.

EXAMPLE

Table 12-1 shows an example of the effect a 6 percent match has on your account if you make $80,000/year:

TABLE 12-1   **Impact of Employer Match**

	You	Employer Match	Total
Annual Contribution (made at the beginning of the year)	$23,000	$4,800	$27,800
Annual Growth Rate	8%	8%	8%
Total After 10 years	$359,800	$75,100	$434,900

This doesn't even factor in raises or bonuses that might happen over the years.

WARNING

Keep in mind that some employers require you to remain with them for a certain period of time in order for you keep the match they gave you. This is called *vesting*, and employers often use this as a retention tool. Remember that your contributions are always yours regardless of how long you have been with the employer.

Automatic investing through payroll

Think about all the financial areas of your life that use automation. For example,

>> Taxes coming out of your paycheck

>> Automatic bill pay through your bank

>> Property taxes and insurance paid through escrow

The easiest way to stick with investing is to make it automatic. The contributions you make to your retirement account come right out of your paycheck, so you don't even have to think about making the contributions to your account. You may not even miss that money because you never see it in your checking account.

TIP

With automatic contributions, you get used to living off only the amount that goes into your bank account, which is a great habit to form.

This strategy of deducting from your pay each period is called dollar cost averaging. You're automatically contributing to your investments on a regular basis, no matter what the market is doing. When the market goes down, you're buying. When the market goes up, you're buying.

Simple investment choices

One paradox of life is that too many choices can hinder you from making decisions because you get overwhelmed. That dilemma is a real thing, and it can happen when you're faced with something like thousands of different investment options.

One way investing through your employer's plan differs from investing in your own account (such as an IRA or brokerage account) is in the number of investments you have to choose from. With an employer plan, you have a list of 10 to 15 investment options, usually in the form of mutual funds.

TIP

Limiting choices may seem like a downside at first, but it does simplify your investment decisions.

Most employers now have online access to accounts, and some even have apps that can make it even easier to check out your investment choices or learn a little more about your options. You'll be able to see things like your balance, rate of return, contributions and other transactions, and the funds you're invested in. You don't need to check it every day, but it's good practice to keep the pulse of what is going on with your account and make changes if needed.

One of the easiest ways to get a quick overview of the investments you have available is to bring up the list of mutual funds (usually under something like "investment lineup" or "available investments") and sort on the headers, which normally include

>> Asset class (stocks, bonds, fixed income, and so on)

>> Expense ratio/fees

>> Historical performance over periods such as 1, 3, 5, and 10 years

TIP

Sometimes you can get a better indication of what the fund is by looking at the asset class of the fund rather than its name.

Not every employer plan is terrific; in fact, some employer plans may be just awful. Fortunately, that is rarer these days with the availability of simple index funds or target date funds. Most plans now offer a choice of investment options such as the following:

>> **Target Date Retirement Fund:** Matches allocation with the year in which you plan to retire. Usually there is a split between stocks and bonds (or other types of safe or fixed income). This is the default option for most plans for automatic enrollment into your employer's retirement plan.

>> **Passive Index Stock Fund:** Usually a stock fund with a low expense ratio (or fees), such as one that follows the S&P 500 index or Total Stock Market Index. You may not have access to the F.I.R.E. favorite VTSAX, but you may find something similar.

>> **Active Stock Fund:** Usually a stock fund with active management and possibly higher fees, but investments in the funds are hand-picked rather than passively following an index.

>> **International or Global Fund:** Has investments not just from the U.S. but also abroad.

>> **Fixed Income:** This would include safer investments with less risk than stocks, such as bonds or money market funds.

TIP

The names of the funds don't always give you a clue about what type of investment they are, which may be confusing. So be sure to take the extra step to click the link (usually next to the fund) that shows you a one-page fund fact sheet that gives the highlights of what's in the fund, including things like fund category, risk level, expenses and fees, performance history, and the portfolio (top holdings and sectors).

TIP

Making your contributions to one fund may get it done. Spreading your money across more funds doesn't mean better performance. You don't necessarily need to do that to achieve your investment goals.

ANECDOTE

I made the mistake of trying to pick four or five different funds and thinking that was helping me. Not really! It just made it unnecessarily complex and confusing. Also, I was overlapping funds that had the same type of investment. After doing a little research, I got it down to one or two funds, which accomplished my investment goals as I approached F.I.R.E.

Making Passive Investing Work for You

Although Warren Buffett made his riches from hand-picking great companies that have been uber successful, he sends the clear message that most people are better off with passive investing.

REMEMBER

Buffett made a $1,000,000 bet in 2008 in which he said the S&P 500 index would beat a hand-picked basket of stocks by hedge funds over a 10-year period (2008 through 2017). The S&P 500 index won for that period, and I don't think it surprised many people. Few investors would bet against Buffett.

TECHNICAL STUFF

Hedge funds actively pick stocks to try to outperform the market.

Passive investing is simply following an index rather than actively hand-picking the investments that will outperform the market (which is rarely the case.)

Passive investing is one of the few areas where less is more:

>> Less time trying to pick investments

>> Less time tinkering with your portfolio

>> Less time worrying about what your investments are doing

TIP

When it comes to income, the only truly passive income is living off your investments and letting the compound growth do all the work.

In this section, I talk about index funds, low investment fees, I-bonds, and dollar cost averaging versus lump sum. These are all areas that can help you follow a very simple and easy passive investing strategy.

Index funds

The simple term "funds" can be a little confusing, so I think it warrants a clearer explanation.

EXAMPLE

An index fund simply tracks the performance of an index — for example, the S&P 500 index, which includes the 500 largest publicly traded U.S. companies. These are names you recognize, like Apple, Amazon, Chipotle, Microsoft, and Tesla.

Other common stock market indexes are

» Total Stock Market Index (all 3,000-plus U.S. companies)

» Dow Jones (30 largest U.S. companies)

» Total World Stock Index (foreign and U.S. companies)

An index fund can come in two flavors:

» **Mutual funds** can only be purchased at the price where they land at the end of each day (the closing price). Some require a minimum in order to buy.

   An example is the Vanguard Total Stock Market Index Fund Admiral Shares (VTSAX). The minimum investment (as of 2024) is $3,000.

» **Exchange Traded Funds (ETFs)** are traded on the stock exchange throughout the day, just like a stock. That means the price may fluctuate throughout the day. Usually there's no minimum to purchase.

   An example is the Vanguard Total Stock Market ETF (VTI), which does not have a minimum.

TIP

The Simple Path to Wealth by J.L. Collins highlights low-cost, broad-based index funds to make your investing simple.

TIP

Check out these books if you'd like learn more about funds:

>> *Mutual Funds For Dummies* by Eric Tyson (Wiley)

>> *Exchange-Traded Funds For Dummies* by Russell Wild (Wiley)

Low fees and expense ratios

Fees eat into the growth of your investments. You may think that higher fees might equate to better performance, but that is rarely the case. One of the best parts of passive investing in index funds is the low fees, which are referred to as expense ratios.

TECHNICAL
STUFF

The expense ratio is how much of a fund's assets are used for administrative fees and other operating expenses.

Any fund will have an overview (usually one page) that includes the fund's expense ratio. It is not the only data point you want to consider when choosing a fund, but fees are a big deal.

Most of the major low-cost brokers have index funds that have nearly zero fees (.03 to .09 percent). Although Vanguard is the F.I.R.E. favorite when it comes to low-cost index funds, some other low-cost providers include Blackrock, Fidelity, and Schwab.

TIP

Employer retirement plans usually have at least one or two low-fee index funds, so do your research when you're making your choice.

No-fee I bonds

I bonds are another low-cost way to have a safe investment because they're a lot less volatile than stocks. The interest rate on a particular I bond changes every 6 months, based on inflation, and there are no fees associated with owning them. Investments like this that keep pace with inflation are a valuable tool to have. They were all the rage in 2021 and 2022 with rates nearly 10 percent when inflation was at historical highs.

TECHNICAL
STUFF

When you buy an I bond (or other U.S. savings bond), you're lending money to the U.S. government in return for getting the money back later plus additional interest (similar to a savings account).

You purchase I bonds directly from the U.S. government at the TreasuryDirect website (www.treasurydirect.gov). You can only purchase up to $10,000 per year (there are a few exceptions).

TIP

With I bonds, the amount you invested doesn't go down like stocks and can provide some diversification.

Dollar cost averaging versus lump sum

When you are contributing to your employer retirement plan every pay period, you're using a technique referred to as *dollar cost averaging.* You are adding to your investments at regular intervals regardless of price fluctuations.

Most people don't have a large amount of funds to invest at once. But if you find yourself in a situation when you can, you may wonder whether it's better to do that or to make smaller purchases over time. It's hard to say because I don't have a crystal ball to know how investments are going to perform. The philosophy of getting the money invested as soon as possible so compound growth can start working holds true here, but the psychological side of investing a lump sum all at once makes some people a little nervous.

If you do have a lump sum to invest (perhaps if you sold a house or inherited the money) and are hesitant to invest it all at once, you could do it in bigger chunks. It would take you a long time to dollar cost average like you do through your paycheck, but it can be done.

EXAMPLE

For instance, if you receive $200,000 to invest, you can divide that into four contribution periods:

>> $50,000 in July 2024

>> $50,000 in October 2024

>> $50,000 in January 2025

>> $50,000 in June 2025

With this method, over a one-year period, you will have all your money in the stock market.

TIP

You can run some of your own comparisons based on the history of S&P 500 performance using the Lump Sum vs Dollar Cost Average calculator at Personal Finance Club (www.personalfinanceclub.com/lump-sum-vs-dollar-cost-average-calculator).

The Three Steps to Investing on Your Own

In this section, I walk you through the steps to investing on your own, including opening, funding, and choosing investments for the account. All three steps are essential to getting your money working for you.

TIP

If you'd like to take a deeper dive int investing, check out *Investing For Dummies* by Eric Tyson (Wiley).

Opening an account

You may feel some anxiety about setting up an investment account on your own. When you do your investing through an employer, they will open it for you. But at some point you will want to invest on your own with an IRA or regular brokerage account.

Brokerage providers (like Vanguard, Fidelity, or Schwab) make it very easy to open an account online. Usually there is an obvious button or link that says Open Account. From there, you simply follow their step-by-step process. It's usually very friendly for those new to investing.

This first step is just for opening the account and you still have to get money in the account and choose your investments.

Funding the account

Once the account is open, you have to get money into the account so you can start investing. The simple way to do that is by connecting your checking account so that you can transfer the funds.

Another alternative is to roll over another brokerage or retirement account to the new account you are opening. Your new provider should have step-by-step instructions for how to do this or a number to call if you have any issues.

Choosing investments

The final step is to choose your investments. If you miss this step, your money just sits in the account without growing.

Choosing investments is much like it is with your workplace retirement account except that you have a lot more choices. Just about every type of investment is available to you, including index funds, stocks, and bonds.

REMEMBER

Don't get bogged down with all the choices you have. You can still keep it simple with an index fund if you want. The account provider will have a (very long) list of investments available, and there should be a search feature if you want to find a particular investment.

TIP

A great resource for investing for beginners is Personal Finance Club (`www.personalfinanceclub.com`), which is best known for their super simple infographics that teach investing and primarily focus on index funds.

TIP

If you have an interest in learning more about investing in individual stocks, a great resource is a nonprofit organization called BetterInvesting (`www.betterinvesting.org`). They provide unbiased investment education and stock analysis tools for long-term investing. This is how I first started learning about the stock market.

Managing Your Investments

Do it yourself (DIY) is the preferred method for most people in the F.I.R.E. community, and there are lots of resources to help you along the way (see Chapter 21). The main reason for doing it yourself is because you can keep things simple with a passive investing approach, and there's not much else to do.

TIP

The approach J.L. Collins describes in *The Simple Path to Wealth* resonates with many people, and it's a book worth reading.

When you set up your own accounts and manage them, you have full control. It can be as easy as using one or more index funds. Stocks and bonds are two major asset classes you want to keep:

>> **Stocks:** More risk and volatility but greater reward. If you need your money in the next few years, you run the risk of the stock market being down when you need it. In the down years of stocks, things can be a little scary, but over the long run, stocks have returned about 8 to 12 percent annually. Take a look at the example of returns for the S&P 500 listed in the "Managing the inherent risk in the stock market" section later in this chapter.

>> **Bonds:** Serve as safety net with less risk than stocks, but the average return is much less (about 1 to 3 percent annually). At some point you need access to funds in your account, so bonds are a way to keep a portion of your funds safe with less volatility than stocks.

A stock is part ownership in a company, and a bond is a loan to the company or government.

Some people may find a target date fund to be another way to put investments on autopilot and let the fund do all the work.

In this section, I cover investing in target date funds, managing risks in the stock market, going beyond index funds in a small way, and using help.

Investing in target date funds

A target date fund is essentially a single fund with a mix of stocks and bonds with an allocation based on your expected retirement date. These types of accounts have become more popular and are offered as an option in most employer retirement accounts.

Target date funds include a collection of multiple funds to get to the desired allocation, so you may end up paying a little more in fees.

Also, when you are ready to make withdrawals from a target date fund, you're not going to be able to choose from stocks or bonds because both are in that single fund. For example, you may want to make a withdrawal of just the bond portion of this fund because the stock market was down, but you can't do that. This lack of flexibility is not ideal, so keep that in mind. It may be a better idea to customize your own mix of stocks and bonds through selecting separate index funds for each.

Managing the inherent risk in the stock market

Stocks may be the first thing that comes to mind you think about investing. There is risk and reward, and the average annual growth of the S&P 500 index is around 12 percent. That doesn't mean that it has returned 12 percent every single year, but with the normal flow of the stock market and the ups and downs, the returns average 12 percent.

Table 12-2 show the year by year returns of the S&P 500 Index from 2019 through 2023 (negative years are in parentheses).

For the most part, those returns look good. Except how would you feel in 2022 when it was down 18 percent? If you were looking at your investment for retirement statement in 2022, you probably saw a lot of red. Years like that can be disappointing and scary, but the important part is to stay the course!

TABLE 12-2

S&P 500 Index Returns

Year	S&P 500 Index Return
2023	26.29%
2022	(18.11%)
2021	28.83%
2020	18.38%
2019	31.74%
5-year Annualized Return	**15.75%**

Source: Money Chimp (www.moneychimp.com)

TIP

My tip is to look at returns for a three- or five-year period rather than for just one year. In that scenario, you tend to feel better, especially when you're in the middle of a down year.

A way to balance out your risk is with some type of safer investment, such as bonds, money market accounts, and cash. These are all less volatile than stocks. But remember that less risk comes with less reward (in the way of growth). These will help smooth out the ups and downs you get with stocks.

Embracing the urge to go beyond index funds

Knowing what to invest in is the toughest part for DIYers, but it doesn't have to be. Stock index funds, bond index funds, or target date funds are simple options.

You may have the urge to try new things or take a little more risk. If you want to stretch yourself a little and look at other more risky alternatives such as single stocks, just keep it small so that it doesn't wreck your finances if things go sideways.

ANECDOTE

Before I ever heard about F.I.R.E., I learned about investing in individual stocks through an investment club supported by the BetterInvesting nonprofit organization (www.betterinvesting.org), which I mention earlier. I was fascinated with being a long-term investor of individual stocks and loved doing research on companies with a community of people that was interested in the same thing. I think this is where I learned how important community was to my education and growth.

You probably guessed that not all my single stock investments worked out in my favor. I've had some dogs. Even with some losers here and there, I haven't given up. I still have a single stock portfolio but keep it very small in relation to my index funds.

TIP

I know most people don't have the same interest or inclination I do to research individual companies. This kind of work is absolutely not required to reach your F.I.R.E. goals. The vast majority of investors are just fine to stick with index funds or simpler and less time-consuming approaches.

Using help

Not everyone is comfortable with taking care of their own investments or sticking with a passive index fund strategy. Having help is okay, and you have a few options.

Just keep in mind that each of the following options comes with some fees that will vary based on the type of help you choose. The fees you pay to them will be on top of the cost of the investments themselves (such as fees within a mutual fund). Here are the primary options:

>> **Robo-advisors:** These are digital platforms that use technology to help get you the ideal risk level and allocation based on the information you provide. Costs will vary, but it is usually much lower than using a full-scale investment advisor. Many brokers offer a robo-advisor option.

>> **Low-fee broker:** These would be providers you may already be familiar with like Vanguard, Fidelity, or Schwab. Usually professionals work for these firms to help you manage assets you have with them for a fee that is usually lower than with a full-scale investment advisor.

>> **Investment advisory firm:** This is usually the most costly option (around 1 percent of the assets they manage). Services from this kind of firm are more one on one and customized. Make sure you don't confuse management of investments with financial planning. Financial planning goes beyond just investments and includes a more comprehensive look at your finances such as cash flow, insurance, retirement, taxes, and estate planning (see Chapter 8).

REMEMBER

If you choose one of these options, you're not stuck with it forever. As you increase your comfort level around investing, you are free to DIY at any time.

4

Decreasing Debt, Expenses, and Taxes

Chapter **13**

Are You Doomed If You Have Debt?

I didn't make Chapter 13 the debt topic on purpose (referring to Chapter 13 bankruptcy), but it's an appropriate pun. Having debt doesn't have to keep you from reaching your F.I.R.E. goals.

TIP

However, you do need to have a plan to address your debt. Because all debt isn't equal, isolating the most detrimental debt needs early attention while other debt needs to be properly managed.

If you are starting your F.I.R.E. journey without debt, you're ahead of the game. According to the Federal Reserve's Survey of Consumer Finances, in 2022, approximately 77 percent of American households had some form of debt. It's a part of most people's financial picture, and this chapter focuses on helping you deal with it on your path to F.I.R.E.

Stopping Debt from Stopping You

Don't let your debt deter your desire to reach F.I.R.E. Emotionally, debt can get you down, and for some people, the mere thought of debt can be paralyzing. It's hard to overcome those feelings, but as you make progress, you will start to see the other side of your debt.

Some of your earliest wins on your path to F.I.R.E. may be around your debt as you get control of it, reduce it, and eventually eliminate it.

The same discipline and skills you're building while tackling your debt help you in many other phases of your F.I.R.E. journey.

REMEMBER

Remember that every dollar that goes toward your debt payoff not only reduces your debt but also does the following:

>> Increases your net worth as it reduces your liabilities

>> Frees up more incoming cash flow to be used toward other wealth-building activities

>> Is a stress reliever and helps your momentum toward F.I.R.E.

The key lesson is that you're moving away from accumulating debt and toward eliminating it.

REMEMBER

Your debt does not need to define your financial life, and not all debt is bad. In fact, there are smart ways to manage debt or use it to your advantage. Here are a couple of examples of helpful debt:

>> Low interest, long-term debt such as a mortgage at 3 percent

>> Student loan debt where you are using the Public Service Loan Forgiveness (PSLF) that is done in ten years

The vision I love to conjure up is that the money you're currently paying toward your debts (which sometimes can be significant) will eventually be directed elsewhere as you pay debt off or down. You can turn what used to be debt payments into contributions toward your savings and investing.

Choosing between Paying Off Debt or Investing

The paying off debt versus investing great debate is one I hear in personal finance and F.I.R.E. circles all the time. In my opinion, it really shouldn't be a debate at all. Don't get me wrong, I love to hear intelligent arguments that point out the merits of each side. But the truth of the matter is you can do both. It doesn't have to be all or none. It's a matter of deciding how much to allocate to each.

Allocating something to each

On the one hand, high-interest debt can be a big drag on your wealth-building for reaching F.I.R.E. On the other hand, you don't want to miss out on compound growth or time in the market with investments. Both sides have equally valid points. One simple social media post can cause people to argue the pros and cons of each side for days.

Table 13-1 shows an example of adjusting the allocation of debt payments and investment contributions over time. A bigger chunk of your dollars would go toward debt payments as you tackle high-interest debt aggressively in the beginning and then move toward a larger amount going to investment contributions. It's good to have both muscles working at the same time.

TABLE 13-1 Allocating Debt Payoff and Investments

	Debt Payments	Investment Contributions
Year 1	80%	20%
Year 2	60%	40%
Year 3	40%	60%
Year 4	20%	80%

Evaluating psychology versus math

The other flavor of this debate surrounds paying off a mortgage versus investing. This points back to the idea of using your own measuring stick, which I discuss in Chapter 3. You can't argue from a psychological point if someone else is arguing the math. Allow me to explain.

TECHNICAL STUFF

Generally, if you have a mortgage far less than the rate of inflation (let's say 2.5 percent), it's mathematically better for your finances to keep the mortgage and invest the funds that could return anywhere from 4 to 12 percent (depending on the investments). If the mortgage was 8 percent, the preferable option is in the direction of paying off the mortgage.

Now enter the psychological side of this equation. If having any kind of debt adds an unhealthy level of anxiety in your life, then eliminating it may be at the top of your list. Even if the math works out better in your favor to do the opposite, it may not be enough to change how you feel. However, being able to sleep better at night will.

TIP

Neither option you choose is going to wreck your finances or derail your F.I.R.E. plans. (It's rare that any other single decision would derail you when it comes to your finances.)

There is no wrong answer. If you've created enough space in your finances to be able to pose a question like this, then you're on the right track.

REMEMBER

ANECDOTE

I have a non-F.I.R.E. confession. When I retired in 2019, I proactively decided to keep the mortgage on my home, and I caught a lot of criticism for it. I made this decision because my mortgage interest rate was super low (less than 3 percent), and I did not plan to stay in the home for much longer. The funds I would've used to pay off the mortgage remained invested. I acknowledge that this is not the right decision for everyone, but it was for me.

Knowing That Credit Doesn't Equal Debt

It's a F.I.R.E. flex to have a high credit score (760+) and to use credit in a way that will help propel your journey. Just to be clear, using credit does not mean you have debt. The way to avoid having debt on your credit cards is to simply pay off the card in full each month before the due date. This concept sounds very simple, but many people equate having credit cards with having debt, although that does not have to be the case.

So why should you be concerned about having a good credit score if you don't want to get into debt? As I discuss in Chapter 5, your credit matters more now than ever before and may be checked for many reasons that have nothing to do with debt, such as

>> Getting and maintaining a security clearance

>> Getting property insurance (car or home)

>> Renting a home or an apartment

>> Applying for a job (typically in financially related role)

TIP

Another F.I.R.E. favorite for use of good credit without accumulating debt is qualifying for the best rewards credit cards (especially travel rewards). This may not be your thing, but the right reward credit card could help offset expenses for some of the fun stuff you do while pursuing F.I.R.E., so don't rule it out. If you want to read more about credit card bonuses and rewards, check out Chapter 10.

Determining Your High-Priority Payoffs

Since all debts aren't created equal, you want to isolate the ones that cost you the most and are impediments along your F.I.R.E. journey. Debts to prioritize for paying off sooner rather than later are ones with high interest, those that are in default, and those with expiring promotional rates.

High-interest debt

Credit card interest rates can easily exceed 20 percent. (Your credit score is one factor used to determine your interest rate.) As I mention in the preceding section, having a credit card doesn't mean having debt. So, if you pay off your card each month, the interest rate doesn't matter because you won't have a balance that will accrue interest.

However, if you have balances with high interest rates sitting on your credit cards, it's a good idea to make it a high priority to pay them off.

REMEMBER

Note: Many credit cards have different interest rates that apply for cash advances and other activities. You can usually find these on your monthly statement.

There are two primary methods to help eliminate credit card debt:

>> **Snowball method** where you pay off the smallest debts first

>> **Avalanche method** where you pay off the highest interest rates first

From a mental standpoint, it may feel better to have quick wins and pay off smaller loans first using the snowball method. However, if you want to do it based on what's going to save you the most money in interest, use the avalanche method.

TIP

The bottom line is that if you've decided to pay off the debt, you're in a great place.

Other high-interest debt you may need to address can be on short-term or nonrevolving debt like payday loans. These aren't mentioned often, but rates on some of these types of loans can be egregious and much higher than on credit cards. They typically are small amounts initially, but high interest and fees can blow up the balance fast. If you have a loan like this hanging around, you want to prioritize it ahead of credit cards.

Debt in default, collections, and judgments/liens

Old debts that may be dragging down your credit score can include

>> Debts in default

>> Debts in collections

>> Judgment or liens against your property

These types of debt aren't fun to deal with, but you should make it a high priority to get them resolved. If your credit score is low (below 700), one of these types of debt could be the culprit. You can start by checking your credit report.

TIP

Medical debt often falls within this category and is one of the main causes of bankruptcy in the U.S. There are usually easy opportunities to set up payment plans with providers or to negotiate a lower price for paying a lump sum.

TIP

Free credit reports from all three credit bureaus are now available every week at www.annualcreditreport.com. These free credit reports used to be offered only once per year, but as of October 2023, the Federal Trade Commission made it permanent to offer them weekly.

Here are a few tips in addressing this category of debts:

>> Check to make sure the debts belong to you and are accurate. If not, you should file a dispute online to have them removed or corrected (credit reports are known for having errors and no one cares more than you).

>> Contact the creditor or collection agency that owns the debt (if it was sold) to work on a payoff agreement. Companies will often settle for being paid a fraction of the original debt.

>> All states have a statute of limitation on the amount of time a creditor has to take legal action against you over debt, so look into what the limit is for your state. Remember that the negative information still stays on your credit report for seven years.

Low or 0 percent offers close to expiration

Credit cards with low or 0 percent promo rates have a huge jump in the interest rate when the offer expires. So if you have a 0 percent or low promo rate credit card or loan, make sure that you are clear on the expiration date. If you don't have a record of it, check the monthly statement or contact the creditor. If it's close to expiring or it's going to jump up to a higher rate, that debt becomes a higher priority, and you want to pay it off before the lower rate expires.

TIP

To avoid these types of offers slipping your mind, set up automatic payments through your bank or credit union and nickname it something like "0% promo" with the expiration date. Now you have a monthly reminder of when this offer is about to expire.

Addressing Low-Priority Payoffs

Not all debt is detrimental to your journey. You can build your wealth and achieve your F.I.R.E. goals as you take care of certain low-priority debt.

There's a psychological side to debt that may make you feel averse to keeping around any type of debt, and that is okay. Use the tips in this section to reduce your mortgage, student loan, and low-interest debt.

TIP

If you are a military service member (or plan to be) you may qualify to have your interest rates reduced to 6 percent because of The Servicemembers Civil Relief Act (SCRA). You have to notify the financial institution that holds your loan that you are in the service because they won't know otherwise.

Mortgage

Home mortgages are probably the loans with the longest terms and lowest rates available. Most are set up over a 30-year term, and we've seen rates as low as under 3 percent over the past decade. I consider low rates to be anything under the rate of inflation.

If you have a mortgage interest rate this low, it makes more financial sense *not* to pay it off and instead invest the funds in other ways where it likely will earn more than 3 percent over the long term.

Here are a few of the benefits of keeping a low-interest rate mortgage on your path to F.I.R.E. versus paying it off:

>> Using the funds for investing to reach your F.I.R.E. number sooner or building your bridge account for early retirement

>> Avoiding tying up all your funds into the home if you expect to sell the house soon

>> Getting a tax deduction on the interest you pay if you itemize your deductions on your taxes (not as common now that the standard deduction is so high)

>> Paying extra toward a mortgage as a forced way of saving because the funds otherwise would not be saved or invested in other ways

REMEMBER

Maintaining a mortgage for these reasons works in a perfect world, but if having a mortgage keeps you up at night, the reality is that you should pay it off to have peace of mind. This is using your own measuring stick to determine what's appropriate rather than using someone else's. No judgment.

Long-term, low-interest debt

Other low-interest or longer-term debts that can be compatible with your F.I.R.E. journey are

>> A home equity loan on your primary residence

>> A loan on a second home

>> A loan on an investment property

>> Private student loans (different from federal student loans)

Again, by keeping a low-interest loan, it frees up your funds to be invested or used in other ways.

Student loans with low interest or forgiveness options

Direct Federal Student Loans (through the Department of Education) have more generous provisions than any other type of loan, so they deserve a section of their own. If you have loans in the federal system, think twice before refinancing into a private loan because you'll be giving up some valuable benefits, including

>> Special provisions declared by the government (like the COVID Pause)

>> Income-driven repayment plans

>> PSLF (Public Service Loan Forgiveness) for government and nonprofit employers

>> Loan deferment or forbearance

>> Forgiveness in the case of death or disability

The interest rates on these federal student loans are not always the lowest. However, the ability to have your payments based on your income can make a huge difference, especially if you have a lower income. The loan forgiveness provisions like with PSLF, which mean that after ten years of making on-time payments the loan will be forgiven, can be beneficial. The bonus is that there is no tax on the forgiven portion of the loan.

TIP

In 2023, there was a new income-driven repayment created called SAVE (Saving on a Valuable Education) that could potentially be even more favorable for those with federal student loan debt. You can find out all about your federal student loan repayment options at https://studentaid.gov/.

Dealing with Loans from Workplace Retirement Accounts

Most financial professionals give stern warnings about borrowing against your 401(k) or other workplace retirement plan. I agree that you should proceed with caution, especially if you have a small balance or are just getting started with your account. Also, if the loan is being used to pay off other debt (like credit cards) it can start a vicious cycle if you end up just running up the debt again.

The maximum loan amount set by the IRS is the lesser of 50 percent of your vested account balance or $50,000. If you have a significant amount in your account, this may only represent a small portion and be less of a concern.

REMEMBER

Employer-sponsored retirement accounts that commonly allow you to take loans include 401(k), TSP (Thrift Savings Plan), 403(b), and 457(b). This type of loan is different than any other type because you're not using someone else's money (like a bank or credit union); you're using your own money. So when you pay back the loan, you're paying yourself back, both the funds you borrowed and the interest.

Ideally, you would have access to other money (like your emergency fund) rather than borrowing from your retirement account, which is typically earmarked specifically for your retirement years. However, we know it's not a perfect world, and according to the U.S. Bureau of Labor Statistics, 30 percent of employees have loans from an employer-sponsored retirement account.

There are typically two types of loans available:

>> **General purpose loan (usually up to 5 years):** Can be used for any purpose, and usually no documentation is required for proof of reason you are taking the loan.

>> **Residential loan (usually up to 10 to 15 years):** For the purchase or construction of a primary home. Typically, you have to provide supporting documentation showing the costs associated with home construction or purchase.

IRAs and Roth IRA accounts do not allow loans.

ANECDOTE

I have a confession: In 2010 (right after the real estate market meltdown), I took a $50,000 loan from my 401(k) to purchase an investment property (a condo near the beach). I decided to do this rather than getting a traditional loan from a financial institution because it was much easier and quicker.

There were some unbelievable deals on real estate at that time, and I wanted to try my hand at property management. The provisions of my company's plan would allow me to continue paying the loan back even if I separated from the company.

After about three years, I decided I didn't want to own a rental anymore, so I sold the property. The appreciation was about 40 percent, and I continued to pay back the loan as agreed (it was a five-year term). The funds from the sale of the property went into a brokerage account and back into the stock market (the type of investment class I enjoyed a lot more than real estate).

I like for decisions to be rooted in facts and education. With proper information, you make better decisions for your situation. Even advice that seems as universal as "don't ever take a loan against your retirement" deserves to be evaluated to ensure that you understand what it means for you.

Table 13-2 lists some pros and cons of borrowing from your workplace retirement.

REMEMBER

The caveat is to always look at the specifics of your employer's Summary Plan Description that governs the plan.

TABLE 13-2 **Pros and Cons of Workplace Retirement Loan**

Pros	Cons
You can use the loan to fund another type of investment, such as buying real estate.	It takes your money out of the market, and you may miss out on potential growth of investments.
You are borrowing against your own money.	You may be prohibited from making new contributions until the loan is repaid.
There is no credit check and easier approval compared to other loans.	It could be an indicator you don't have enough other non-retirement resources.
When paying back the loan, the interest also goes into your account.	Amounts of loans are limited to the lesser of 50% your vested account balance or $50,000.
It's better than taking a hardship or other type of withdrawal where the money is out of the account for good.	The loan may be due if you separate from your employer and the remaining amount is treated as a distribution and subject to early withdrawal penalty. Note that some employers may allow you to continue making payments through the custodian even after you have separated from service.

REMEMBER

Not all employers allow loans against the retirement plan, and they are allowed to define the parameters of the plan any way they want (as long as it complies with the IRS rules).

Table 13-2   Pros and Cons of a Retirement Loan

Pros	Cons
You can use it as a loan to fund another type of investment such as buying real estate.	If you lose your job or quit, the balance may be due, and you may owe an additional penalty if you fail to give that money back.
You are borrowing against your own money.	You may be prohibited from making new contributions until the loan is paid.
There is no credit check and easier approval compared to other loans.	You could be in trouble if you don't have enough money after you default; it's a non-replenishable resource.
When buying back the loan, the interest also goes into your account.	Amounts of loans are limited to the lesser of 50% of your vested account balance or $50,000.
It's better than taking a hardship or other type of withdrawal where the money is out of the account for good.	The loan may be due if you separate from your employer using the default; the amount is due and should be set aside. Know that some employers may allow you to continue making payments but it gets complicated even after you have separated during that time.

Not all employers allow loans against the retirement plan, and they are allowed to define the parameters of the plan any way they want (as long as it complies with the IRS rules).

Chapter **14**

Do You Have to Cut All Your Expenses to the Bone?

I don't like budgeting. There, I said it. You may not be a big fan of it either. That "b" word often conjures up negative thoughts, especially if you know you need to make some changes. Although reducing your expenses is one of the key components in reaching F.I.R.E., there are many ways to achieve this besides buying into the myth that you have to cut everything to the bone. That sounds miserable, and misery is not what you're going for if you want to stick with anything for the long haul.

You do need to know where your money is going and live on less than you earn. But even the most well-intentioned F.I.R.E. plans won't survive if you attempt to annihilate every expense without regard to the value and happiness certain things bring you.

REMEMBER

Here are a few things to remember about your expenses:

» Resist the urge to increase your lifestyle as your income rises (avoid lifestyle creep), and you should be fine.

>> Make sure that your expenses don't escalate faster than your income.

>> The bigger the gap between your expenses and your income, the sooner you will reach F.I.R.E.

TIP

If you are overwhelmed with debt or feel your spending is out of control, getting your expenses in check is an important early step in your journey.

This chapter helps you focus on spending your money on the things you value, reducing the big expenses that have the most impact, and finding smarter ways to lower or cut your expenses.

Prioritizing What You Value

I've heard some smart people say that if you want to see what's important to someone, just look at their bank account or credit card statement. Those transactions tell a story of where your money is going.

EXAMPLE

If there are lots of flights, hotels, and ride-sharing charges on your statement, that probably means travel is a big part of your life.

Although reducing your overall expenses is a key part of building wealth, you can do it in a strategic way. Not all spending is created equal because there are some things that you value more than others. Value-based spending means aligning what's important to you with how you spend your money.

REMEMBER

There are only two ways to fix a budget:

>> Increase income

>> Reduce expenses

Of these approaches, focus on the one that you're better at. If you choose to reduce expenses, just remember that you can only reduce expense so much. You have a lot more room to increase your income (see Chapter 10).

TIP

When you reflect on your spending, examine each area where you put your money and think about whether it represents what really matters to you.

WARNING

Cutting out expenses that bring you joy is a quick way to burn yourself out and can be a deterrent to your pursuit of F.I.R.E.

Don't neglect the other side of the coin, which is not spending on things you don't value. Here's a few examples of what I mean:

>> You may have no interest in watching TV, so you save on streaming services.

>> You may have no desire to drive a new car, so you can save a ton by buying an older vehicle and possibly paying cash for it.

>> You may be flexible with where you want to live, so you can choose a location where housing and other expenses are less expensive.

TIP

As you review your expenses, try assigning each of them a high or low value. This will make it more obvious where you can make adjustments without feeling deprived.

Considering the cost of making memories

I recall that in the early days of the F.I.R.E. movement there was more focus placed on radical expense cutting, but I've felt a shift over time toward enjoying the experience while on the journey. You should feel inspired to create memories, not stress when it comes to managing your expenses. Being intentional about spending money on certain things can bring you more happiness than just cutting everything out.

EXAMPLE

For instance, installing a fence so that your kids can play with the dogs in the back yard where you can easily keep an eye on them may make you feel safer and more at ease.

You may have heard of the extreme frugality and minimalism that sometimes gets attributed to the F.I.R.E. lifestyle. Though there are some people who subscribe to this (and are probably pretty good at it), a life of deprivation is not what F.I.R.E. is about. Even on the path to F.I.R.E., you still want to live life and be able to savor the moments along the way. Doing so doesn't have to break the budget, but even if you do go a little over budget from time to time, what price tag do you put on making memories like these:

>> Celebrating birthdays or graduations with friends and family

>> Taking time to do activities with your kids while they're young

>> Vacationing with the special people in your life

None of these are free, but they're also things you don't want to skip out on. Whatever price tag you put on them, it's simply a matter of adding the appropriate amount to your planned spending.

I made a deal with my daughter when she got her first job at 15. I agreed to match whatever she saved toward getting her first car. I wasn't anticipating her saving much at that age, so she surprised me when she had saved nearly $4,000 over the course of a year. I was glad to do the match as promised but the real win was that my lessons on saving actually stuck.

Measuring with your own stick

I've mentioned throughout this book the importance of using your own measuring stick so that you don't compare your standards with those of others. Spending your money in the way that's best for you is one example of this. Here are some example scenarios:

EXAMPLE

>> Someone brags about how much they saved by having a roommate who covers half their mortgage. This is a great house hacking move that cuts housing expenses for someone who doesn't mind having a roommate. However, this may be an unrealistic prospect for you and your lifestyle.

>> Some of your friends are paying for lawn mowing service and may think it's odd that you don't. But if you love maintaining your own grass and take pride in getting perfect lines when mowing your own lawn, you may never want the expense of hiring someone else to do it.

Your own values and priorities are what matter. What works for you may not work for another person, and vice versa. There are many ways to reduce expenses and the rest of this chapter will give you some ideas.

Evaluating the Big Expenses

An honest evaluation of your largest expenses will go a long way in determining where adjustments may be needed. These also tend to be ongoing basic expenses that take a huge bite out of your budget. I don't think you need to completely cut out any of these expenses. Often a little creativity goes a long way in coming up with a happy medium.

TIP

Think about the areas where you're willing to be flexible without adding unnecessary stress or anxiety to your life.

Housing, transportation, and food are almost aways at the top of the list. You should also include taxes, which sometimes are overlooked as an expense you can control (read more in Chapter 15). Also, if you have kids, child care gets to be a huge drag on your budget, too.

Housing

Housing costs can eat up your budget in short order. Your housing expenses generally should represent about 28 percent of your gross income. This is a benchmark that includes principal, interest, taxes, and insurance (PITI). When you're getting approved for a home loan, this amount will vary by lender (most will gladly approve you for a lot more).

Many people rationalize the high expense of owning a home as an investment, which brings up the never-ending debate of renting versus buying. You will have your own set of reasons why you want to do one or the other, but be sure to do a realistic comparison that takes into account things other than the rent payment versus the mortgage payment.

After owning a house for the past 20-plus years, I have come to realize that home ownership goes far beyond the mortgage payment. Here's a list of costs associated with most homes:

» PITI (principal, interest, taxes, and insurance)

» PMI (private mortgage insurance)

» HOA (homeowners' association) fees

» Trash/recycling fees

» Lawn and landscaping care

» Indoor/outdoor maintenance and repair

TIP

If you want to run your numbers to compare renting and buying, check out the Home Rent vs. Buy Calculator at www.dinkytown.net/java/home-rent-vs-buy-calculator.html.

REMEMBER

The tax deduction for the property tax and mortgage interest is not used as much anymore because the standard deduction is much higher than it used to be. For example, for 2024, the standard deduction for married filing jointly is $29,200.

ANECDOTE

I'm not attempting to convince you to rent instead of buy. I've been a long-time homeowner and do not regret it one bit. But for my next move, I'm leaning toward renting for a while because I want more flexibility and less maintenance at this stage of my life.

A few of the other factors in how big of a chunk your housing costs will be include

>> **Cost of living for the location:** San Francisco, California, will be much higher than Nashville, Tennessee.

>> **Mortgage interest:** Rates were about 3 percent in 2020 but have risen to about 8 percent in 2024.

>> **How much of a down payment you put on the home:** A lower down payment means a higher monthly mortgage and possibly mortgage insurance.

>> **A fixer upper versus move in ready:** A home that needs a lot of work is going to come with more additional expenses than a home that is fine just as you purchase it.

REMEMBER

Remember that your decision doesn't just stop at the math. Things like being near family or near better public school districts could be important factors that impact your quality of life.

Transportation

Transportation can be a big expense, although it was probably a bigger expense before the COVID-19 pandemic in 2020. Long commutes were a big factor when everyone went into the office, but if you now work from home, you may have more flexibility to reduce your transportation costs.

Depending on where you live, these costs could include

>> Public transportation such as bus, train, or subway

>> Ridesharing services like Uber or Lyft

>> Parking

>> Maintenance, insurance, and gas for a personal vehicle

TIP

Check with your employer to see if you have access to a Commuter flexible spending account. These accounts allow you to set aside pre-tax dollars to cover commuting costs such as public transportation and parking, which are typically available for those that live in big cities like New York or Chicago.

The biggest transportation expense is usually for personal vehicles. Buying a new car every few years is probably the biggest drain, plus there are costs of interest on loans if you finance the vehicle. The value is also likely to go down more quickly because cars experience their fastest depreciation in the first few years of ownership.

ANECDOTE

My non-F.I.R.E. confession: I learned about vehicle depreciation the hard way when I purchased a new 1989 blue Ford Probe while I was in college (I know, horrible decision). I was barely able to make the monthly payments. Less than a year after getting the car, I tried to refinance it and got the awful news from the bank that I owed more on the car than it was worth. That was the first and last new car I ever bought. It was a hard lesson, but at least I learned it early.

I've since learned much smarter ways to buy a vehicle. There are many approaches to lowering your car expenses while still driving a nice reliable vehicle. Here are a few things to remember:

>> Buying a used car is almost always cheaper than buying a new car, and it won't depreciate as quickly.

>> Doing a little research goes a long way to making sure you get the best deal (online shopping for cars makes it very easy).

>> Shopping around for the best loan rate if you are financing the car can help you get lower monthly payments.

>> Buying a car is almost always more cost effective than leasing. (The one small exception is if the vehicle is for business purposes.)

ANECDOTE

My non-F.I.R.E. confession: I drive luxury cars that use premium gas. I still find ways to keep my costs in check by buying used and paying cash. I also put only about 7,000 miles per year on the car. I'm well aware that I could further reduce this expense if I got a cheaper car and invested the difference in VTSAX (the ticker symbol for the Vanguard Total Stock Market Index Fund). I intentionally included this in my budget, and I still reached F.I.R.E. This probably isn't a popular choice, but I defer to the philosophy of using my own measuring stick.

Food

All people have to eat, but food costs vary wildly from person to person. That said, this is probably one of the most flexible and easily controllable of the big expenses. An immediate adjustment can include some low-hanging fruit like

>> Reducing how often you go out to eat

>> Shopping at a low-cost grocery store, such as Aldi (a F.I.R.E. community favorite)

>> Buying in bulk at a wholesale club like Costco or Sam's Club

>> Using grocery rewards perks or coupons

>> Using a credit card with hefty rewards at grocery stores

>> Cooking at home more or meal prepping (making multiple meals at once to eat later)

Don't underestimate the financial impact of making a few food-cost adjustments you may not even notice (except that you have a little more money in your bank account).

You may overlook some options that aren't cuts so much as they are a way to do things smarter, such as these ideas:

>> **Alcohol:** Beer, wine, and cocktails are much more expensive at restaurants than at home. You may also find that the products at a grocery store may be priced differently than those at a wine and spirits store.

>> **Meal service subscriptions:** These services can get costly after the initial promo period. Having a subscription means that you are automatically charged even if you don't really need a box in a particular week. Take a second look and make sure you are still getting value out of it. If you continue with the service, make sure to skip the deliveries you don't need so you're not charged unnecessarily.

>> **Food delivery:** Oh, my, these have gotten out of hand! Just about everyone has used DoorDash or Grubhub for restaurant food delivery, and it used to be very cheap to do. Now many places charge more for menu items and a delivery fee. And don't forget about the tip for the delivery driver! It's a similar story for ordering groceries online. There are times when convenience trumps cost, but shifting a habit may make a difference.

>> **Food waste:** I hate throwing away food, and I'm sure you do, too. Buying fresh foods often means things go bad before you can use them. You may save more money by buying smaller quantities and shopping more often. This is especially true if you will be leaving home for an extended period of time.

Taxes

Taxes are often overlooked, and you may even think it's not something you have control over. Consequently, I made sure to include a section for taxes in this this section as a "big" expense.

The higher your income, the more taxes you may be subject to paying. However, there are ways to reduce your taxes, some of which you can do while doing other wealth-building activities on your path to F.I.R.E. Here's just a few:

- Pre-tax deductions for contributions to employer-sponsored retirement plans such as a 401(k), 403(b), or Thrift Savings Plan (TSP)

- Pre-tax deductions such as traditional IRA and Health Savings Account (HSA) contributions and the student loan interest deduction

- Tax credits such as the child tax credit and lifetime learning tax credit

- Favorable capital gains rates on growth on regular brokerage accounts

- Deductions for business expenses for self-employed people or small business owners

TIP

A little tax planning can help ensure that you are minimizing your tax liability. Whether you do your own tax return or hire a professional, you are ultimately in control.

TECHNICAL STUFF

One big pro where taxes are concerned if you own your own home is the favorable capital gains tax treatment when you sell the home. If there is a gain (over what you originally paid for it) when you sell your primary home, it's tax free up to

- The first $250,000 of gain for a single person

- The first $500,000 of gain for a married couple filing jointly

TECHNICAL STUFF

This is referred to as a capital gain exclusion and generally requires home ownership and residence for at least 24 months within the previous 5 years.

The topic of taxes is wide ranging, and you can find multiple references throughout the book. You can find the basics in Chapter 5 and more details about controlling your taxes in Chapter 15. You may also want to check out *Reducing Your Taxes For Dummies* by Eric Tyson (Wiley).

Child care

If you have options like family members or a stay-at-home partner, child care costs may not be much of a concern. But if you have young children and you don't have those options available to you, child care can take a big chunk of your income. I know it's hard to think about cutting costs when it comes to your little ones, but there are a couple of options to help with the cost of child care. Both are related to taxes:

- **Dependent Care FSA:** This type of flexible spending account allows you to use pre-tax dollars to pay for child care expenses.

- **Childcare Tax Credit:** This tax credit helps you pay for the care of your child or children.

Being Smart Rather Than Just Cutting

Creativity comes in handy when managing your expenses. If there are areas that you don't want to cut, you can always compromise with some type of adjustment or happy medium.

All expenses aren't created equal, so being smart and strategic gives you better results than attempting to cut everything across the board. The goal is to be realistic with the changes you make so that you find your budget easier to stick with.

Finding a budgeting method that suits you

Basic budgeting has gotten a little easier than it used to be because you can use apps. Back in the day, people just used a yellow pad and drew a line down the middle to create two columns. Though the methods for tracking a budget are different, the goal is the same: planning how you spend your money.

The key is to find a type of budgeting method and tool that suits you. You may naturally keep your costs down and always look for the best deal; if you do, you're at an advantage. Even if you do that, you still have to get a sense of how much you spend each month because you need that number to calculate your F.I.R.E. number (25 times your expenses).

ANECDOTE

I do my budgeting a little backward: save and invest first and then live on what's left. I've always been a better saver than a budgeter, so I worked from the area where I was stronger.

You can try my backward budgeting method or start with one of these common methods:

>> **Zero-based budgeting:** Every dollar of income is assigned a place to go.

>> **50-30-20 budgeting:** Separating your income into three categories:

- 50 percent needs
- 30 percent wants
- 20 percent savings

REMEMBER

If you are new to budgeting and tracking your spending, remember that specific categories are better than broad categories. For example, instead of having a single category for food, break it out in more detail:

>> Groceries

>> Alcohol

>> Restaurants

Specific categories allow you to more easily evaluate areas that you may want to change or adjust.

The tool you use to budget is probably more important than the method. Having an automated system like an app or software may be the easiest of all. One example is the You Need a Budget (YNAB) app, but there are many others. Most have a free version that you can use, and some have a small monthly fee for access to more features.

F.I.R.E. people love spreadsheets, so many do their budgets with one. If you use this method, you have the flexibility to customize your expense categories and other datapoints you want to see that may not be available in a prebuilt tool. If you have reservations about connecting your financial accounts with a budgeting app or software, using a spreadsheet may be a better option for you.

REMEMBER

After you establish your budget and get a clear picture of how much you need to live on each month, remember that your life and finances don't stay the same forever. When changes happen, make adjustments as needed.

Shopping and re-shopping

By "shopping and re-shopping," I don't mean buying new clothes for your wardrobe. I'm talking about comparing and reevaluating essential expenses that you may be able to reduce by simply shopping around.

Some of the service providers you have year after year may take you for granted. Most companies don't offer you a discount as an existing customer. Most deals and promos go to new customers companies are trying to acquire, and you may have been lured by this when you first started with your provider.

Companies know that people don't like the hassle of changing and stick around for years or decades without question. When you wake up about your finances like I did, you can make some early wins in lowering your expenses.

TIP

As you shop around, you also may have some luck with asking your current provider to meet or beat the better offers. They don't want to lose your business, so you may as well give them an opportunity to keep you as a customer.

Here are just a few of the areas you can start with:

>> **Insurance:** If you have not changed your car or home insurance in the past couple of years, you may be paying more than you need to. I mean, have you seen the number of commercials and advertisements for insurance companies lately? It is very easy to compare companies online (including ratings). You can use a comparison website (like PolicyGenius, www.policygenius.com) or just go directly to a few of the providers you want to consider.

>> **Home utilities:** In some states, you are allowed to choose your electric or gas provider. In 2024, there are 30 U.S. states that offer retail energy choice. If you live in one of these states, you may have the opportunity to shop around for a better rate. Some of the providers in this space also offer new customer incentives.

>> **Internet:** How long have you had the same internet provider? This is another auto bill pay item that may not be on your radar. You can compare your costs or check with your current provider to see if there are lower cost plans. Sometimes it's as easy as asking, especially if the market you live in has lots of competition.

>> **Cellphone service:** The cellphone industry is forever changing with new players in the space. Lots of competition helps bring prices down. Some services are now less than $20/month, and most of the major carriers offer a low-cost option. It's worth a call or going online to see what your options are if you have not shopped around in the past couple of years.

Finding the hidden expenses

We live in a subscription-based world. Many companies have shifted to a subscription-based model because it's more profitable to them and less likely that you'll make the effort to cancel your subscription.

A subscription audit may be in order. There are some apps to help you with this, but you can also list the subscriptions you have to decide which you can do away with. Here is an example of some common ones:

>> Microsoft Office 365

>> Apps signed up through your smartphone

>> Cloud services

>> Webhosting and related services

>> Streaming TV and music services

>> Gym memberships

>> Memberships to groups or organizations

>> Online shopping subscriptions (like Amazon Prime or Walmart+)

>> Free trial subscriptions you forgot to cancel

I call these "hidden expenses" because most of them are automatically renewed and can be nearly invisible to you. The company probably required you to connect your credit card or bank account when you signed up so that you don't even have to think about paying the fee. How convenient for them! They simply send you a nice e-mail notification every month to confirm that you have been billed.

TIP

Another way to keep subscriptions from flying under your radar is to review your credit card or bank account online. Just do a quick filter of your recurring transactions. You may even spotlight other errors or issues that you weren't looking for that could save you money.

ANECDOTE

When my daughter conducted a review of the transactions on one of her credit cards, she noticed some variable small charges several times a month that she did not recognize. Turns out, this had been happening for a year and added up to the tune of nearly $1,000! It was a case of fraud, and the charges were not hers. Luckily, the credit card company went back and refunded the entire amount, and she learned a big lesson.

Managing investment fees and other professional services expenses

Investment fees and similar professional services can be annoying if you don't know exactly what you're paying for and how much you're being charged. I'm all for using professional help, but transparency is a must.

These types of fees usually fall in the realm of financial services such as

>> Investment products with expenses and fees, such as with a mutual fund or exchange-traded funds (ETFs)

>> Insurance (usually whole life or similar) where the person offering it may be paid a commission

>> Investment management where the person offering it may be getting a percent or flat fee on the account being managed

Most of these services have very low-cost alternatives. Some can be had for free. Because these can be large ticket costs over your lifetime, it pays to do a little research.

TIP

I talk more about using financial professionals in Chapter 8.

Striking the right balance

Minimalism and frugality are two traits that you will hear a lot about in the F.I.R.E. community, and some people are champs at it. They often overlap, and although they're sometimes perceived as negatives, done strategically, they can be very helpful on your F.I.R.E. journey.

Here's how I describe the two:

>> **Minimalism** is simplifying your possessions and decluttering your physical spaces.

>> **Frugality** is using resources sparingly and avoiding waste and excess.

TIP

When handled the right way, they help you reduce your spending, but the other components of the wealth-building formula (increasing your income, savings, investing, and so on) can't be overlooked.

These attributes can get a bad rap because the media and some critics of the F.I.R.E. movement tend to harp on them. Critics often talk about excessive minimalism and frugality, and those qualities are not exclusive to the F.I.R.E. movement.

Although minimalism and frugality are common in the F.I.R.E. community, if you don't hold these traits, no worries. They are not required to reach F.I.R.E. Simply being intentional about your spending and reducing your expenses are what matter. Make sure your efforts are centered around your values and that you are not depriving yourself. Enjoy your journey!

IN THIS CHAPTER

» **Taking advantage of the most tax-favored accounts**

» **Maximizing the power of a brokerage account**

» **Ensuring that you get tax credits you deserve and making the most of deductions**

» **Minding your taxes while minding your own business**

» **Breaking down Social Security and Medicare taxes**

» **Identifying types of tax-free income**

Chapter **15**

Can You Really Control Your Taxes?

This chapter is not meant to turn you into a tax expert, but it will take you beyond the basics covered in Chapter 5. Optimizing your taxes is one of the areas on your F.I.R.E. journey that will have a massive impact and lighten your efforts in other areas of your finances.

REMEMBER

There's a big difference between tax filing and tax planning. *Tax filing* is that annual event that may amp up your anxiety every April, but *tax planning* is something you think about months and years ahead. Planning is the focus of your F.I.R.E. journey. Even if you use a CPA or other pro to file your taxes each year, you're still the one ultimately in control of how you manage your taxes.

Taxes are one of the biggest budgetary line items that you may be overlooking. That may be because they're a big confusing blur that you shy away from. I know dealing with taxes isn't fun, but saving money is. This chapter can help you build your knowledge and understanding of the world of taxes and why it matters so much on your F.I.R.E. journey.

Taking Advantage of Tax-Advantaged Accounts

Tax-advantaged accounts are the solid base for getting your wealth-building and F.I.R.E. journey started. With them, you not only get your compound growth working but you also minimize your taxes (either now or later).

TECHNICAL STUFF

You may have heard these called "qualified accounts." That's a more formal term used by the IRS and in the financial industry.

TIP

The tax benefits of these accounts are so attractive that they all have annual contribution limits. Fortunately, the amounts inch up each year to offset inflation. See Table 15-1 for the 2024 annual limits for each type of account and the catch-up contribution for those age 50 and older.

TABLE 15-1   **2024 Retirement Contribution Limits**

Retirement Plan	Limits	Limit for Catch-up at 50+
401(k), 403(b), Thrift Savings Plan (TSP) workplace retirement accounts	$23,000	$7,500
Traditional IRA and Roth IRA	$7,000	$1,000
457 workplace retirement accounts (most)	$23,000	$7,500

Tax-advantaged accounts are mostly retirement accounts that have age (typically 59.5) requirements and stipulate when you can withdraw the funds without a tax penalty. Even with those parameters, these accounts are still powerful for those seeking F.I.R.E. because there are ways to access these funds before the traditional age. (Read more about that in Chapter 17.)

You can argue the merits of the tax treatment of different types of accounts, but the real power comes with having a mix. Tax-advantaged accounts will fall into these categories:

>> Save on taxes now through traditional IRAs or workplace retirement

>> Save on taxes later through Roth IRAs or workplace retirement

>> Save on taxes both now and later through some 529s or health savings accounts

The common thread for all tax-advantaged accounts is that the money in the account grows tax-deferred. That means that if you buy, sell, or change the investments within the account, there are no tax implications as long as all the action happens inside the account.

TIP

This is very different from a regular brokerage account, which I talk more about later in this chapter.

Saving on taxes now

A traditional IRA or workplace account allows you to reduce your income and pay less in taxes during your working years (see the following example). The biggest impact happens with an employer-sponsored plan like a 401(k), 403(b), or TSP because you're allowed to contribute more to those accounts than to any other tax-advantaged account. (Refer to Table 15-1 for the contribution limits.)

EXAMPLE

$80,000 (gross salary) – $20,000 (401(k)contribution) = $60,000 that's taxed

TECHNICAL
STUFF

Though rarely talked about, the IRS allows an "all-in" contribution limit (from you and your employer) each year that goes beyond the numbers I list in Table 15-1. For 2024, this all-in limit can go up to $69,000 (not including the $7,500 catch-up contribution for those age 50+). This is ideal for high-income earners or late starters who want to catch up.

The dangling carrot with these employer-sponsored accounts is the typical company match of about 3 to 6 percent. That's a big incentive to start with this account. Your goal would be to get to the IRS maximum, but until you can put away a sum that large you should put away enough to get the maximum company match.

A traditional IRA may also reduce your taxes now, but there are some differences from the employer-sponsored accounts:

>> The maximum amount you can contribute is much lower (in 2024 it's $7,500 and an additional $1,000 catch-up).

>> There are income limits that determine how much (if any) you can deduct on your taxes. The amount varies based on your filing status and whether you have access to a workplace retirement plan.

REMEMBER

Traditional IRAs have the same tax impact as traditional workplace retirement plans, but you want to take advantage of any employer match at work before making contributions to a traditional IRA. When you're getting the maximum match, you can choose to contribute to your IRA or continue contributing up to the IRS maximum to your employer plan.

TIP

The benefit to the IRA is that you have more options and more control over the investments in it. (See Chapter 12.)

Getting the tax benefit now may matter more if you are a higher-income earner than a lower-income earner. Assuming you have earned income as a household, there are no income limits to *contribute* to a traditional IRA, but there are income limits on the tax *deductibility*.

Saving on taxes later

Roth IRAs can be very powerful when it comes to early retirement (before you're 59.5 years old) because you have a pot of funds (the contribution portion of the account) that don't require you to be traditional retirement age to use. Those contributions are always tax and penalty free, with no strings attached.

That means you can take the contributions out

>> At any time

>> At any age

>> For anything

REMEMBER

Remember you did not get a tax break up front on those contributions, which is why there is no tax to withdraw them. However, this applies to contributions only. Growth on the account is taxed if you withdraw it before you turn 59.5 years old.

REMEMBER

Just because you can take the contributions out doesn't mean that you should. The longer you leave money in an account, the bigger it becomes with the power of compound growth. The goal for F.I.R.E. is to keep the money growing rather than depleting the funds.

Roth accounts have the same rules as traditional workplace retirement plans and traditional IRAs, except with a Roth IRA, the tax break happens at the end when you withdraw the money.

Roth accounts do not allow you a deduction in the year that you make the contribution, but when you're ready to take the money out of the account, it is completely tax free, no matter how much it grew, as long as you meet these two criteria:

>> You are 59.5. If you're younger, the growth portion of the account will be taxed.

>> You've had a Roth IRA for at least five years.

EXAMPLE

Here's an example using a Roth IRA:

$7,000 Roth IRA contributions at the beginning of each year

8 percent annual growth

15 years

$205,000 total account value will come out tax free if you are 59.5 and have had a Roth IRA for at least five years.

TIP

Although you can withdraw your direct contributions at any time for anything with no penalty, your earnings (growth) on the account are handled differently, so keep that in mind.

REMEMBER

Remember, Roth IRA contributions are much lower than a workplace retirement account, as mentioned earlier in this chapter.

A Roth IRA is an ideal account for your early years when you may have lower income. Because you're in such a low tax bracket (probably 10 to 12 percent), you may as well take advantage of it. Your income will likely start to increase as you move along in your career, which means that during your peak earning years, you will probably be in the higher tax brackets (24%+). Also, increases in your income may disqualify you from contributing directly to a Roth IRA (although there are no income limits for Roth employer-sponsored retirement).

TIP

If you cannot contribute directly to a Roth IRA because your income is too high, you should start looking at the option of a traditional IRA. However, you may not be able to take the deduction. So what's the point of contributing to a traditional IRA if you can't take a deduction for it? Essentially this is what leads high-income earners to do a workaround called the "backdoor" Roth.

With a backdoor Roth, someone who makes too much to contribute directly to a Roth IRA makes indirect contributions by contributing to a traditional IRA and then converting it to a Roth IRA. An extra step is required with this process, but now the person has funds in a Roth IRA that will not be taxed upon distribution.

WHICH IS BETTER: ROTH OR TRADITIONAL IRA?

There are spirited debates around whether you should make contributions to a Roth IRA or traditional IRA. Mad Fientist (www.madfientist.com) has a detailed post titled "Traditional IRA vs. Roth IRA — The Best Choice for Early Retirement" that takes a look at the options through the lens of a F.I.R.E. person. There's lots of banter in the comments section that is great food for thought.

The main difference between these two types of IRAs is saving on taxes now or later. Most F.I.R.E. people will be in a lower tax bracket when they retire than they are during their higher earning years while they're working. This makes the case for leaning toward contributing to a traditional IRA, but the beauty of Roth money has tremendous benefits for F.I.R.E. as well (as mentioned earlier). You have to decide which will work best for your situation. You may decide to have a mix of both, so don't get boxed in to do all of one or all the other. Having both is kind of ideal because you have more flexibility once you retire.

Here are some things to note about how a backdoor Roth works:

>> You contribute to a traditional IRA but can't take a tax deduction because you're above the income limits.

>> You convert to a Roth IRA and pay taxes if there's any growth on the account.

REMEMBER

You can withdraw your direct contributions at any time. Even if you have Roth money within an employer retirement plan, you simply can roll it over to a Roth IRA and it works virtually the same.

Saving on taxes now and later

Health savings accounts (HSAs) are one of the obsessions of the F.I.R.E community, and they're deserving of all the love they get (if you have access to one). This account's superpowers give you triple tax savings: as it's going in, as it's coming out, and while it grows. Contributions to HSAs are tax free and reduce your taxable income, which means you can reroute dollars that would normally go toward taxes back to yourself.

This almost seems too good to be true, and there is a catch: You have to be on a qualified High Deductible Health Plan (HDHP), also referred to as an HSA-eligible plan, to contribute to an HSA. This type of plan isn't right for everyone, but it's worth running the numbers each year during open enrollment to decide if it can work for you.

TIP

Although HSA-eligible plans have high deductibles, they also usually have much lower monthly premiums. Be sure to factor that in when you're deciding whether this option makes sense for you.

REMEMBER

You do not have to choose an insurance plan with an HSA every year. It's not a once-in-a-lifetime election. You can go year by year to decide if it works for you and choose a different plan if it doesn't make sense in a particular year. Even if you only have an HDHP/HSA for a few years, it can still serve as a great asset to your F.I.R.E. plans.

Many people think that HSA-eligible plans are just for the young, healthy, or wealthy.

TIP

Although it's true that these groups are likely to benefit from this type of plan, other consumers can benefit as well. You won't know until you run the numbers. Bear in mind that having a HDHP/HSA plan may require a behavioral shift that may take some getting used to.

EXAMPLE

For example, if you are used to paying $15 each time you go to a specialist, it may feel weird to now pay $85 because of your HSA-eligible plan. Because you have lower monthly premiums, however, you still may be paying less overall.

When you put funds into your HSA account, you can use your HSA dollars for typical medical expenses, but if you really want to optimize it for F.I.R.E., consider using it for the following:

>> Because there is no age limit and the withdrawals are tax free, use it for qualified medical expenses during the bridge time between early retirement and reaching age 59.5.

>> The years of retirement (after age 65) when you're likely to have more health care costs

Table 15-2 shows how the tax advantages of an HSA stack up to other retirement accounts.

QUALIFIED MEDICAL EXPENSES

Some lesser-known qualified expenses are

- Some health insurance premiums (COBRA, insurance while collecting unemployment, long-term care insurance)

- Common over-the-counter healthcare (pain relievers, feminine hygiene products, and medical supplies)

- Psychiatric care and mental health services

- Fertility treatment or birth control

- Lactation expenses (such as breast pumps)

- Medicare premiums (Part A, B, C, and D only, not medigap)

- Dental, vision, hearing expenses

Publication #969 is the official IRS publication on HSAs (www.irs.gov/forms-pubs/about-publication-969). For a user-friendly list of qualified expenses for HSAs, check out www.hsalist.org.

TABLE 15-2   ## Tax Treatment of HSA Versus Retirement

	Traditional	Roth	HSA
Tax-free growth	Yes	Yes	Yes
Tax-free going in	Yes	No	Yes
Tax-free going out	No	Yes	Yes (for medical)
No FICA Tax (If payroll deduction)	No	No	Yes

Saving on state taxes

College savings for you or your kids may enter the picture. One way to save is with a 529 college saving account, which is usually cosponsored by the state. For these accounts, there is no federal tax break on the contributions, but most states offer a tax credit or deduction (for states with income tax). Direct plans are those you manage yourself, as you would a 401(k) or other workplace retirement account. You choose from a menu of investments (like index funds).

In the past, you only got the tax break if you used the plan in your state, but some states have dropped that requirement. Be sure to check the requirements for your state.

The account grows tax deferred, so there are no tax implications if you make changes within the account.

When the account is used for qualified college expenses, the distributions are tax free. The list of qualified expenses goes beyond tuition and books. Other categories include

>> Housing (does not have to be on campus)

>> Internet service

>> Computers

>> Software or other required supplies for school

>> Student loans (up to $10,000 total)

>> K-12 tuition at qualified elementary or secondary schools (up to $10,000 per year)

In addition, you can transfer the funds to other family members to use for qualified education expenses. Most states make this easy to do with an online process.

529 plans can be a great way to share money with multiple family members while you are living. I did this with my 10 nieces and 1 nephew after my daughter did not use all the funds in our 520 account. I basically threw out a challenge for any of them that made it to their last year of college or similar education by offering to pay $5,000 toward their tuition and fees.

One big concern people have about these plans is about overfunding it. In the past, this was a concern because there was a penalty for withdrawing funds for reasons other than to pay for qualified education expenses. Recent changes in the law have mostly laid this concern to rest by providing an attractive option. You can roll unused 529 college savings funds to a Roth IRA in the name of the beneficiary. This solution isn't a silver bullet, but it's a compromise and a great way to get a young person started with a Roth IRA. Here are the requirements to use this option:

>> The account must have been open for 15 years.

>> You can roll over an amount equal to the allowable contribution (essentially, it's a funding source for that year)

>> You can roll over only up to $35,000.

TIP

To help find the best 529 plan for you, personal finance expert (and friend of the F.I.R.E. community) Clark Howard publishes a great list by state at Clark.com/529.

Understanding Tax Benefits of Regular Brokerage Accounts

A brokerage account is a grossly underutilized account that can offer a unique set of benefits on your F.I.R.E journey. I stop short of calling it a tax-advantaged account because I don't want you to confuse it with the retirement accounts I mention earlier in this chapter. Here, I'm talking about a *taxable brokerage* account because you are subject to tax on the growth portion when you sell investments within the account.

Here are some of the F.I.R.E. powers that regular brokerage accounts have:

>> No age limit or early withdrawal penalties that most other retirement accounts have.

>> There are no annual contribution limits.

>> You only pay taxes on the growth and that is at a lower tax rate than your regular income.

>> You can take advantage of gains or losses within the account (tax gain harvesting or tax loss harvesting).

>> When someone inherits the account from you, the beneficiary doesn't pay any taxes on the contribution or the growth portion.

Pay capital gains taxes

If you sell investments in a brokerage account, you are subject to taxes on the growth. However, the tax rate you pay falls under what's called capital gains. There are two types:

>> **Short-term capital gains** are when you have held the investment for 12 months or less; they are taxed at regular income rates.

>> **Long-term capital gains** are when you've held the investments for longer than 12 months. Long-term capital gains are taxed at a lower rate than your regular income tax rate (such as from wages or self-employment).

The tax rate on long-term capital gain can be as little as 0 percent, and it goes only up to 20 percent for very high-income earners! Contrast that with the regular income tax brackets, which can be as much as 37 percent.

TIP

For information about the long-term capital gains rates, visit www.irs.gov/taxtopics/tc409.

Here's an example of how long-term capital gains work in action:

EXAMPLE

>> You have retired early (or are taking a sabbatical) at age 45 and your tax filing status is single.

>> You sell $35,000 of investments from your brokerage account ($11,000 is contributions; $24,000 is growth).

>> Your other taxable income is $15,000 (subject to regular income tax).

>> The $24,000 in growth of your brokerage account is the only part that is taxable, and it will be taxed at 0 percent capital gains for federal income tax (may be taxed at a higher tax for state income tax) . . . you're a champ!

Even if you are a high-income earner, the difference between the tax rates for capital gains and regular income tax can make a huge difference.

TIP

Another nice bonus is that the long-term capital gain income amount is based on your "taxable income." This is the number on your tax return that is calculated after taking your standard (or itemized) deduction.

So, what if you have a loss? If you combine your gains and losses from your brokerage account and you still have a loss, you can deduct up to $3,000 worth of losses per year. If you have more than $3,000 in losses, you can carry that loss forward into future years.

A brokerage account also allows you to use strategies called tax loss or tax-gain harvesting:

>> **Tax loss harvesting:** Selling investments within a brokerage account to take advantage of tax loss (up to $3,000/year). You can use this loss to offset capital gains that you may have on other investments, or you may want the $3,000 deduction for the year.

>> **Tax-gain harvesting:** Selling investments within a brokerage account to take advantage of the favorable tax rates on the gain. Remember that the first bucket for long-term capital gains is 0 percent, and the next is only 15 percent.

The strategies in this section are some advanced moves to optimize your taxes that you'll hear discussed in the F.I.R.E. community. Be sure they're not the only driving force for your investment decisions.

Inheriting brokerage accounts

Brokerage account benefits get even better when it comes to inheritance. Whether you are inheriting the account or planning to leave an account for someone else to inherit, the favorable tax treatment is like having tasty chocolate without the calories.

The person inheriting the account pays no tax on the contributions or the growth. (Conversely, if the original owner of the account sold the investments, they would have to pay capital gains on the growth.) This special provision is called step-up in basis.

A *step-up in basis* means that the person inheriting the funds will not have to pay taxes on the growth of the account like the owner would have to if it was sold prior to death. The new basis of funds in the account gets reset to the full amount inherited as of the date of death.

See more about the inheritance of brokerage accounts in Chapter 7.

Giving Yourself Some (Tax) Credits

In most cases, tax credits are more valuable than tax deductions because they have a direct result on reducing taxes owed. However, the value of deductions depends on your tax rate.

Tax credits reduce the amount of taxes you owe. For example, if the amount of tax you owe is $2,000 and you have a tax credit of $900, you only owe $1,100 ($2,000 – $900 tax credit = $1,100).

Table 15-3 show the difference between tax deductions and tax credits with some examples.

One tax credit people often tend to overlook when they're making a lower income is the Saver's Tax Credit for making contributions to certain accounts, such as these:

TABLE 15-3   ## Tax Credit Versus Tax Deduction

	Tax Deduction	Tax Credit
Reduction from	Your income	Your tax owed
Examples	Traditional IRA contributions	Child Tax Credit
	HSA contributions	American Opportunity Tax Credit

>> Traditional or Roth IRA

>> Employer-sponsored retirement plan, such as 401(k), 403(b), Thrift Savings Plan, Governmental 457(b), SEP, and SIMPLE

>> Achieving a Better Life Experience (ABLE) account, if you're the designated beneficiary

The Saver's Tax Credit is worth 50 percent, 20 percent, or 10 percent of a maximum contribution of $2,000 (or a total of $4,000 if you're married filing jointly). The credit is based on your adjusted gross income. In 2024, you can make up to $73,000 if you are married filing jointly. It's not a huge amount, but it's a nice bonus if you have a lower adjusted gross income. There are changes coming to this credit in 2027 that include a higher-income threshold.

TIP

Here are some other common tax credits:

>> **Child Tax Credit** for lower-income earners with children

>> **Child and Dependent Care Credit** for the care of children or other dependents

>> **Adoption Credit** for adopting a child

>> **Earned Income Tax Credit** for lower-income workers

>> **American Opportunity Tax Credit** for college tuition and related expenses (limited to the first four years of college)

>> **Lifetime Learning Credit** for college tuition and related expenses

>> **Health Insurance Premium Tax Credit** for those purchasing coverage from the Health Insurance Marketplace (www.healthcare.gov) or an equivalent state exchange

>> **Clean Vehicle Tax Credit** for purchase of an electric or fuel cell vehicle

>> **Foreign Tax Credit** for taxes paid to a foreign country

There are many other obscure tax credits (both personal and business) that can reduce what you pay to the IRS. Remember that tax credits reduce your tax liability.

TIP

The IRS has a comprehensive list of tax credits and deductions at www.irs.gov/credits-and-deductions-for-individuals. Most tax credits have income limits that are adjusted annually.

Bunching Donations: A Wise Way to Itemize

The standard deduction has increased significantly from what it was before 2017 because of the Tax Cuts and Jobs Act (TCJA), which nearly doubled the amount. Taking the standard deduction makes your tax filing less complicated and requires less record-keeping. It only makes sense to itemize if all your deductions added together are more than the standard deduction. Table 15-4 shows the standard deduction rates for 2024.

TABLE 15-4

Standard Deduction 2024

Filing Status	Standard Deduction
Single or Married Filing Separate	$14,600
Head of Household	$21,900
Married Filing Jointly (including surviving spouses)	$29,200

REMEMBER

Remember that even when taking the standard deduction, there are several above-the-line deductions you can take without itemizing. Here are a few of the most common ones:

>> Student loan interest

>> Contributions to an employer retirement plan (traditional only, not Roth)

>> Contributions to a health savings account

>> Contributions to a traditional IRA

With the standard deduction being so high, how on earth could you do better by itemizing? In most years you probably won't. However, you can selectively switch between taking the standard deduction and itemizing.

EXAMPLE

Clearly, you should itemize when you have years where your deductions add up to be more than the standard deduction. Here are a few ways to use some strategic tax planning to deduct a lot more in years by itemizing:

» **Pulling forward property taxes:** Some counties in the U.S. allow you to pay property taxes early. For instance, my county taxes are due in January, but I could easily pay a month early to bring it into December of the prior year. Note that state and local taxes, including property taxes, are currently limited as itemized deductions to $10,000 per year for federal income taxes.

» **Making donations every other year rather than each year:** If you make donations every other year, bigger chunks will fall into the same year. You may make an unusually large amount of donations in a given year that helps bump up your deductions. Think about when you are moving or doing renovations. You may make daily trips to donate items as you're clearing things out. Also, if you regularly donate to organizations, considering doing larger amounts every other year versus every year. Your donation schedule may look something like this if you want to donate about $10,000 a year, but get $20,000 in deductions:

- $10,000 in January 2024

- $10,000 in December 2024

- $0 in 2025

- $10,000 in January 2026

- $10,000 in December 2026

» **Donor-advised funds:** This is an account that you set up for charitable giving. With it, you take the deduction in the year you add funds or investments to the account. You can divvy out the funds to the organization(s) you choose over time (even many years in the future). Even though you can direct where the funds go, you can't take them back once they're in the donor-advised fund account. You can do an internet search for *donor-advised fund* to get more information.

Finding Advantages for Small Business and Self-Employment

Being self-employed or having a small business is a scary prospect for some, especially when it comes to taxes. Even if you are a full-time employee, you may have a side business or self-employed gig that can be a way to dip your toe into the world of running your own business. It doesn't have to be all or none.

I bring this up because there are some tax benefits to self-employment and small businesses that can be a huge advantage while you are approaching financial independence and after you retire early. It gives you yet another option where you can do things on your terms and not be tied to an employer.

ANECDOTE

I must admit that the most fun part of starting my own side business (while I was still working full time) was going "deduction hunting." That is what I call uncovering all the tax deductions I was eligible for because I call myself a business owner. In reality, I barely earned $6,000 in revenue that first year and had enough expenses to offset nearly all of it.

Now it's your turn to go deduction hunting for expenses if you are self-employed or have a small business (no matter how small). There are many business-related expenses that you likely incur already, such as internet and cellphone service, health insurance premiums, and professional memberships that you may be able to deduct at least a portion of.

REMEMBER

Remember that the amount of self-employed income you report for tax purposes is the earnings you bring in minus your tax-deductible expenses.

Here's an example:

EXAMPLE

>> Earnings: $20,000

>> Deductible expenses: $12,000

>> Net income you are taxed on: $8,000

Think about all the products and services you spend money on to keep your business going. Some may not be so obvious, but when you go deduction hunting, you will start to identify more and more.

ANECDOTE

My small business is focused on financial education, and I often conduct workshops where I give away $2 bills in a clear plastic sleeve with my company logo on the back. For years, I did not count them as a business expense, but I later realized that this would fall under a business expense much like pens or other promotional items with my logo on it.

TIP

Generally, the IRS says a deductible business expense must be both ordinary and necessary. Of course, what's ordinary and necessary varies by industry, but try to avoid any extravagant or over-the-top expenses (you don't want to trigger an audit). Here are just a few to get you going:

>> **Qualified Business Income (QBI)** to deduct 20 percent of qualified business income

>> **Insurance premiums** for costs of medical and dental insurance as well as long-term care (up to a certain amount)

>> **Self-employed retirement contributions** (see the end of this section)

>> **Home Office Deduction** for using part of your home (whether you own or rent) for business (usually does not apply to W-2 work)

>> **Memberships related to your business** such as to professional organizations or associations, civic organizations, trade organizations, or public service organizations.

>> **Education expenses** related to your trade or business used to improve skills or required by law for keeping your license (such as continuing education courses)

>> **Tax preparation fees** for software or the cost of hiring a tax professional

This is quite a roll call of small business tax deductions, but you're just getting started. Under each of these areas, there are many unique items that apply to you that are not going to be specifically listed in the IRS rules or examples (like my $2-bill scenario).

TIP

The IRS has a guide to business expense resources (www.irs.gov/forms-pubs/guide-to-business-expense-resources), or you can check out the list of F.I.R.E.-friendly tax resources at the end of this chapter.

One of the largest deductions is the tax-advantaged retirement accounts (traditional pre-tax dollars only) with similar limits to larger employer sponsored plans like 401(k) and 403(b). Here are the most common:

>> Solo 401(k)

>> SEP (Simplified Employee Pension) IRA

>> SIMPLE (Savings Incentive Match Plan for Employees) IRA

Understanding FICA Taxes

When you had your very first job, you probably noticed this line item on your paycheck right away. It's a deduction so automatic that no one probably explained it to you, but seeing the amount it reduced your take-home pay was probably a big disappointment.

The FICA (Federal Insurance Contributions Act) tax funds two major government programs in the U.S.: Social Security and Medicare. A percentage of each paycheck is deducted for these programs:

>> Social Security: 6.2 percent

>> Medicare: 1.45 percent

>> Total FICA tax: 7.65 percent

Your employer matches this amount. If you're a taxable self-employed worker or have business income, you pay as both the employee and the employer (7.65% × 2 = 15.3%).

FICA taxes seem unavoidable, but you can minimize them. Here are just a few items that are not subject to FICA tax:

>> Health/dental/vision insurance premiums

>> FSA

>> HSA

Social Security

Social Security is a social insurance program that offers income support to eligible retirees, survivors, and people who have disabilities.

There is a maximum amount of income that you pay Social Security on. Once you hit that max for the year, you no longer pay the 6.2 percent in tax, so it may seem like you got a little raise in your take-home income until the new year starts. That amount for 2024 is $168,600. So for a person who earns $180,000, only the first $168,600 is subject to the Social Security tax, which means $11,400 in earnings is not taxed for Social Security.

Medicare

Medicare is a health insurance program that provides coverage for eligible individuals, primarily those age 65 and older, but also certain individuals with disabilities.

Even though Social Security tax applies only up to a certain amount of income, Medicare doesn't have the same limitation. The Medicare tax is 1.45 percent, so using the example of a person who earns $180,000, that full amount is subject to the Medicare tax.

In addition, high-income earners have an additional 0.9 percent Medicare tax (some call it a surtax). The income threshold amounts are

>> $250,000 for married filing jointly

>> $125,000 for married filing separately

>> $200,000 for all other taxpayers

TECHNICAL STUFF

This additional Medicare tax is used to help fund the Affordable Care Act tax provisions.

Paying Attention to Tax-Free Income

Some things in life really are tax free. I know it feels like every dime of your earnings gets taxed. Most of it does, but not all. It's important to identify what is tax free so you can push more of your income in that direction.

Roth distributions

Roth IRA accounts are universally loved by the F.I.R.E. community and the personal finance space at large. I mean look at the tax treatment on that Roth! The community loves those attractive tax-free funds when it's time to take the money out.

See the "Saving on taxes later" section earlier in this chapter for more information about contributions, earnings, and conversions. In this section, I want to talk about the distributions from a Roth IRA.

Distributions from Roth always come out in this order (set by the IRS):

1. Contributions
2. Conversions
3. Earnings

Let's look at each of those individually.

Contribution portion

REMEMBER

Earlier in this chapter, I mention that the contributions you make directly to a Roth

>> Are tax free

>> Are penalty free

>> Don't have a required holding period

>> Don't have age restrictions

Conversion portion

After your contributions are withdrawn, distributions move to pre-tax traditional IRA funds you've converted to a Roth IRA. The conversion itself is subject to tax. Once the converted money is in the Roth, you need to wait five years before you can withdraw the converted amount without paying the 10 percent early withdrawal penalty.

REMEMBER

Each conversion has a separate five-year clock. After five years, you can remove the funds you converted (not the earnings) without penalty. This gives you an opportunity to stagger (or ladder) your conversions and the ability to withdraw funds as each conversion five-year clock expires.

TECHNICAL STUFF

This is what's referred to as a "Roth Conversion Ladder." It's one of the many ways to get funds out of your retirement account without penalty before you turn 59.5. (see Chapter 17).

TIP

No matter when you did the conversion during the year, the IRS counts from January 1 of that year.

EXAMPLE

Here's an example:

>> You convert your traditional IRA to a Roth IRA on November 30, 2024.

>> The clock for the five-year rule "started" on January 1, 2024.

>> You can withdraw the converted funds without penalty as of January 1, 2029.

Growth portion

This is the last bucket in the ordering rules. You must meet both of the following requirements for the growth portion of your Roth IRA to be withdrawn tax- and penalty-free:

>> You've reached age 59.5.

>> You've had your account open and funded for at least 5 years.

It's best to think of the growth portion as funding for your later retirement (post 59.5) so that you can avoid any penalty or tax.

TIP

Your Roth IRA can get big if you started it early (say right out of college) and you have Roth workplace retirement plans that you roll over to a Roth IRA after leaving the company.

Life insurance proceeds

If you are the beneficiary of life insurance, you get those funds tax free. This can be a significant advantage because receiving the lump sum all in one year would result in nearly half going to federal and state taxes.

EXAMPLE

If you receive $500,000 in life insurance proceeds, you have to pay exactly $0 in taxes. Conversely if you had $500,000 in regular income that had an average tax rate (federal and state) of 35 percent, you'd have a $175,000 bill.

Makes it worth checking your state's unclaimed property records to see if you have a rich auntie who may have left you some life insurance.

Profit from sale of primary home

There are many pros and cons of owning a home, and the taxability of the profit from the sale of a home falls solidly in the pro column.

If there is a gain (over what you originally paid for it) when you sell your primary home, that profit is tax free up to

>> The first $250,000 of gain for a single person

>> The first $500,000 of gain for a married couple filing jointly

EXAMPLE

If you purchased a home in Nashville, Tennessee, for $150,000 fifteen years ago and sell it this year for $475,000, these are the tax implications:

$475,000 sale price − $150,000 purchase price = $325,000 profit

$250,000 is tax free for a single person; the rest is taxed at capital gains tax rates.

$325,000 is tax free for a married couple (filing jointly); they are eligible for a maximum of $500,000 tax free.

Not too shabby! Clearly the IRS rewards home ownership.

Of course, there are a few of those pesky IRS tax rules you must follow to enjoy this generous provision:

>> You have to have owned and lived in the home for at least 24 months out of the last 5 years leading up to the date of sale.

>> The 24 months can fall anywhere within the five-year period, and it doesn't have to be a single block of time.

>> If you don't meet the full 24-month requirement, there are exceptions or partial tax exclusions available (outlined in IRS publication 532, www.irs.gov/forms-pubs/about-publication-523).

TIP

If your F.I.R.E. plans include selling your primary home, the profit could be a smart pot of tax-free money. It can be especially helpful if you plan to rent, downsize to a smaller home, or move to a lower cost of living area.

Inherited non-retirement assets

You may have heard of something called federal estate and gift tax. It sounds like it could eat up any money you inherit, but an estate has to be really big for this to even apply. And when I say *big*, I mean more than $13.6 million per person in 2024. Few of us fall into that asset range, so you may easily escape that tax grab.

According to the 2017 Tax Cuts and Jobs Act (TCJA), after 2025 the federal estate and gift tax exclusion amount is scheduled to drop to pre-2018 levels (about $6 million).

As of 2023, there were 17 states that hit you with inheritance or estate taxes. The state taxes still mostly impact larger estates.

Here are some common assets that you may inherit that are tax exempt:

>> Non-retirement investment accounts

>> Bank and credit union accounts (savings, CDs, and so on)

>> Real estate

>> Vehicles (cars, RVs, boats)

>> Personal possessions (such as household items or jewelry)

>> Cash

Finding F.I.R.E.-focused Tax Experts

There are people who have reached F.I.R.E. and were able to get their effective tax rate at or near $0. I was able to do it for a couple of years, but my efforts pale in comparison to the couple at Go Curry Cracker (www.gocurrycracker.com) blog. They have published the details of their $0 tax returns for over a decade for all the world to see. It's like a work of art! This is an example of the transparency of the F.I.R.E. community that helps others.

Other people can help you navigate your way through the tax stuff on your F.I.R.E. journey. Some people are F.I.R.E. super fiends when it comes to tax planning. They're the geniuses who crunch the tax code, crush the IRS status quo, and create tax content that has blown my mind over the years. Check out these people for sound tax suggestions:

>> Mad Fientist at www.madfientist.com

>> FI tax guy at https://fitaxguy.com and on YouTube @SeanMullaneyVideos

>> Retirement Planning Education with Andy Panko at https://retirement planningeducation.com and on YouTube @RetirementPlanningEducation

5

After F.I.R.E.ing: Things to Do after Retiring Early

Develop a plan with a checklist of things to do before you leave your job and start your post-F.I.R.E. life

Figure out where to find income to live on after you retire early (including funds in some retirement vehicles) and understand the health insurance options available for early retirees.

Know the advantages you may have if you're a late starter on your F.I.R.E. journey and plan for the advanced years of your retirement.

Chapter **16**

Planning a Graceful Exit from Your Job

Y ou've come so far and set yourself up for the ultimate peak — the financial freedom to leave your job. You've hit your F.I.R.E. number (see Chapter 4) and no longer have to depend on a paycheck or trade your time for money or any of the 50 other things that come with working a day job. This will have you grinning from ear to ear and maybe experiencing a little disbelief that you've reached F.I.R.E.!

Putting together a to-do list prior to leaving your job will help you stay on task as you plan your departure. It's one of the most fun lists you'll ever put together and perhaps the last big project before you leave the company. You can do some tasks far in advance, whereas you'll have to assess others in the months preceding your official retirement date.

In this chapter, you find out what you need to do as you count down to F.I.R.E., how to write your F.I.R.E. resignation letter, and how to walk away from your job with grace.

REMEMBER

If you love your job, you may not want to leave quite yet. The "retire early" part of F.I.R.E. is not required; just because you *can* leave doesn't mean you *have* to. You're still in a unique and powerful position. You continue earning money and benefits from your job and know that you are financially able to walk away any time.

Counting Down to Early Retirement

After you've announced that you'll be retiring early, you'll get lots of questions, strange looks, and doubtful remarks from coworkers and bosses. Some of the smart ones will invite you for lunch or coffee so they can pick your brain about how you were able to pull this off. I even had someone who was two levels above me ask me to have coffee with him after he had heard about my plans to retire early. I was happy to do it and admittedly a bit flattered. Though I was leaving the corporate hierarchy, decades of conditioning left me with a mindset that those in positions above me were somehow smarter than me.

But that obviously wasn't true! I was the one retiring early, and now you're setting yourself up to do it, too. In the following sections, I walk you through your F.I.R.E. countdown so that you have an idea of what you should do in the time leading up to your retirement.

Creating a checklist for an organized departure

Logistically, a checklist or some type of road map will help you stay organized and get you through this important transition. Most people are tethered to work way more than they think, as I found out when I was decoupling my personal life and my work life.

TIP

You can start this list even before settling on an exact date and giving your official notice. In fact, you will get very busy as your departure approaches, so you may find it more helpful to front-load as many of your tasks as you can, perhaps starting a year or so prior. Examples of things you can do in advance include becoming part of communities or organizations outside of your job or starting to build up the funds you plan to live on after you retire (see Chapter 17).

Thinking far in advance may be hard at first, but if you maintain a running list, things will start to flow. Thoughts may even pop into your head in the middle of your workday. (Just a quick note: All those daydreams about your life after F.I.R.E. have a way of filling your mind while you're at work.)

Segmenting your checklist by date is the most effective way to stay on track. I split mine into three time frames:

>> 1 to 2 years before

>> 6 to 12 months before

>> 3 to 6 months before

TIP

Use whatever format you like to maintain your checklist: paper, app, computer, or cloud-based document. I used my notes app on my iPhone because I loved adding things as they popped into my head. In the team meeting, I may have looked like I was texting on my phone, but I was really adding something to my Early Retirement Checklist.

Your checklist is a living document that you may add to or change as you reach the goals on the list. The following sections are a guide with things you want to be sure to include for different time frames and topics.

One to two years before retiring early

This may be the toughest list because you're quite a bit away from retiring (as I mention earlier in the chapter). How do you even know you're ready? When you start thinking more about your post-retirement endeavors than your current tasks at work, that's a good sign that it's time. Even though you may not have an exact date yet, you may have an idea of the year, and it's time to get the ball rolling. Make sure to do the following one to two years before retiring early:

>> Strengthen/engage social and professional connections outside of work.

>> Reevaluate projected sources of retirement income and expenses.

>> Identify income sources that you can live on until you reach the no-penalty age for most retirement accounts.

>> Evaluate options for health insurance and healthcare programs.

>> Check ACA Exchange (www.healthcare.gov) pricing and projected income needed to earn subsidy for the state you will reside in after retiring (see Chapter 18).

>> Evaluate/adjust asset allocation/diversification (stocks, bonds, and so on).

>> Evaluate/adjust tax diversification of assets (Roth IRA, traditional IRA, health savings account (HSA), brokerage accounts (see Chapter 15 for details).

>> See if you have pension benefits from current or prior employers (even if they were frozen) and understand rules/options.

>> Make sure you understand how your commission/bonus payout works when you separate from the company.

>> Review and confirm your earnings history (consider doing this annually) at www.ssa.gov; see Chapter 6 for details.

>> Review projected social security benefits and run assumptions of $0 future income at SSA.gov; see Chapter 6 for details.

Six to 12 months before retiring early

Things are starting to get real as you get within a year of your planned retirement date. You still may not have an exact date or have officially revealed that you are retiring to coworkers or your boss, but there is a lot you can get done in this period. Consider the following tasks 6 to 12 months before retiring early:

>> Start lifting others up on your way out (as I explain later in this chapter).

>> Get copies of awards/recognitions you've received while at the company.

>> Reserve paid time off (PTO) for cash payout or make a plan for using the PTO days.

>> Reevaluate options for health insurance and healthcare programs.

>> Make sure any bonuses and incentives are earned, paid out, or fully vested.

>> Make sure you have plenty of available credit and a good mix of card types (low interest, no foreign trans fee, rewards, and so on).

>> Make sure to get as much of the retirement plan employer match as possible before you retire.

>> Front-load 401(k) if retiring earlier in the year.

>> Max out HSA by front-loading (if allowed) to take advantage of payroll deduction (no FICA tax); see Chapter 15 for details.

>> Get online access to retirement, payroll, health and HSA accounts outside the company portal.

>> Make sure you have a copy of the summary plan agreement (the document that explains the rules and provisions of the plan) for retirement accounts for reference.

>> Get a mortgage or refinance while you are still working if you plan on financing a home.

Three to six months before retiring early

Even several months before retiring, you may not have made it official. That's probably a wise decision because anything can change. But at this point, you're so close that you can probably see the light at the end of the tunnel. Stay on track with your plans and do the following three to six months before retiring early:

>> Determine the time of the month you'd like to retire (your health insurance typically goes to the end of the month no matter when your last day is within the month).

- » Estimate COBRA payments and understand the rules.

- » Re-shop all recurring expenses that tend to fly under the radar (car insurance, home insurance, cell, internet, tv, utilities, subscription services).

- » Get records of performance evaluations, salary history, company policies, and so on.

- » Make sure you have external access to the payroll program (if allowed).

- » Make sure you have external access to employer-sponsored retirement accounts.

- » Make sure you have external access to employer stock or equity compensation plans.

- » Remove personal items from your work computer or phone.

- » Make sure all personal accounts are tied to your personal e-mail and phone number rather than your work e-mail and phone number.

- » Get personal phone numbers and e-mail addresses from those you want to stay in touch with (do this prior to notification of resignation).

Custom items for your checklist

TIP

There will be a few areas you need to customize for your plans. Think about the special situations or circumstances that will apply to you — for example, your plan for paying off your home or getting approved for a home equity line of credit. These circumstances may not apply to everyone but be important to you. Make sure to include those items on your checklist as well; just add them with a time frame that makes sense to you. Here are a few examples from my list:

- » Pay cash for a good reliable car that will require little to no maintenance costs (one to two years before).

- » Earn employer matching for qualified charitable donations (three to six months before).

- » Earn wellness bonus to get company HSA contributions (three to six months before).

- » Take two volunteer days benefit offered by company (three to six months before).

- » Check pricing and eligibility for health insurance at the university I was planning to attend (6 to 12 months before).

Picking your departure date strategically

Sometimes you don't get to choose when to leave a company. For example, I was once notified that my position was being eliminated, and I still remember how I felt at the time. I was in my 20s and my boss and the human resource person invited me into one of the meeting rooms. It shouldn't have, but this took me by surprise. They explained that the company was downsizing my department and made me sign an agreement in exchange for six weeks' severance. This felt awful, and I thought that it was somehow a negative reflection on me and my performance.

I had no control over what was happening to me. They called all the shots, and it was all on their terms: the terms of my separation, the final weeks of pay, and even the dates. Twenty years later, I emerged as what felt like a superwoman after I learned about F.I.R.E.! Now, the game has changed, and I got to separate from my company on my terms.

Now it's your turn. You get to choose whatever date you want as your early retirement day, and *you are in control*. Think of it as your new "birthday." It's a great feeling and you've earned it.

REMEMBER

As you begin to narrow down your date, being strategic about your choice will serve you well. Here are a few things to consider before you select your date:

>> **Company benefits:** Be sure you are not giving up valuable benefits such as a pending reimbursement for training or education.

>> **Bonus payouts:** Set your retirement date after scheduled bonus payouts if you believe you've earned a bonus but you won't receive it if you leave the company before it's paid out.

>> **Company vesting of retirement or other compensation incentives:** Consider the timing if you're close to being vested in your stock options or workplace retirement and you want to get the full company benefit.

>> **Health insurance effective dates:** Coverage typically remains in effect until the last day of the month regardless of what day of the month you leave.

>> **Potential big changes with the company:** Whispered rumors of upcoming layoffs could work to your advantage (severance, unemployment eligibility, and so on).

>> **Personal plans such as time with family or travel:** If you have a big trip planned for the summer, it might work out to retire just before then.

TIP

These considerations can also apply when you are changing jobs.

I ended up choosing December 6, 2019, as my official retirement date, when there were no layoffs in sight. Then boom . . . the COVID pandemic hit only three months later and there were lots of layoffs. The moral of the story is that it's hard to pick the perfect time because no one can predict the future. Just pick a date based on what you know at the time and stick with it.

Writing Your F.I.R.E. Resignation Letter

Most resignation letters are short and to the point. They are usually no more than a sentence or two that ends with the employee's last day of work and that's about it. Most don't mention what you're doing next or why you're leaving. The assumption is usually that you are going to work somewhere else.

But your F.I.R.E. letter conveys a grander message and deserves much more. This will represent your written transition point of being free from depending on a paycheck from a job. That's a big statement right there, and you've worked hard for this.

Saying more than just "I quit"

The time has finally come for you to draft the departing words from your employer, and it should say a lot more than "I quit," especially because you're not quitting but leaving on your own terms to do more of what brings you joy. Think of it like graduating from working a regular job to your life after F.I.R.E. Let the gravity of that sit for just a moment. You used clarity, focus, and lots of courage to set your own retirement date rather than following the traditional cadence. A decision that momentous deserves a worthy resignation letter.

TIP

You don't have to share all of your plans or reasons for leaving, but conveying that the terms of your departure are the culmination of a meaningful, well-thought-out plan is powerful.

You may not have admiration for the job you're leaving (and it may even be the reason for speeding up your F.I.R.E. date), but remember that you have turned the tables and now hold most of the power. You are the one setting the parameters of this final project at work; have fun with it.

Figure 16-1 shows the full text of my F.I.R.E. letter from 2019, but here is a portion that summarizes how big of a deal this was to me and shows the deep thought I put into this decision

I know my 40s is a little early to retire and some may even say I'm giving away the Golden Ticket. I've certainly spent many months (maybe even years) imagining such a divergence from the norm and ultimately came to this conclusion: I could follow a traditional path or blaze my own; I choose the latter.

---

1 of 1

Date.   September 25, 2019

To: ███████████, Director
             [Company Name]

Dear ██████,

With a great deal of thought, I have made the bittersweet decision to retire from ████████ after 20 amazing years. I am thankful for my time with the company, which fueled my growth; and more importantly, my human spirit. I know my 40s is a little early to retire and some may even say I'm giving away the "golden ticket". I've certainly spent many months (maybe even years) imagining such a divergence from the norm and ultimately came to this conclusion: *I could follow a traditional path or blaze my own; I choose the latter.*

My next step? Well, change is always scary, and this is no exception. I have aspirations of being at the forefront of educating and inspiring people to better understand their finances and raising America's Financial IQ. I know, I know...big dreams! But it's the culmination of many years of following my passion for financial literacy. I'm also very excited to be starting a Master's Degree program ranked as one of the top Graduate programs in my field of interest. It's quite a shift for me but will strengthen my ability to give back to society in a way I never imagined.

I thoroughly enjoyed the many colleagues and friends I've been fortunate enough to work alongside. As the longest tenured ████████████employee on our team, I believe this opens the door for other talented professionals with new perspectives, to join the team and further its success. Also, one of my farewell deeds has been lifting up as many others as I can on the way out and that has been the most fun of all!

██████, you have an exceptional work ethic and leadership style that has motivated me both in my career and personal life. I'm very lucky to have been in this group for so long and will always treasure the many lessons I have learned. I wanted to give you as much notice of my departure as possible in an effort to reciprocate the courtesy and kindness you have extended to me over the years. I'll have this letter serve as my official notification and will remain with the company through **December 6th, 2019**. It will be my pleasure to assist with a smooth transition for my replacement and our customers.

The past eight years with the ████████████ Division have been the best of my 20 year tenure with the company and its impact; immeasurable. Further, I believe I'm in a unique position to reach higher, be better and do more. [1st/2nd/3rd level boss], I'll simply leave you with two of the most powerful words in the English language: *Thank You!*

Respectfully,

██████, ████████
[Company Name] (Ret., 2019)

FIGURE 16-1:
My F.I.R.E. letter.

Making your letter frame worthy

The gravity of reaching F.I.R.E. is huge. This is a triumphant moment that deserves to be memorialized and frame worthy. Writing my letter was cathartic, and I had some emotions I hadn't expected once reality set in that this transition was going to change the trajectory of my life. Ten years prior to retiring early, I never imagined it would be possible. Moving the needle from poverty to reaching F.I.R.E. in my forties — what a feeling!

My original letter was several pages long, but I wrote it and re-wrote it many times. After several versions, I finally got it down to one page and that was a win! I just became more intentional with my words and was mindful in how much I wanted to share at that point. I knew I would keep the letter for years to come and you will probably want to hold on to yours as well.

Here are a few things you may want to include in your letter to make it frame worthy:

>> Mention a few of the things that are important to you as it relates to why you might be leaving.

>> Get across what you really want your employer to know and remember as your parting words.

>> Name individuals where it matters to you (especially anyone that may have had a positive impact on your time with the employer).

>> Share your mission or big audacious dream that you want to shout to the world.

Deciding when to give your official notification

After scribing the perfect F.I.R.E. letter, the big question is: When's the right time to give it to your boss? So far in this chapter, I've been talking about the ambiguous future retirement date. There has not been a firm date or official notification in place. In this section, things shift because it's time to pick a date.

Some F.I.R.E. people struggle with making their early retirement plans official. I was one of those people. I took nearly two years from the time I started contemplating retiring early to the time I gave my official notification to my employer.

The timing of your official notification is important, and you don't want to unintentionally give up valuable benefits, as referenced earlier in this chapter.

You can handle vacation, sick time, and PTO, in a couple of ways:

>> Some people decide they want to get paid out for the time and just leave the company. That is what I did and was paid for about three weeks of PTO after I left the company.

>> Others take that time off in the months or weeks preceding their separation of service, so they are technically still employed during that period (just on vacation). I call that "vacationing out."

The federal government is known for its generous benefit of allowing employees to roll vacation and sick time from year to year. I had a friend who accumulated over 100 days of paid time off that she used in the months preceding her last day of official work. She spent that time living it up while still enjoying all the benefits of a full-time employee. I didn't have such generous PTO, but we all can only work with what we have.

Consider any lump sum payouts, bonuses, or vesting of equity compensation (like stock options) that may require you to still be employed with the company to collect.

TIP

These provisions can be found in your employer's documentation and it's something you definitely want to investigate before handing in that F.I.R.E. letter. There could be thousands of dollars at stake.

Peek around the corner to see if there are any whispers of possible layoffs or downsizing. If there is, you might be able to negotiate a severance or other favorable terms that will give you a little extra bonus on your way out. Negotiating on your way out may also be an option for you in other circumstances depending on your company and position. It never hurts to verbally broach the topic with your boss before giving your written notice.

TIP

If you are terminated from your job (from a layoff, downsizing, job elimination, and so on), you may also be eligible for state unemployment benefits in addition to any lump sum severance. Massachusetts, for instance, has one of the highest maximum weekly benefits of $1,015/week as of 2022. Some states (like Tennessee) have as little as $275/week. Amounts and rules will vary by state.

Walking Away Gracefully

There are lots of people who hate their job, their boss, or their employer. It's often what leads people to seek F.I.R.E. in the first place. Now that you've reached F.I.R.E., you may see things through a different lens than you had previously.

Instead of feeling stuck because you need the paycheck, you can walk away when and how you want. You've set up a safety net that will allow you float out of there with dignity and grace.

Giving ample notice

You can give more than the standard two weeks' notice if you want to be nice and give your employer a little extra time to find a replacement or make other arrangements.

WARNING

The timing of your announcement is up to you. Keep in mind that once you officially submit your F.I.R.E. letter, word will travel fast at work and the wheels will be in motion. Also, once you submit the letter to your employer with your date of separation, they can and will hold you to it. So, there may be no going back . . . this is it!

ANECDOTE

I gave my boss a "soft" notice by verbally sharing my plan to retire early about six months before I was intending to leave. I was careful not to give a specific date at that point, but he did ask for at least two weeks' notice (no problem). This verbal notice wasn't binding, and I could change my mind at any time before providing a notice in writing.

I turned in my official letter about two months prior to my chosen separation date. I printed the letter, slid it into a flat yellow envelope, laid it on my boss's desk, and walked out of his office. I wanted to give him time to read and digest it without me standing there. He came to my desk about 20 minutes later to give me a hug and said congratulations, which was a nice gesture that helped make the next two months easier for both of us. I was happy to do as much as I could to leave things in good shape. (I hope your boss responds with a similar reaction and supports you on the way out. It would actually be in their best interest.)

Offering a transition plan

After receiving your official notice, your boss may be a little shocked and perhaps even beg you to stay. This could put you in a position of strength to negotiate even a sweeter deal, sort of creating your own separation agreement.

Even if you don't want to extend your time with the company, you could offer to help with a transition plan — particularly if you are in a specialized leadership role.

REMEMBER

You are not obligated to train your replacement or be involved in what happens after you leave. However, many people feel some sense of duty to help their employer, especially if they were treated well. I felt this type of affinity for my boss. Several years prior, he hired my daughter as an intern while she was in college and treated her with kindness and respect. I always remembered that, and I was happy to do as much as I could to help with the transition.

Your transition plans will look quite different than mine, but here are a few things I included:

>> Introducing and endorsing my replacement to long-time clients

>> Documenting some of my best practices

>> Resolving issues with trouble accounts

TIP

If your experience with your employer was negative or toxic, you may want to skip the whole transition plan, but it's best not to burn bridges. You may not want to ever work for them again, but how you leave is a reflection of who you are. You want to maintain your grace, even in a not-so-rosy situation. The upside is that your ability to walk away on your own terms has a way of putting you in a pretty good mood.

Lifting up others on the way out

Even in the worst work environments there are some great people whom you respect and admire. Whether the person is a coworker, your boss, or a random person who always seemed to be working their butt off, you may have a desire to lift them up on your way out. Taking the time to spread a little kindness or sharing your appreciation with those people will keep your good mood going and build goodwill among those you're leaving behind.

ANECDOTE

The security person at the building where I worked was unbelievably perky every morning. I don't know how she did it, but it made me feel a little better even if I was in a rotten mood. Before leaving, I made a point of telling her I was retiring early and how much I appreciated that she was one of first smiling faces I saw every morning and that just about everyone else I know felt the same way.

TIP

Within your work group, there could be an opportunity for you to speak up on someone's behalf because you feel they're doing a great job but never get the attention they deserve, or you can even recommend the person you think is most worthy of taking over your position (and brag about them a little in the process).

Why would you want to do all this for people you may never see again? The fact that you may never see them again may very well be the point. You have nothing to gain, so what you say and do on your way out will be perceived as truly genuine. Knowing that you're about to embark on your post F.I.R.E. life, you can either focus on the bad or the good you're leaving behind. A big part of the good is usually the people. You may as well sprinkle a few good deeds on those people that you'd like to see succeed.

ANECDOTE

A few months before I left my company, there was a newly created position in our group that equated to a promotion for someone within my team. Several of my coworkers applied. I probably would have, too, but I obviously had no interest because I was leaving. I thought of one person definitely didn't deserve it and one who absolutely did. So, I advocated for the person I thought was best for the position by doing these things:

>> Writing a letter of support to explain why I recommended her for the position

>> Helping her strategize and prepare for the interview process

>> Making sure she knew why I thought she was the best person for the role, even if she wasn't the final choice (she did get the job!)

Sharing your plans publicly

You've laid out your exit plan for retiring early by

>> Creating and reviewing your checklist

>> Giving official notice to your boss

>> Sharing your good news with your friends and coworkers

>> Starting your countdown

For some, that might be it, but for others, there is a public crowd you want to share your good news with. Do you have a blog, podcast, YouTube channel, or social media accounts? Talking about your plans publicly through that type of media means that everyone can see it — your audience, your connections, and even your employer. You will inspire many with your news, and there is nothing like sharing how you are feeling in the moment. You will get lots of questions, and some of them will be about how you did it.

REMEMBER

Be mindful of sharing too many specifics (like the name of your employer) before you actually leave your job.

ANECDOTE

I was conservative in my approach to sharing publicly before I officially retired. Out of respect for my employer, I decided to hold off with the public announcements. I didn't blog about it, give interviews, or share it on my social media. It was probably unnecessary for me to do that, but it's what I felt was right at the time because I wanted to leave in a way that kept things on friendly terms and leave the door open for the possibility that maybe one day they would become a client for my future endeavors. There would also be the remote chance that I would change my mind and decide to go back to work, so I tried to avoid burning bridges. However, behind the scenes, I was capturing the moments by recording short videos on my phone and preparing other ways that I would share after I retired.

About a week before my official day, I blasted the news all over my social media! I was almost done with the job and so excited to share it with the world. I made my announcement about me, not my employer, and presented it as a celebration. It felt unbelievable!

Celebrating with a FIREment Party

Just like a birthday party, graduation, baby shower, or bridal shower; reaching financial independence and retiring early is deserving of a celebration. Let's call it a FIREment party, shall we? This big day started feeling a lot like my new birthday.

REMEMBER

Most good bosses will want to honor and celebrate you just as they would a person retiring at a traditional age. This makes sense if you spent many years with that employer, but it doesn't need to be the only way you celebrate.

I love the idea of a FIREment party that is independent of your employer. You can bring together friends, family, and colleagues from prior employers that represent snapshots in your career. Throughout our jobs and professional careers, you build many relationships; work is a big part of your life.

ANECDOTE

I recently had a good friend have a FIREment party, and it was what I wish I had done. Her party was planned by a few of her friends (not her current employer). It was like piecing together a timeline of her life and all the people she'd impacted over the years, including her kids.

I had been with my employer for nearly 21 years, so it meant a lot that my boss insisted on celebrating my early retirement. That many years with one employer is becoming increasingly rare, and it still sounds wild that I stayed there so long. On the other hand, I know it was a big contributor to the financial part of my journey to reaching F.I.R.E.

ANECDOTE

My FIREment party took place about two weeks before my last day. I had about 30 people from my company, mostly within my department. They also allowed me to make a list of people to invite. I included my daughter and a couple of other nonwork friends. I admit, it was great to hear the kind words from my coworkers and leaders in our group, especially with my daughter being there. I said a few brief words —mainly to express gratitude. Though things were by no means always perfect at my job, my thoughts were mostly filled with the good times. I gladly accepted the very nice gifts, and, in my mind, it closed the chapter of this part of my life.

Chapter **17**

Planning Your Post-F.I.R.E. Income and Health Insurance

The F.I.R.E. community gets all kinds of pity from people who think we're just out of luck when it comes to having money to live on. That's because the conventional thinking is that income can only come from retirement accounts that require you to be 59.5 or older. Epic myth!

The truth is that F.I.R.E. people — who are some of the smartest people I know — do their homework. So, this question of how to create income to live on in early retirement has been asked and answered a hundred times over. It takes a little planning and forethought, but rest assured there are many ways to do it, as this chapter explains.

Applying the Infamous 4% Rule

Simply put, this "rule" says that 4 percent is the amount you can withdraw from your investments portfolio each year (adjusted for inflation) with little chance of it running out in retirement. In other words, the first year you make a withdrawal, it will be 4 percent. The next year, it will be that same amount plus an extra sum to account for inflation.

Many opinions about how to apply the 4% rule exist, but don't let that confuse you or discount it as a reference point. Think of it as a guideline that may require some adjusting. The main adjustment for F.I.R.E. is obviously the fact that you are retiring much younger than the traditional age on which the 4% rule was based.

TECHNICAL STUFF

The 4% guideline is based on research done in the 1990s by Bill Bengen, using historical returns and inflation.

Here's an example:

EXAMPLE

$50,000 in estimated annual spending in retirement

$50,000 × 25 = $1,250,000

$1,250,000 is your F.I.R.E. number

4 percent of $1,250,000 = $50,000 (+ amount to adjust for inflation each year) to live on when you retire

WARNING

As you can guess, there are lots of assumptions factored in to this 4% rule that can make the difference in how well it works. That is the genesis for much of the debate. Here are some factors to consider:

>> The 4% rule factors in inflation, but how much? Some people say 2 percent; others say 3 percent.

>> The 4% rule factors in growth of investments, but how much? Some say 6 percent; others say 8 percent.

>> Taxes are *not* factored in, which may increase your estimated expenses in retirement. If you have tax-efficient investment vehicles, taxes may not be much of an issue.

Despite the uncertainty of this guideline, the 4% rule is still commonly used because it is simple and offers a good point of reference. Even if you're retiring early (like in your 40s), I think the 4% rule is still a good estimate to use because there are lots of positives that aren't considered in the rule that could make your portfolio last even longer. Those possibilities include additional income that may offset what you actually need to withdraw from your retirement portfolio. Here are some examples:

>> Income from part-time work or passion projects (mostly during early retirement years)

>> Passive or semi-passive income from royalties, commissions, or real estate

>> Pension income (during later retirement years)

>> Social Security income (during later retirement years)

TIP

You can use a calculator to help you figure out your F.I.R.E. number based on the 4% rule. Check out these sites for a few calculators:

>> Mad Fientist FI Laboratory at https://pages.madfientist.com/fi-laboratory

>> FIRECalc at https://firecalc.com/

>> Playing with FIRE calculators at www.playingwithfire.co/calculators

In addition, your retirement account or brokerage provider usually has a retirement calculator.

Being the Engineer of Your Income

When you reach F.I.R.E., you are in a unique position to engineer the flow of your income and where it comes from. This also allows you the flexibility to control your taxes on that income. This is a stark contrast to what you were probably used to if your income came from a full-time day job. You had no say in when you got paid or when bonuses hit.

In this section, I cover creating your own paycheck, living off your investments, and understanding the importance of diversifying the taxes on your investments.

Getting your "paycheck"

WARNING

You may feel nervous because during retirement, you may not see a regular paycheck deposit in your bank account like you have for decades. The predictability is no doubt something you will miss.

Without an employer to deposit money on a regular basis, where does your "paycheck" come from? You now make your own through the sources you have so diligently worked to build throughout your F.I.R.E. journey. That may be

>> Royalties, commissions, or other type of passive income

>> Real estate income

>> Investments you draw from

You can structure your paycheck from these and other types of income. You set up your own schedule for tax withholdings (as long as it follows IRS guidelines). You can "get paid" on a schedule that works for you — it doesn't have to be every two weeks as it may have been with your job. You may prefer monthly, quarterly, or even annually.

Annually may not give you enough flexibility throughout the year to shift if needed. This is especially true for taxable transactions like withdrawing from your retirement accounts or selling investments in your brokerage account.

My first full year of retirement was 2020. Everyone knows what happened in early 2020: the pandemic and the unprecedented economic and financial implications that came with it. Because I was creating a paycheck for myself on a quarterly basis (rather than annually), I was able to shift my finances for the rest of the year to be more beneficial for tax purposes.

Living off your investments

At some point you will be living off your investments and putting the 4% rule I talk about earlier in the chapter to the test. You spent most of your life in accumulation mode, but now the tables are turned, and it's time for decumulation.

The financial shift is obvious: You will need access to a portion of your investments to live on. The behavioral aspects of this process are less obvious. You may find some things require an adjustment, such as

>> Taking distributions rather than making contributions

>> Deciding how much to withdraw

>> Allocating your portfolio for retirement

It's said that decumulation mode is harder than accumulation mode. My theory for why this is true is that you have spent decades creating the habit of contributing to your investments, and it can be challenging to withdraw from them.

When you're planning to live on your investments, you can do it yourself or seek a professional who focuses on retirement income planning to help you (see Chapter 8).

Understanding the importance of tax diversification

Diversification of the tax treatment of your accounts is as important as diversification of the investments themselves. After retirement, you may need to decrease or increase your taxable income in a given year to optimize your tax situation.

One reason you may need to adjust your taxable income is to qualify for subsidies for health insurance via the Health Insurance Marketplace (www.healthcare. gov). (Read more later in this chapter in the "Getting Health Insurance for Early Retirement" section). If your income is too high, you may not qualify for a subsidy.

As I mention in Chapter 5, there are a few ways that investment accounts are treated in regard to taxes:

>> **Traditional:** Pretax at the time you make the contribution but taxed when you withdraw the funds

>> **Roth:** Taxed at the time of contribution but not taxed when you withdraw

>> **HSA:** Pretax at the time you make the contribution and not taxed when you withdraw as long as it's for qualified medical expenses

>> **Brokerage account:** Only the growth is taxed, but those gains are at a lower rate than your other income

If you had a high-income year from some sources but you still need funds, you may choose to pull from one of the accounts that has tax-free distributions, such as a Roth IRA or HSA.

Conversely, if you had a low-income year, it may be advantageous to withdraw from an account that has taxable distributions (traditional) or take advantage of the favorable long-term capital gains from a brokerage account.

Being able to strategize and make sound decisions based on the tax treatment of different accounts in retirement is powerful. The best way to do that is to have a mix of pre- and post-tax vehicles. So, the great debate between Roth and traditional IRA contributions is settled: You need both!

Building a Bridge: Strategies for Early Retirement

The bridge period is the time in retirement when you can't access the funds in your retirement accounts without penalty (or you have limited access) because of your age. For instance, if you retire at 40, you're limited to what you can withdraw from certain retirement accounts until you turn 59.5. (There are exceptions I talk about later in this chapter).

I probably would have reached F.I.R.E. 20 years sooner if I had a nickel for every time someone has asked me, "What do you live on in early retirement if you can't touch your retirement accounts until you're 59.5?" The short answer is there are lot of bridging strategies for getting access to your funds without penalty so you can live on them in early retirement. This is one reason I suggest having some nonretirement accounts if you plan to retire early, and it's what I help clarify in this section.

Using a liquid savings account

A liquid savings account gives you easy and immediate access to your money to live on in early retirement. Because it's a bank account, it's not going to grow like a stock investment, but it's also not in as much danger of going down either. Examples of credit union or bank accounts that work for this purpose are

>> High-yield savings account

>> Money market account

>> Certificates of deposit (CDs) with a term that matches when you need it for early retirement

In 2024, you can find interest rates on these accounts near 5 percent, which is the highest they've been for more than a decade. Just remember that rates change. The main goal is having money available when you need it.

You can start building this account years before you plan to retire. I know it might be hard to look at a large pot of money that is not earning anywhere near what it could earn in the stock market, but I can tell you that it will give you peace of mind to know that it's there and stable.

REMEMBER

Your entire nest egg isn't in this liquid fund. Depending on your other sources of income, a reasonable amount to have in this account is enough to cover your first one or two years of retirement (and more if you prefer). You don't want anything to get in the way of you and your early retirement.

Accessing funds in a brokerage account

A brokerage account frees you from age restrictions, and you can invest inside of it (and will typically have a better return than a bank account over long periods of time). Though you can invest the funds, keep in mind the time horizon that you'll need part the money. For instance, if you need a certain amount of money in the next two years, you probably shouldn't have that part invested in the stock market because there's the risk of those investments going down.

REMEMBER

For investments in a brokerage account, you are only taxed on the growth of the investment. You can choose which investments you want to sell and when you sell them.

REMEMBER

If you have held the investment for more than a year, you will get the favorable long-term capital gains tax rate (see Chapter 15).

Withdrawing Roth IRA contributions

If you have a Roth IRA, direct contributions you made to the account come out first when you make a withdrawal. This is advantageous if you need to access the money during your early retirement because contributions are always tax free and penalty free. In addition, there's no required holding period for them, and you can make the withdrawal regardless of your age.

WARNING

Keep in mind that since the withdrawals come out of this tax free, there are also advantages to letting this account grow bigger and longer. That way, you have even more tax-free money.

Another way to use a Roth IRA before you turn 59.5 is to start a Roth conversion ladder. This is where you take traditional IRA funds and convert them to a Roth IRA. The conversion is subject to tax, but once the converted money is in the Roth, you can withdraw the converted amount after five years to avoid the 10% early withdrawal penalty.

REMEMBER

Each conversion has a separate five-year clock before 59.5. After five years, you can remove the funds you converted (but not the earnings) without penalty. This gives you an opportunity to stagger (or ladder) your conversions and the ability to withdraw funds as each conversion five-year clock expires.

I talk more about Roth IRAs later in this chapter.

Using income-producing assets like real estate

There are plenty of people who reach F.I.R.E. through real estate and have lots of love for owning property. If you are one of them, you won't mind the work that goes along with it. Managing property gives you more freedom than a full-time job, but it's not entirely a passive endeavor, although some property owners run their business like a well-oiled machine and there's very little work for them to do.

If you've been hard at work building your real estate empire for F.I.R.E., you have set yourself up nicely. Whether you have long-term or short-term rentals, the income you receive each month can serve as your bridge. Every dollar you bring in means that you don't have to pull from your other accounts.

If you have an asset that produces income, it likely is appreciating in value as well.

Taking on projects or part-time work

Once you've reached F.I.R.E., you have earned the freedom of time that you can use any way you want. Being in "early retirement" doesn't necessarily mean you quit working altogether. Sometimes it's a matter of doing what you love on your own terms.

You have passions that you may want to continue pursuing, and some of those skills or types of expertise may be very valuable to others — valuable because you can earn money by doing projects or consulting, doing part-time work, or running a small business.

If you've reached F.I.R.E., you've earned the time and freedom to choose.

One of the greatest assets that gets grossly underestimated is the human capital of an early retiree. If you retire in your 30s, 40s, or 50s, you have the currency of youth and much more potential to earn income than someone in their 70s.

Any income you earn serves as a bridge in your early retirement years and reduces the amount you need to withdraw from your accounts, so funds left in the accounts can continue growing. Also, bringing in earned income means that you are eligible to contribute to retirement accounts such as an IRA (as long as you meet the other guidelines for contributing).

TIP

Some part-time jobs (such as at Amazon or Disney) may even offer health insurance, giving you another perk that could save you a chunk of money.

Taking Early Distributions from Tax-Advantaged Accounts without Penalty

Finding ways to get money out of tax-advantaged accounts without early withdrawal penalties seems like a genius hack or loophole of some kind. The IRS carves out lots of exceptions to the dreaded 10 percent penalty, so you have to look for one that can work for you.

In this section, I cover some of the most important techniques for F.I.R.E. seekers. Money from these methods can serve as bridge funds, as I discuss in the preceding section.

ANECDOTE

When I was preparing for my big CFP exam, my favorite area related to the rules around getting money out of retirement accounts early. It came easy for me because I had spent a lot of time digging into this subject while planning to F.I.R.E.

HSA distributions

Health savings accounts (HSAs) technically aren't retirement plans, but they are tax advantaged, and you can use them like a retirement account. Because HSAs don't have an age minimum like retirement accounts do, you're in the clear no matter how early you retire.

The benefit HSAs have over both Roth and traditional accounts is that there is never a 10 percent early withdrawal penalty as long as the funds are used for qualified health expenses.

TECHNICAL STUFF

Qualified health expenses include dental, vision, hearing, and many other areas of healthcare that are not usually covered under a health insurance plan (see IRS pub #502).

REMEMBER

If you have accumulated receipts from health expenses over the years, you can make distributions to reimburse yourself any time. Keeping receipts digitally is the best way to maintain them for a long period of time.

ANECDOTE

As an early adapter, my HSA became one of my superpowers for F.I.R.E. When my employer first started offering them in 2008, I barely understood what the account was. However, as soon as I realized the tax investing benefits and how valuable it could be to me in early retirement, I went full speed ahead. By the time I retired in 2019, my HSA had grown to more than $150,000!

Roth IRA withdrawals

As I talk about in Chapter 15, direct contributions you've made to a Roth IRA are always tax and penalty free. By the time you're ready to F.I.R.E., you may have decades of Roth contributions that you can access.

EXAMPLE

Here's an example:

From age 16 to age 35 (20 years) you contributed $5,000/year.

$5,000/year × 20 years = $100,000.

That's $100,000 you can withdraw without a 10 percent penalty and without taxes.

Even if you have a workplace retirement plan — like a 401(k) — with Roth funds, you can roll that over to a Roth IRA, and the contribution portion will be tax and penalty free.

Here's what that looks like:

From age 22 to 35 (14 years) you contributed $12,000/year to the Roth portion of your 401(k).

$12,000/year × 14 years = $168,000 in Roth contributions.

After you retire, you roll over your 401(k) to a Roth IRA ($168,000 in contributions plus the growth).

You can withdraw that $168,000 in contributions in early retirement without a 10% penalty and without taxes.

TIP

If I could give anyone a personal finance tip to use very early in their career, it would be to start contributing to a Roth IRA as soon as possible. Even if your income is from a part-time job at a fast food restaurant. At the time you're reading this, you may be well beyond that point, but perhaps your kids, nieces, nephews, or other young people in your life can benefit from that tip.

REMEMBER

Remember that growth and conversion portion is handled differently than contributions and may be subject to tax and/or penalty.

Even if you have most of your money in a traditional IRA, you can still do a series of conversions to a Roth IRA using the Roth conversion ladder method I explain in the "Withdrawing Roth IRA contributions" section earlier in this chapter.

Understanding the rule of 55 for workplace retirement accounts

The rule of 55 does not refer to the highway speed limit. Instead, it's something that may help you get to your retirement sooner than you thought you would. News headlines may have led you to believe that F.I.R.E. is mainly for the millennials in their 20s or 30s. I'm here to tell you that's not the only group who can F.I.R.E.

Retiring in your 40s or 50s is still much sooner than the traditional retirement age of 60-plus. This means that getting access to some of your retirement accounts without a penalty before 59.5 may be a concern.

One provision that you should consider in your planning is the Rule of 55 which allows for penalty-free withdrawals if you're 55 or older in the year you separated from your employer. This rule applies to these workplace retirement plans:

>> 401(k)

>> 403(b)

>> Thrift Savings Plan (TSP)

REMEMBER

You must defer to the rules of the employer plan, which are usually outlined in the summary plan description. Even though the IRS rules allow withdrawals before the age of 55, not all employers may allow this provision.

This rule applies in the calendar year in which you turn 55. So, if you are 54 at the time you separate from your employer, you may still qualify if you turn 55 by December 31 of that year.

EXAMPLE

For example:

You are 54 in 2025.

You will turn 55 on December 5.

Since you will turn 55 by the end of 2025, you will qualify for the rule of 55 any time during the year if it's available through your employer.

Your reason for separation from the company does not matter.

REMEMBER

Here are a few other important points you want to keep in mind when using the rule of 55:

>> It applies only to your employer at the time you leave your job. If you have old employer plans that you left behind, they won't be eligible unless you roll them over to your current employer. The downside is that many employer plans don't allow the "rule of 55" distributions from the incoming rollover portion,

>> To get the rule of 55 benefit, the funds must stay in the workplace retirement account and not be rolled over to an IRA.

>> The IRS requires your employer to withhold 20 percent in federal taxes from your distributions.

>> You can keep withdrawing from your rule of 55 retirement plan even if you get another job later.

TECHNICAL STUFF

If you retire before you turn 55 (say at age 40) and return to work, you can roll over your old workplace retirement into your new workplace retirement plan (if allowed by the provider). If you leave that job after you turn 55, all the funds in that account would fall under the rule of 55. As mentioned earlier, some employer plans don't allow "rule of 55" distributions from the incoming rollover portions.

PUBLIC SAFETY WORKERS GET A FIVE-YEAR BONUS

Public safety employees can use this rule five years earlier, at age 50. That's a nice bonus for our public safety workers, which include

- Police officers and some other law enforcement members
- Firefighters
- Emergency Medical Technicians (EMTs)
- Air traffic controllers

Again, just make sure your employer's plan allows this provision and check the details.

Taking advantage of 457(b) workplace retirement

457(b) plans have F.I.R.E. written all over them. It's the only employer-sponsored retirement account that lets you take distributions when you separate from service without a penalty and regardless of age. So, what's the catch? The IRS doesn't allow just any employer to offer these types of plans. You're in luck if you work for any of these types of organizations:

>> State government

>> Local government (like a county or city)

>> Tax-exempt 501(c) organization (like a nonprofit hospital)

457(b) plans work nearly the same as other employer-sponsored retirement plans like 401(k)s or 403(b)s except there is no 10 percent early withdrawal penalty after you leave the organization. That makes this type of plan ideal to use in early retirement.

Another unique provision on 457(b) plans is that you can have one in addition to having other employer sponsored plans. For instance, you can contribute to both a 457(b) and 403(b) at the same time, which means in 2024, you can contribute a max of $46,000:

403(b): $23,000

457(b): $23,000

Total: $46,000

You can essentially double what you can contribute to workplace retirement plans. If you contributed $46,000 across both accounts for 13 years, you'd get to more than $1 million (see Table 17-1)!

TABLE 17-1 **Growth of 403(b) and 457(b)**

	Total of 403(b) and 457(b)
Annual contribution	$46,000
Assumed rate of return	8% (compounded annually)
Total value after 13 years	$1,000,000

REMEMBER

These plans are usually available to law enforcement, teachers, and medical personnel at nonprofit hospitals (including doctors), but remember it is the employer and not the position or profession that qualifies you to participate in a 457(b) plan. For instance, if you're a civil engineer who works for a state government that offers a 457(b) plan to its employees, you are allowed to participate in that plan.

WARNING

Non-governmental 457(b) plans (such as those offered by a nonprofit organization) have a few more restrictions than governmental plans. Be sure to review your employer's plan provisions.

TIP

If you work for an employer that offers a 457(b) plan, you have a powerful tool that can supercharge your F.I.R.E. journey. A teacher who blogs at Millionaire Educator (millionaireeducator.com) shares how he and his wife maximized their retirement savings by using a 457(b) plan along with their other accounts to reach F.I.R.E.

Making early withdrawals from an IRA

IRS Rule 72(t) is a brilliant yet little-known provision that I had no idea about until I started poking around at the start of my F.I.R.E. journey. This is a rule that allows you to avoid the 10 percent early withdrawal penalty by setting up regular distributions from your IRA using Substantially Equal Periodic Payments (SEPP). That name is a mouthful, but it's not quite as complex as it sounds.

There is no age requirement to set up periodic payments using Rule 72(t) for your IRA, but you must continue the longer of:

» Five years

» Until you reach 59.5

This sounds like you may have to lock up your IRA for a long time if you're starting young (say in your 40s), but you do not have to include all of your IRAs. You're allowed to isolate just the IRA dollars you want to include as part of the periodic payments (using a separate account). This gives you flexibility that might look something like this:

You have $400,000 across all your IRAs.

You can choose to have only a portion of that (say $150,000) for the 72(t) period payments.

You establish a separate IRA for the $150,000 and follow the IRS rules to set up the 72(t) periodic payments from that account (or use a tax or financial pro to set it up for you).

The rest of your IRAs ($250,000) are not impacted by the 72(t) period payments because they remain in a separate account.

There are three different methods you can use to calculate your payments, which depend on your life expectancy:

- >> Fixed annuitization method
- >> Fixed amortization method
- >> Required minimum distribution (RMD) method

The maximum percent of the balance you can use to set up the 72(t) is 5 percent, unless 120 percent of the Federal Mid-Term exceeds that amount. For 2024, 120 percent of the Federal Mid-Term rate was 5.25 percent.

The IRS provides instructions on how to figure this, but you also can do it with a 72(t) calculator, such as the one at dinktown.net. Here's an example using a $150,000 IRA owned by a 45-year-old:

First year of distribution	2024
Account balance	$150,000
Age	45
Applicable life expectancy	41 years
Maximum annual distribution (must continue until age 59.5)	$8,976.55
Method used	Fixed amortization method
Interest rate used	5.25%

Setting up the 72(t) periodic payments is almost like creating your own annuity without the worry of big fees. You also get to manage the investments yourself.

Although 72(t) can solve the problem of early withdrawal penalties, there are a few things to be careful about:

- >> You can't add additional funds to the 72(t) SEPP IRA.
- >> If you don't follow the payment schedule that has been set up, you will have to pay the 10 percent penalty for the current year and all previous years you made distributions under the 72(t) plan.

>> If you don't follow the payment schedule that has been set up, the 72(t) SEPP is treated as no longer in effect.

These are some harsh penalties, so it's important to ensure that you are following the rule on this one. You should plan for the tax implications of the withdrawals from the account.

TIP

72(t) SEPP is a good strategy in the right situation, but there are a lot of moving parts. Make sure you do your homework thoroughly or consult a professional who is familiar with the stipulations.

Here are a couple of great resources that can help you out:

>> FI Tax Guy article on 72(t) payments: `fitaxguy.com/retire-on-72t-payments/`

>> `72t.net` website (72t.net)

>> IRS website section on SEPP (`irs.gov/retirement-plans/substantially-equal-periodic-payments`)

Getting Health Insurance for Early Retirement

One of the main reasons people say they delay retiring early is health insurance. That's because in the U.S., people are used to acquiring health insurance through their employers. Most other countries don't have this issue, and health insurance may not be as much of a concern.

ANECDOTE

I can say from experience that thinking about getting health insurance on my own was terrifying. I used it as a crutch to delay retirement. Once I finally convinced myself to do independent research (rather than listening to the conflicting information I was getting from others), I was pleasantly surprised at all my options.

The only way to help alleviate your health insurance concerns in early retirement is to start doing a little digging, and I help you with that in this section. There is a sea of confusion, but you'll quickly realize (just as I did) there are lots of options to consider, and one of them will likely be right for you.

TIP

The F.I.R.E. community isn't the only group of people that face the dilemma of getting health insurance that isn't tied to an employer. Small business owners and self-employed people have dealt with this for a very long time, and they have found plenty of solutions that you can take notes from. Talking to other people who've been down this road can help you find answers.

Health Insurance Marketplace

The Health Insurance Marketplace (www.healthcare.gov) that resulted from the Affordable Care Act (ACA) is the most common health insurance option for early retirees. It's certainly worth consideration for anyone seeking F.I.R.E.

TIP

To avoid any confusion, this type of insurance is also referred to as

» Obamacare

» The Healthcare Exchange

» Marketplace Health Insurance

REMEMBER

Regardless of what you call it, it's the Federal program that offers health insurance plans that you can buy on your own.

The insurance plans and providers vary widely by state and, to an extent, by county, but you can easily search your location without even signing up for an account. Just go to www.healthcare.gov and enter your zip code. Aside from your location, these other factors affect the cost of your insurance:

» Age

» Income

» Family size

» Tobacco use

Marketplace plans use four main health categories:

» Bronze

» Silver (this is the category that gives you extra savings on things like deductibles, copays, coinsurance)

» Gold

» Platinum

If you are planning for F.I.R.E., the premium tax credits (also referred to as ACA subsidies) are a big deal. A subsidy could save you thousands of dollars each year if you're able to control your taxes as I discuss in Chapter 15. Keeping your income low can qualify you for big health insurance subsidies. With tax credits, your monthly premiums can go as low as $0. An advantage is that the qualifications for ACA premium tax credits only look at income, not assets.

EXAMPLE

If you have assets of $500,000, you could still qualify for tax subsidies as long as your income meets the requirements.

WARNING

If your estimated income is lower than a certain amount (138 percent below poverty level for most states), you may be pushed to Medicaid, which is a very different program than the ACA. The primary difference is that the ACA does not have an asset test and is only based on your income (not assets).

The following example uses the Health Insurance Marketplace Calculator at KFF (also known as the Kaiser Family Foundation (`www.kff.org/interactive/subsidy-calculator`). I used these criteria:

>> 40 years old

>> Single person, no kids

>> $30,000 income

>> Not a tobacco user

>> Resides in Georgia

EXAMPLE

Monthly cost without premium tax credit	$476
Estimated premium tax credit:	$421
Cost for a Silver plan	$56
The most you have to pay for the second-lowest cost Silver plan	2.23% of income

An income of $30,000 may seem low, but remember that if you have reached F.I.R.E. and live on investments or other income where part of it may be tax free, it is possible. Try running scenarios for yourself with a calculator like the one I used.

Even if you do not qualify for subsidies, you can still buy your health insurance off of the exchange if you don't have affordable health insurance available through an employer.

Using your own measuring stick is very important here. I used to get so scared when people would say "Oh, I pay $1,500 a month for my health insurance; the cost is outrageous." Turns out, this person has a spouse and five kids and lives in New York City. I was one person living in Ohio, so my cost was significantly different.

Health insurance broker

A health insurance broker is very similar to a mortgage broker. They represent multiple providers and work on your behalf to find an appropriate plan. They are typically paid a commission by the insurance carriers, not by you. They may also include the options available on the Health Insurance Marketplace.

A broker is a good option if you don't want to do all the research on your own. It is possible that the health insurance broker will know of providers you may not have thought of.

Health insurance varies by location, so be sure to choose one that knows your area.

COBRA

COBRA (Consolidated Omnibus Budget Reconciliation Act, whatever that means) is one option that most people think of as being an expensive way to get health insurance.

COBRA gives workers and their families who lose their health benefits the right to choose to continue group health benefits provided by their group health plan for limited periods of time.

It's likely you can find coverage that's cheaper than COBRA using one or more of the options in this section, but you may have reasons for wanting to use COBRA, such as

>> To continue with your health providers in a certain network

>> Because you like your plan benefits

>> Because you've already paid your deductible or out-of-pocket maximum and expect additional medical care in that year

>> Because you're close to the end of the year and only need COBRA for a short period

When you leave your employer, you get a quote to continue coverage without your employer's subsidy under COBRA, that can be shocking. The jump in cost to you is usually because under COBRA, you pay the entire premium yourself (no more employer subsidy). You also may be required to pay a 2 percent administrative fee.

EXAMPLE

Table 17-2 shows an example of a $700/month premium before and after COBRA.

TABLE 17-2

COBRA Premium Example

	Your Cost	Employer Subsidy	Total
Cost of insurance premiums while employed	$200/month	$500/month	$700/month
Cost of insurance premiums under COBRA (no longer employed)	$700/month (plus a 2% admin fee)	$0	$714/month

COBRA is temporary, so it is not a solution you can use for years (or decades) during early retirement. You commonly can use it for up to 18 months after you separate from service, but there are other reasons you or your dependents may qualify for coverage for up to 36 months (see Table 17-3).

TABLE 17-3

COBRA Coverage

Qualifying Event	Person Losing Coverage	Max COBRA Coverage Period
Separation of service (for reasons other than gross misconduct) or reduction in hours of employment	You, spouse, dependent child	18 months
Divorce or legal separation	Spouse, dependent child	36 months
Death of employee	Spouse, dependent child	36 months
Loss of "dependent child" status under the plan	Dependent child	36 months
Employee enrollment in Medicare	Spouse, dependent child	36 months

TIP

You have 60 days after your employer's health insurance ends to enroll in COBRA. Even if your enrollment is delayed, you will be covered by COBRA starting the day your prior coverage ended (it's retroactive). Of course, you still have to pay the premiums for those months.

Part-time job

Some people say that if you're working a part-time job, you aren't really retired. I say otherwise.

REMEMBER

You define your own retirement, which can mean that at some point, you take on a part-time job. For many, the reason for that may have something to do with getting low-cost health insurance.

Many F.I.R.E. people have taken part-time jobs, and it can make sense for you. As I describe in the previous section, you can have huge savings on your health insurance premiums through an employer. Health insurance may not be the only reason to get a part-time job; there are other benefits:

>> Pay

>> Discounted company stock (for larger companies)

>> Company product and service discounts

Here is a small list of companies that extend their health insurance benefits to part-time workers:

>> Amazon

>> Chipotle

>> Costco

>> Disney

>> Starbucks

There are many more. Many companies put health insurance information on the benefits section of their websites. There may also be small businesses in your community that offer health insurance to part-time employees.

TIP

If you serve in the National Guard or military reserves, you may also be eligible for some level of Tricare health insurance (insurance for military personnel). You can find more information about TRICARE at https://tricare.mil.

College, military service, or other organization

Your affiliations with certain organizations can earn you the possibility of qualifying for health insurance. In this section, I share some of those possibilities.

College

If attending college is part of your F.I.R.E. plans, you may qualify to have health insurance through the college or university you're attending.

TIP

The premiums are usually very low for students because of the low-risk pool. Most students are young and healthy with very low healthcare costs.

Many schools even have health services on campus where you can get wellness or minor care services. Every school has their own guidelines for eligibility, so be sure to check the school's website under student health insurance. Also, there may be different rates for international students.

Vets

If you're a service member retiring early from the military, you're in a great spot when it comes to health insurance if you qualify for some type of retiree TRICARE. Visit https://tricare.mil for more details.

TIP

If you are considering the military as a career choice, the benefits are unmatched (including the health insurance). It's a great path to reaching F.I.R.E. while serving our country at the same time.

Other organizations and options

Your membership with professional organizations or a group like a chamber of commerce may give you access to health insurance. In addition, some professions such as doctors, dentists, financial planners, and accountants in small businesses may have organizations that support these professionals within their community and have self-employed or small business health insurance plans available at group rates.

REMEMBER

Remember, you pay fees to be a part of some of these organizations so you may as well take advantage of the benefits. Even if you are no longer practicing full time after you reach F.I.R.E., you may still want to maintain your membership.

A few nontraditional options for healthcare worth mentioning are used by some in the F.I.R.E. community. You can look into these:

>> **Healthcare sharing programs:** These are private healthcare programs that may be used in lieu of or along with insurance. They are often religion based.

>> **Direct Primary Care (DPC):** DPC is not insurance but direct care from physicians who provide primary wellness that may be used in lieu of or along with insurance.

>> **Local Farm Bureau:** This organization provides health care programs that vary by state in their rules and offerings. Be sure to check your state.

Relocation: Moving to another country

Healthcare in the U.S. is notoriously expensive compared to many other countries, which is why health insurance is a must-have. Many in the F.I.R.E. community love travel, so the option of relocating to another country comes up often. A little geo arbitrage (taking advantage of lower costs of living in an area other than where you currently live) can go a long way. Health insurance is not usually the sole reason to move to an international destination, but the healthcare component can be a factor.

The caution here is that the healthcare system in the U.S. versus other countries is not apples to apples, so you should do some research on the location you are considering. I discovered this after spending time with some of my Canadian F.I.R.E. friends at a Camp Mustache in Toronto in 2023. After comparing notes with them about health insurance, it became more of a list of pros and cons rather than one country's system being better than the other.

TIP

If you are looking for one more reason for saving in an HSA account, here it is. You are allowed to use your HSA dollars for healthcare outside the U.S. So, if you pay out of pocket for services in another country, you can reimburse yourself through your HSA funds (see IRS pub # 502 for more information).

REMEMBER

Most U.S.-based health insurance does not allow for care in other countries or greatly limits it.

Chapter **18**

Planning for the Later Retirement Years

There are many phases of F.I.R.E., but once you hit retirement, you can think of it in terms of two major parts:

» **Early retirement:** The time after you F.I.R.E. and you're younger than 60. During this period, restrictions on certain accounts may limit when you can access the funds.

» **Normal retirement:** The years after you've turned 59.5 have fewer restrictions around accessing some of your retirement accounts.

When you're on the F.I.R.E. path, most of your focus is likely on the early part of retirement because you're departing from the norm by starting retirement at a younger age, which requires a little more creativity and planning than a traditional retirement plan.

No doubt some of the biggest challenges come in the early retirement years, but in most cases, you will spend many more years in normal retirement.

EXAMPLE

Figure 18-1 graphs the years you'll be in each phase if you retire at 39 and live until 90. You'll spend

20 years in early retirement (age 40 to 60)

30 years in normal retirement (age 60 to 90)

Years in Early and Normal Retirement

Age 40–90

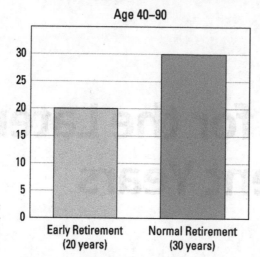

FIGURE 18-1:
Years in early
and normal
retirement.

In these later years, many more financial doors open for you than in your younger years, but planning for that phase is still not simple. This chapter highlights some important areas about planning for those later years, some of which may prompt you to revisit your approach to your early years.

Playing Catch Up

ANECDOTE

I didn't get introduced to F.I.R.E. until I was almost 40. At that point, I just knew it was too late for me even to consider it after hearing about people that were reaching F.I.R.E. in their 20s and 30s. Besides, I wasn't even close to what I should have had in my retirement accounts according to the financial experts I was listening to, so I became hyper-focused on catching up to where I thought I should be to retire at the normal age. As it turned out, all that fast running got me where I wanted to go far sooner than I ever imagined: I reached F.I. at 46 and retired early at 49.

You may have many reasons for feeling that you're behind. Here are some examples:

» A daunting divorce

» Excessive debt

» Captivity in lifestyle creep

» Anemic retirement savings

You may have many other reasons for feeling that you're behind, and you would not be alone in most of them. Here's a little encouragement to make you feel better: The 30 to 40 years that you were told it would take to reach retirement can be more like 10 to 15 years.

REMEMBER

F.I.R.E. is not only for people leaving their jobs in their 20s and 30s (although that's what usually gets the media attention). The worst thing that could happen when you start your F.I.R.E. journey is that you will be wiser and more prepared when it comes to your finances. If you end up retiring closer to the traditional age, it is still earlier than most.

In the following sections, you find out how to make headway even if you're starting late. I talk about being beyond the bottleneck of high expenses, entering your peak earning years, being more likely to have a pension, having higher contributions limits for your retirement accounts, and having more years of paying into Social Security.

You may be beyond the bottleneck of big expenses

When you are just starting your career in your 20s, you're likely to have a lower income and higher expenses that make it hard to create the gap you want to be able to save and invest. People can have a lot of competing priorities in those early years, such as

» Child care if you have children

» A mortgage for your first home

» Student loans

» Car loans

Often, these big expenses all seem to happen around the same time. If you also had the type of lower salary that's often associated with an entry-level position or first job, you may have felt it was hard to get ahead at that point in your life.

Fast forward 15 or 20 years and the picture changes and starts to look more like this:

>> You're earning a higher salary that may be double or triple where you started.

>> Kids are grown and out of the house (or close to it).

>> Home is nearly paid for or has more equity.

>> Student loans are paid off.

>> Cars are paid off, or you can pay cash for them.

By the time you hit your 40s and 50s, these expenses may lessen and create space for more of your income to go toward saving and investing. As you start to think more about your personal finances and discover that you can reach financial independence much sooner than you thought, this helps you move faster toward your goals.

You may be near your peak earning years

The more time you spend building your skills, perfecting your craft, and gaining experience in your career, the greater your income. By the time you hit your 40s and 50s, you may be at the top of your game and in your peak earning years.

Rising to a higher income may come from a lot of different ways:

>> Moving up the corporate ladder

>> Running your own business

>> Owning income-producing assets such as real estate

>> Passive income investments

This higher income gives you more room to increase your savings rate, invest more, pay off debts, or do other wealth-building activities. When your income outpaces your expenses, you are in a powerful position.

WARNING

You may encounter lifestyle creep, where your expenses increase at or faster than the pace of your income. As your income increases, try to increase your savings rather than increasing your spending.

You may have benefits from a workplace pension

With traditional pensions in the U.S., employees who work with a company long enough would earn a guaranteed monthly payment from their employer after they retired. Those types of plans are nearly gone but shouldn't be forgotten. This is a resource that you may have that younger workers may not.

Many employers have online access to pension accounts now, so you should check your account. (You can contact your benefits department to get information or instructions on how to gain access to your account.) Look for the following information:

>> Your lump sum balance (if that option is available with the plan)

>> Estimates on what the monthly payments would be

>> The summary plan description that will give you all the rules of the pension

TIP

Once you get this information, you may want to include the lump sum amount in your net worth and F.I.R.E. numbers. If you don't have a lump sum option, you may want to factor the estimated monthly payout into your plans as income you don't have to take from your other investments.

You may be able to make catch-up contributions to retirement accounts

Catch-up contributions are like a bonus that can be a big help in your later years. If you're feeling behind, picking up your pace if you have more disposable income and fewer expenses can be quite helpful.

There are limits to how much you can put toward catch-up contributions each year. Table 18-1 outlines the 2024 limits.

TIP

The rule of 55 is a feature of some 401(k), 403(b), and TSP accounts that may be helpful in your catch-up plan. I give a full description of this rule in Chapter 17.

You have paid more into Social Security

Many people question the viability of Social Security because of the headlines announcing that the trust fund is running out. However, most experts agree that the program will still be around, although benefits will be reduced if no changes are made by 2034.

TABLE 18-1   **2024 Retirement Contribution Limits Catch-Up Amounts**

Retirement Plan	2024 Limits	Limit for Catch-up at 50+
Workplace retirement such as 401(k), 403(b), Thrift Savings Plan	$23,000	$7,500
Traditional IRA and Roth IRA	$7,000	$1,000
457(b) workplace retirement (most)	$23,000	$7,500
Health savings account (HSA)	Individual: $4,150 Family: $8,300	$1,000 (at 55+ rather than 50+)

REMEMBER

Part of Social Security benefits are funded by younger workers paying into the system (via FICA taxes).

TIP

If you are a worker in your 40s or 50s, here are a few things to know about Social Security:

>> You've likely worked the required 10 years to qualify for benefits.

>> You're probably close to the 35 years of earnings that Social Security uses to calculate your benefit amount. Really early retirees (people who retire in their 20s or 30s) may not have that many years of work, which means they'll receive a slightly lower benefit.

>> Your estimates (which you can get by creating an account at www.ssa.gov/) are more accurate as you get closer to retirement age.

TIP

Whether you want to factor Social Security into your retirement plans is up to you. At minimum, it could be a powerful backstop for you in your later years of retirement. (Read more about Social Security later in this chapter.)

Projects, Pensions, and Passive Income

In this section, I talk about passion projects, pensions (even the frozen ones), and passive income that can be a boost to your finances in your later years.

Doing passion projects or consulting

Here's where your years and decades of perfecting your craft can really come in handy. At this point, you may have acquired highly valued skills that afford you the opportunity to call some of your own shots, and you may be able to earn some money by putting those skills to work. Here are some examples:

>> Branching out and starting your own business

>> Consulting for your current employer after you leave or doing other independent consulting

TIP

If you're not already doing work you're passionate about, you may now be in a position to make a switch and do something you may want to retire "to."

REMEMBER

Remember that the "retire early" part of F.I.R.E. is not required. If you're feeling behind, your focus may center around being in a position to find more meaningful work that you enjoy.

Thawing out a frozen pension

Companies and organizations that froze their pensions in the past decade or so may have stopped new contributions from employees, but that doesn't mean the existing funds just disappear. If you worked for an employer that had a pension, your account still exists in accordance with the plan provisions, unless you have separated from service and cashed it out.

TIP

Many employers with frozen pensions offer employees a lump sum option once they leave employment.

If you met the required tenure for a pension with your current or former employer, it has some value and is worth checking out. The balance of your account may have grown consistent with the rates defined by the plan, even though you weren't contributing to it anymore. You may have the option to take monthly payments once you retire or take a lump sum.

TIP

Before you jump at a chance to take a lump sum, make sure to examine the options for monthly payments. The numbers may work out the same actuarily, but there are some other benefits you should take into consideration with the monthly payments:

>> You typically get a fixed monthly amount for the rest of your life that can serve as stable income, requiring you to pull less from your other investments.

>> Some plans offer an annual inflation adjustment or other provisions that you cannot get with other investments.

>> Most pensions allow you to start monthly payments as soon as you turn 55 without incurring the 10 percent early withdrawal penalties.

WARNING

The big concern for many people with taking monthly payments over a lump sum is the risk of the pension plan going bankrupt or not being able to fulfill its funding obligations. If you are concerned about this with your pension, then taking a lump sum may trump all other factors.

TECHNICAL STUFF

The Pension Benefit Guaranty Corporation (PBGC) is a federal agency that may recover some funds for participants when a pension plan goes bankrupt, but it has limitations.

Setting up passive or semi-passive income

Setting yourself up with passive income can help you rest a little easier as you get into your later years of retirement.

REMEMBER

Truly passive income matters more as you get older because you may be ready to slow your pace. Things that fall in the category of truly passive income are

>> Dividends from investments in retirement accounts

>> Interest or coupons from treasury bonds (like I bonds) or other types of bonds

>> Interest from bank accounts like certificates of deposit (CDs)

>> Commissions or royalties

Semi-passive income may still demand some time, work, or supervision. Those would be things like

>> Real estate investments

>> Owning a small business

REMEMBER

Every dollar of income you earn from passive or semi-passive resources means that you will not have to draw down your nest egg.

Uncovering the Truth about Social Security and F.I.R.E.

When I was working out my F.I.R.E. plan, I did not include Social Security. I was hearing so many confusing and negative opinions (often oozing with political undertones), so I decided to disregard it.

ANECDOTE

After retiring in 2019, I finally had the time and head space to do my own research and satisfy my curiosity. After gaining a bit more knowledge and putting the pieces together from independent and reputable sources, I realized I had been overly pessimistic about Social Security.

REMEMBER

This section is not meant to influence you one way or the other, but it will give you insight on the basics through the lens of F.I.R.E. Whatever you decide about Social Security (and anything else), you will do far better by making your decisions rooted in knowledge and facts than by going solely on the views of others who may not share your same circumstances.

Understanding the state of Social Security

There is some truth to the pessimism around Social Security. Here's some information straight from the Social Security Administration actuaries:

"The Social Security Board of Trustees estimates that, based on current law, the Trust Funds will be able to pay benefits in full and on time until 2034. In 2034, Social Security would still be able to pay about $800 for every $1,000 in benefits scheduled." (Source: Social Security Administration, 2023)

This probably doesn't give you a warm feeling, and some people go so far as calling the system broke or busted. To fix it, Congress can make changes to the current system by raising taxes or cutting benefits (or making other adjustments), but only time will tell if they take those measures.

Meeting the requirements for Social Security

It seems every expert I've heard says that Social Security starts by mentioning 35 years of work. Yuck . . . who's working for 35 years? Probably not me, you, or others in the F.I.R.E. community. But then they mention that you only need *10 years* to qualify. Okay, that's doable!

Some critics contend that you are ruining your Social Security benefits if you retire early, but that's just not the case. If you've worked for at least 10 years, you will likely qualify for benefits. If you don't factor Social Security into your F.I.R.E. plans, the sum you receive will seem like a bonus.

Take a look at some of the details of Social Security benefits:

>> You only need 10 years of work or 40 credits.

>> One credit equals $1,730 FICA earnings in 2024 (it's adjusted for inflation each year).

>> You can earn a maximum of four credits per year ($1,730 × 4 credits = $6,920 for the year). Most people can earn this amount by working a part-time job.

>> You can continue earning credits even after you leave your full-time job (earnings may come from projects, part-time work, or net earnings from self-employment).

>> Even if you retire in your 30s, you will likely have benefits (assuming you worked enough to earn credits starting when you were 18).

EXAMPLE

If you have worked full time making about $60,000 per year for at least 10 years, you likely qualify for about $1,000/month in Social Security benefits. This amount is adjusted for inflation, and it's secure passive income you'll receive every month for the rest of your life.

Social Security can be a nice backstop in your later years of retirement, even if you end up receiving an amount lower than your projected benefits (based on the Social Security trust funds running out).

TIP

Another reason to check your Social Security account is to confirm the accuracy of your earnings reported each year. There are sometimes mistakes, and it's easier to have them corrected soon after they happen rather than waiting years later.

Deciding whether to include Social Security in your plans

I don't regret not including Social Security in my F.I.R.E. plans, but running a few worst-case scenarios did help me realize that it will be a powerful backstop in my later years. Even if you decide not to include it, you should at least be aware of how it works and your projected benefits.

To at least get an idea of what your estimated benefits are, create an account at www.ssa.gov/. There, you can see your projected benefits from age 62 to 70 (see Figure 18-2).

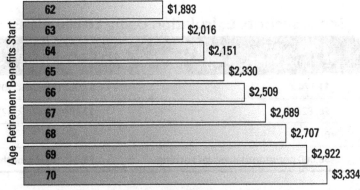

**Personalized Monthly Retirement Benefit Estimates
(Depending on the Age You Start)**

Age Retirement Benefits Start	Monthly Benefit Amount
62	$1,893
63	$2,016
64	$2,151
65	$2,330
66	$2,509
67	$2,689
68	$2,707
69	$2,922
70	$3,334

FIGURE 18-2:
Social security
estimates
example.

**TECHNICAL
STUFF**

Even though there's a quick reference to your estimated benefits, you may also want to know the moving parts behind it. Bear with me as I nerd out for just a moment and attempt to simplify how your benefits are figured. This could help you strategize about the accumulation phase of Social Security. Here's how your benefits are calculated:

1. Adjust annual earnings for wage inflation.

2. Add 35 highest years (use 0 for years with no earnings).

3. Divide by 420 months (35 years × 12 months = 420).

This is your Average Indexed Monthly Earnings (AIME).

4. Take AIME and apply it to the buckets (also called bend points) to get a Primary Insurance Amount for the normal retirement age of 67.

Here are the buckets for 2024 (these are adjusted for inflation each year):

» 90 percent of the first $1,174 ($1,174 × .90 = $1,057)

» 32 percent of the next $7,078 ($7,078 × .32 = $2,266)

» 15 percent: Above $7,078

As you can see, the first bucket gives you the highest return of your monthly earnings. By the time you reach the last bucket, you get only 15 percent of that segment of your earnings back in benefits.

EXAMPLE

Table 18-2 shows an example of a person who has AIME of $8,000 a month:

TABLE 18-2 ## Social Security Calculation Using $8,000 AIME

Bucket	Average Indexed Monthly Earnings (AIME)	Primary Insurance Amount (at 67 benefit)
1st (90%)	$1,174	$1,057 ($1,174 × .90)
2nd (32%)	$6, 826	$2,184 ($6,826 × .32)
3rd (15%)	0	0
Total	**$8,000 per month average earnings**	**$3,041 total monthly benefit**

Adjusting your projected earnings to account for early retirement

When you visit your Social Security account online, you can adjust your future earnings to make it more realistic if you plan to retire early.

REMEMBER

Your default estimates assume you will continue to earn the same as you have in the most recent year until you start your benefits.

Here are a couple of online calculators that will help you estimate your Social Security benefits:

>> Open Social Security at https://opensocialsecurity.com

>> Social Security Calculator at https://ssa.tools

REMEMBER

Remember that when you are at the point of filing for your Social Security benefits, the later you wait, the more your monthly benefit will be (up to age 70). Your statement in your Social Security account will show you the different amounts.

TIP

People have long debated the best time to take Social Security. I don't believe that everyone should wait until they're 70 or take it as soon as they can at 62. The actuaries have done the math based on average life expectancy. The advantage you have over the actuaries is that you can factor in demographics and other individual considerations that may impact *your* life expectancy. Those may include gender, ethnicity, tobacco use, health status, and other family members (such as minor or disabled children) who may gain benefits based on your record.

EXAMPLE

I have a friend who is in her 60s. She legally adopted her four-year-old grandchild a few years ago. She decided to start taking her Social Security benefits at 62, which also allowed her grandchild to receive benefits.

Considering additional Social Security filing strategies

Social Security is not just limited to benefits paid to you for retirement. If you have a spouse or ex-spouse to whom you were married for 10 years or longer, you may have some additional strategies at your disposal.

For instance, if you are married, you and your spouse may not want to start your Social Security at the same time. It may be better to let one account grow and take it later. The calculators I mention earlier in this section can help you run some scenarios.

Even if you don't factor your Social Security benefits into your F.I.R.E. plans, be sure to consider the other benefits of the Social Security system that could impact your family, including benefits for

>> Spouse

>> Ex-spouse (if married 10 years)

>> Children

>> Surviving spouse or children (in the event of your death)

TIP

Your Social Security statement includes projections for these other situations.

REMEMBER

Remember that part of the Social Security system also includes disability.

Revisiting Your Estate Plan

As you get older your life may become more complex. Your finances may need a little more attention as your nest egg gets bigger.

Chapter 7 covers the ins and outs of your estate planning, but as you get older, things may start to change as your children become adults, you exit or enter marriages, and your plans for what should happen with your estate change. As a result, you may need to make some updates to your estate documents, and you may even want to consider getting professional help.

EXAMPLE

For instance, if you used to have a simple will or beneficiary designations to distribute your assets, you may now want to consider a trust.

Even if you aren't in need of any changes, it's good practice to revisit your estate plan every few years.

Considering Long-Term Care Options

As you enter your 50s you should start considering long-term care options. In the U.S., care for the elderly can get very costly, so long-term care insurance may be needed.

The three main options are

>> Self-pay (typically for people with a higher level of assets who have the cash flow to cover the high cost)

>> Long-term care insurance (typically for people with moderate assets who would need help to cover the cost).

>> Medicaid (a government program for people with low-income and assets)

TIP

If you plan to get long-term care insurance, the premiums will likely rise as you get older.

BUILDING YOUR LEGACY

I believe that the F.I.R.E. community as a whole represents a legacy of its own where we (you, me, and others in the movement) can have a profound impact on how people think about financial independence and living a happy life sooner.

As you build your assets while on your F.I.R.E. journey, you have done something great for you and your family. Even better is a legacy that goes far beyond finances. With age and experience comes wisdom, and your question is how you share that. I'm talking about things like:

- The lessons you are passing on to your kids or grandkids (or other generations coming behind you) that you have learned

- The knowledge and habits you share with your family, friends, or community

- The content or resources you create that others will learn from and better themselves because of the work you put in

6

The Part of Tens

Become familiar with some concepts that the F.I.R.E. community highly values and discover why they are such hot topics.

Make your happiness the center of your journey and align your values with your approach to pursuing F.I.R.E.

Get to know some influential voices who have helped shape the F.I.R.E. movement.

Chapter **19**

Ten Hot Topics in the F.I.R.E. Community

I n the F.I.R.E. community there are lots of tactics and strategies that help fuel your journey. Some are deemed to be critical components that many people are nearly obsessed with. They are hot topics I hear repeated all the time and you will, too. In this chapter, I share the ones that stand out.

Building Community

The F.I.R.E. community is a small sliver of the population, so it's no wonder we gravitate toward each other. The way we think about finances is quite different than most people, and you might not have many friends or family who even get the concept of F.I.R.E. You may find yourself seeking out like-minded people either online or in a local community. There are plenty of options. Your preferred social media or community platform is a good place to start.

TIP

Being around others who espouse the same thinking is how we have fun, and it helps us grow. Some of the F.I.R.E. philosophies go against the norm of spend, spend, spend, and we openly talk about money when others think it's taboo. We nerd out on advanced money topics while others shy away. We want to talk about our finances all the time when everyone else around us would rather not. To get your fill and charge your battery, community is key.

Reducing Expenses

Although there seems to have been a shift to focusing on value, reducing and keeping your expenses in check in areas that don't really matter to you is one of the ways to get some quick wins when you're early in your F.I.R.E. journey. Reducing expenses can create more room to spend on the things that do matter. The goal is to be intentional with your cash flow — aligning your spending with what you value. Read more about expenses in Chapter 14.

Being a DIYer

This book literally has "do it yourself" (DIY) written all over it! This was born out of realizing how simple some financial stuff has become; it's so simple, you can DIY. A good example for many in the F.I.R.E. community is investing. To many people, it seems complex, but keeping it simple with something like a low-cost index fund and automating the contributions makes it an easy thing to DIY rather than paying someone else to do it.

TIP

DIY has a lot to do with control of both your time and money by taking care of certain tasks on your own. You will decide what's worth it and what's not.

Increasing Savings Rate

Savings rate is a key metric of building wealth regardless of how much you make (see Chapter 4). It is a function of creating a gap between your income and expenses. Your savings rate is simply the percentage of your income that you are saving and investing. The higher your savings rate, the sooner you reach F.I.R.E.

Those on the path to F.I.R.E. keep up with their savings rate and increase it along with their rise in income. It doesn't have to be 50 percent or more, but remember that the conventional recommendation of saving 10 percent is for those seeking to retire at the traditional retirement age (in their 60s), not people who want to retire decades earlier.

Using Spreadsheets

Ask most people in F.I.R.E. community what they use to track their finances (see Chapter 4), and many will say a spreadsheet. I think this probably started because most of the pioneers in the F.I.R.E. moment were engineers or tech pros.

The real reason people often use spreadsheets is that going down the F.I.R.E. path is a departure from the traditional time frame that many financial calculators are built around. Some calculators don't even let you put in a retirement age younger than 55. The customization freedom you have with spreadsheets gives you lots of flexibility.

Investing in VTSAX

When I saw "VTSAX and Chill" on a T-shirt, I knew it was an obsession, but the message was valid. Keep investing simple.

TECHNICAL
STUFF

VTSAX is the ticker symbol for the Vanguard Total Stock Market Index Fund, which measures the investment return of the overall stock market. It's a mutual fund (a basket of stocks) that includes more than 3,500 U.S. stocks, including well-known companies like Apple, Amazon, and Tesla. F.I.R.E. people love it because it is simple, has a low fee, and represents the total U.S. stock market.

Many feel that it's simpler to stick with one and done, meaning investing in just one index fund is sufficient. It doesn't make for an entire investment portfolio, but for someone who doesn't know where to begin, it's a good way to start learning that investing doesn't have to be hard. VTSAX happens to be a Vanguard fund, but every fund company offers a similar version of this total stock market index fund.

Putting Money in HSAs

Health savings accounts (HSAs) are great in general but are valued even more by people retiring early. You have to be on an HSA-eligible plan to make contributions, but the characteristics of this account are like no other. Beyond just the triple tax savings you hear about (tax free going in, while it grows, and coming out), you do not have to be a certain age to take the money out like you do with some other tax-advantaged accounts as long as you're using it for qualified medical expenses. A few of the other features that F.I.R.E. people get excited about with HSAs are

>> You can invest the money in the account.

>> You don't need income from a job to contribute like you do with other tax-advantaged accounts.

>> You can reimburse yourself for qualified medical expenses at any time in the future (like after you retire early or in your older years).

Converting to Roth IRAs

TECHNICAL STUFF

Funds in a Roth IRA account can be a great bridge for early retirement because the contribution portion can be withdrawn anytime for anything, tax and penalty free.

Traditional IRAs don't work the same, but you can convert those funds to a Roth IRA — something called Roth conversions. The taxable funds you convert (generally) cannot be distributed from the Roth IRA without a 10 percent additional tax (penalty) until the earlier of five tax years or age 59.5. After you meet one of those requirements (typically, it's five years for F.I.R.E. people) you are free to withdraw the converted funds for anything (the growth is handled differently).

So why does the F.I.R.E. community get obsessed about Roth conversions? Because retiring early may put you in a very low tax bracket that makes it advantageous to do this because you can end up paying little or no tax. You can do a series of these and start a "laddering process" (called a Roth conversion ladder) that provides for funding a long early retirement. Read more about Roth IRAs in Chapters 15 and 17).

TIP

Roth conversions are a bit on the advanced side of things, but its why I say the F.I.R.E. community is filled with brilliant people who love talking about these strategies. The best explainer on this is by one of my favorite bloggers, Mad Fientist. Visit www.madfientist.com and look for the "How to Access Retirement Funds Early" article.

Investing in Real Estate

This is another big subset of the F.I.R.E. community because owning rental real estate can create a way to both speed up your F.I.R.E. journey by increasing your income and create passive (or semi-passive) income in early retirement. Having this type of income stream could minimize what you need to take out of your investment accounts.

REMEMBER

Real estate investment can be long term (annual leases with tenants) or short term (like Airbnbs). It can also include what some call "house hacking." For instance, you may own a multi-family unit, live in one of the units, and rent out the other unit(s). There are other clever maneuvers for house hacking.

TIP

One of the most popular real estate investing platforms is BiggerPockets (http://www.biggerpockets.com/)

Using Travel Hacks and Travel Rewards

F.I.R.E. people often love to travel. It's one way to express a sense of freedom (and fun), but it's not cheap. It can get even more costly when it involves mega travel, like overseas trips or periods of extended travel (a week or more).

Travel rewards enable F.I.R.E. people to travel on the cheap, especially when someone can "hack" the travel rewards system. The bonuses and rewards you can get from credit cards can be significant, and the word gets around about which cards have the best bonuses. Airfare and hotel rewards often have incredible deals, primarily for opening new accounts.

WARNING

The big caveat for taking advantage of these reward credit cards is to pay the balances off every month so you do not incur any interest charges (which would negate any rewards you would earn). Used efficiently, this can be a great way to make the F.I.R.E. journey even more fun.

Chapter **20**

Ten Tips to Make Your F.I.R.E. Journey Fun

I wouldn't have gone down the F.I.R.E. path if I'd been told I had to give up certain things, and neither would you. Remember that each person's journey is unique to them. You will customize your path to F.I.R.E., and it should revolve around what makes you happy and gives you joy. It may take some time to design what this looks like for you, but this chapter gives you some tips that will help get you on your way.

Explore Your Why of F.I.R.E.

This can be one of the hardest parts of your journey. It's easy to figure out what you don't want to do (such as being tied down to a job you don't like), but zeroing in on the things you are most passionate about and want to retire to may take a little more thought. Knowing what's on the other side of F.I.R.E. will help motivate you.

The exploration of finding your "why" can be fun. You may not have ever been able to clear your mind and really think about what you'd want to do if money were no object. You don't have to figure it all out in a day, but you'll enjoy the process. I sure did! It was so much fun trying new things. When you do this, you get to focus more on what matters to you and take steps to start designing your own life.

Give Yourself Grace

You'll run into roadblocks and make some mistakes on your path to F.I.R.E., but roadblocks and mistakes are both teaching tools that sometimes help us learn lessons better than pure success can. So don't be hard on yourself when things don't go perfectly. You can't anticipate everything. Just take complications as teachable moments. (Someone once told me that if I didn't make mistakes, I wasn't even trying.)

Start Learning What You Are Most Curious About

I get asked the question all the time: Where's the best place to get started with F.I.R.E.? Of course, some personal finance stuff is boring and may not exactly get you excited, so my answer always is to start with what you're most curious about. Having curiosity is a great motivator and will keep you digging.

Because people tend to procrastinate on things they don't like, starting with what you're most curious about makes it easier to get started. Much of personal finance is interrelated, so answering one question will lead you to many others. Before you know it, you will be deep into the perpetual learning process, and since there's always something new, it doesn't stop.

Learn in the Style That Best Fits You

Knowing your learning style can be a game changer as you navigate your F.I.R.E. journey. Some people love reading (blogs, books) and that's the way they learn best. Others may hate reading books or blogs but do great if given the same information in an audio book, podcast, or video. Give some thought to your preference. Figuring out what works best for you will help make learning feel more like entertainment than an assignment.

TIP

Many content **creators** are now multi-platform because they know people like to consume information in different ways, so if you find a podcast that seems valuable, but you're not into listening, see if that creator also has a blog.

EXAMPLE

One of my favorite podcasts, Journey to Launch (www.journeytolaunch.com), had been in this audio format for over five years, but the host, Jamila Souffrant, recently wrote a book (*Your Journey to Financial Freedom*, Hanover Square Press). The book format probably introduced a whole new audience to her work because some people prefer to consume content by reading books rather than listening to podcasts.

Align Your F.I.R.E. Plans with Your Values

Sometimes your values may not exactly align with the F.I.R.E. community or its approaches. That's okay. There is no money-saving tactic that is worth putting your own values in question. The goal is not to be the fastest to the F.I.R.E. finish line but to move in the right direction. Fulfillment along the way wins out.

EXAMPLE

Maybe you take a lower paying job at a nonprofit because you're passionate about its mission. Or maybe you provide financial support for other family members. Both of these examples may slow down your path to F.I.R.E., but the tradeoff of your values to get there sooner probably would not be worth it.

Focus on the Things You Enjoy That Support Your F.I.R.E. Goals

I don't like to recommend giving up what you enjoy to pursue F.I.R.E. Some things are just too important or too much fun to ditch, but you can often do those things and still move toward F.I.R.E. There can be ways to integrate what you enjoy into your F.I.R.E. plans.

EXAMPLE

If you love travel (as many in the F.I.R.E. community do), you can do it in smart ways, like using travel rewards or picking destinations strategically. You can even start teaching others about traveling and perhaps find some way to monetize it.

Don't Cut Expenses for Things You'll Be Miserable Without

Some of the words that used to be firmly connected to F.I.R.E. were *frugality* and *minimalism.* While being frugal and minimalistic can help on your path, going overboard can make you miserable. Being miserable for years as you make your way to F.I.RE. is kind of missing the point of getting to your happy place. It's important to keep expenses in check, but balance that with spending on the things you value.

What you value will be different from what others value, and that's okay. You may choose to live in a high cost of living area like San Diego, California, whereas someone else may choose to live in a low cost of living area like Hickory, North Carolina, and tout it as the best way to save money. If you'd be miserable in Hickory, North Carolina (no family there, it's not close enough to the beach, and so on) it could be a huge drag on the way you feel on your F.I.R.E. journey because you won't be happy.

Find Communities and People That Feed Your F.I.R.E. Journey

Whatever your niche is, there's a community that matches it. Even though your current social circle may not have anyone that shares your desire to F.I.R.E., you don't have to do it alone. There are many others who are not only like-minded but probably at the same place as you on the journey. Seeking out those people can give you the support system you need to make the journey a lot more enjoyable.

TIP

ChooseFI has an extensive list of different communities based on locale or shared interests (www.choosefi.com/community). You can also do an internet search for in-person events such as Camp FI, Camp Mustache, and EconoMe or other local meetups.

TIP

There is even a growing cohousing community in Georgia that is aligned with the F.I.R.E. movement called EAGLE (Efficient And Generous Living Environment). EAGLE Cohousing (www.eaglecohousing.com) was started in 2016 by CampFI founder Stephen Baughier (see Chapter 3).

Celebrate Your Wins

You'll reach milestones along the way, such as paying off all your debt or getting to your first $100,000 net worth. Mental milestones are important, too, such as no longer being afraid to invest in the stock market. Celebrating your wins is a way to acknowledge your hard work and progress. That feeling can be very powerful, and the refresh will keep you motivated toward your big win of achieving your time freedom. Read more about celebrating your wins in Chapter 9.

Your F.I.R.E. Path Does Not Have to Be Flawless

The biggest thing I learned after reaching F.I.R.E. is this: Precision is not required. I wish I had learned that lesson sooner! I debated at times whether I should contribute to a Roth IRA or a traditional IRA or if I should switch my cellphone plan to a cheaper carrier. I realized that no single decision I made could wreck my finances or F.I.R.E. plans as long as I understood the big picture: living on less than you earn and investing the difference. I was probably too hard on myself, and I don't want you to feel the same way.

Chapter **21**

Ten Big Names to Know in the F.I.R.E. Movement

Y ou will be incredibly encouraged when you explore the inspiring and diverse voices I share with you in this chapter, many of whom have been around for more than a decade. These are people who have helped shape the F.I.R.E. movement. They share their knowledge on a variety of different platforms, and I know you will find at least a few that you will want to carry with you on your F.I.R.E. journey.

Vicki Robin

I consider Vicki Robin to be the godmother of the F.I.R.E. movement because she was talking about it before it was even an acronym. She and coauthor Joe Dominguez wrote about financial independence in the *New York Times* Bestseller *Your Money or Your Life* (Penguin) in 1992. Their book has been revised several times since then, with the most recent version being published in 2018.

It's still one of the most recommended books for those new to the F.I.R.E. movement. Times have changed over the decades, but Vicki and her philosophy of intentional living still resonates with the F.I.R.E. community.

J.L. Collins

This guy is affectionately referred to as the godfather of F.I. He's considered royalty in the F.I.R.E. community, primarily because of his hit book *The Simple Path to Wealth* (JL Collins LLC). It's required reading if you want to understand how simple investing is when you use index funds like VTSAX (Vanguard Total Stock Market Index Fund) that you hear so much about. Collins's writing helped strip away the fear of investing for many people.

The contents of this book started as a long, multipart series (The Stock Series) he wrote on his blog (still available on his blog, https://jlcollinsnh.com/stock-series/). It was meaningful to me because he originally wrote his stock series for his daughter to teach her about investing.

Mr. Money Mustache

Funny name, smart guy. Mr. Money Mustache is one of the early pioneers who started a F.I.R.E. blog and has gotten a ton of coverage from big financial media. He may have been one of the first voices you heard talking about F.I.R.E. His blog (https://www.mrmoneymustache.com/) has been around for over a decade, and his slogan is "Financial Freedom Through Badassity." The most-talked-about article is "The Shockingly Simple Math Behind Early Retirement," which explains how you can build wealth and reach financial independence in about ten years by focusing on your savings rate.

Here's a little social proof of what a big deal he is: There are annual retreats named after him called "Camp Mustache." He's not affiliated with the events, but the organizers and attendees are fans of the Mr. Money Mustache blog and interested in F.I.R.E. I had lots of fun when I joined my fellow money nerds at a Camp Mustache in the United States and one in Toronto, Canada.

Mad Fientist

Mad Fientist was the crazy financial scientist who blew my mind and convinced me F.I.R.E. was possible. I'm a fan of anyone who can be as brilliant as he is and still have a sense of humor. Just by looking at his website (www.madfientist.com) you can tell that he has done some hilarious experiments with money and shares the results with the rest of the F.I.R.E. community.

His big topics are related to some advanced F.I.R.E. strategies and tax avoidance (the legal kind). He also has some customized tools and spreadsheets (he's got mad skills!). One free tool he shares is FI Laboratory, which helps you calculate your financial independence date and chart your progress. He doesn't post or release podcast episodes very often, but when he does, they can be epic. I'll choose quality over quantity any day.

ChooseFI

ChooseFI is the podcast and platform that I think is responsible for bringing together the largest community of people seeking financial independence, and it has a worldwide following. This group has brought on just about every big-name F.I.R.E. luminary as well as everyday people willing to share their personal stories.

The website (www.choosefi.com) is a great place to start if you're looking to connect with a group or local community of other like-minded people. As of 2024, it had over 600 episodes of its podcast and a Facebook community with more than 100,000 members.

Our Rich Journey

Our Rich Journey is a family of four that kicked the high cost of living in San Francisco and moved overseas to a much less expensive area. The couple, who reached F.I.R.E. before they'd reached their 40s, has two school-aged daughters. Their platform is great for anyone wanting a little inspiration on their F.I.R.E. journey, but it may be especially helpful to those considering becoming expats or who have kids.

Sure, they teach others about financial independence on multiple platforms but it's their massive YouTube channel that so many flock to (www.youtube.com/@OurRichJourney). They are masters at explaining the F.I.R.E. concepts they used on their journey, and sometimes their daughters join them.

Millennial Revolution

Kristy and Bryce are a millennial couple from Toronto, Canada, who quit their jobs to travel the world when they were 31. Kristy is captivating when she talks about growing up in poverty in China, where her family lived off of 44 cents a day. It's hard to imagine that she was able to reach F.I.R.E. at such a young age, but she did.

The couple share their journey on their blog (www.millennial-revolution.com) and in many interviews, but there's no comparison to the massive response to their book *Quit Like a Millionaire* (TarcherPerigree). The book is a great resource to read or listen to, especially if you came from an underprivileged background or immigrated from another country to the U.S.

rich and REGULAR

I remember Kiersten and Julien when they first started blogging, at https://richandregular.com/. Their voices added to the diversity and changing of the faces of F.I.R.E. By sharing their story, they opened the eyes of a lot of African Americans to the possibilities of F.I.R.E. and introduced them to financial independence community.

Kiersten and Julien document their focus of leaving their jobs and creating a life of their own in their book *Cashing Out* (Portfolio). Their life of financial independence included Julien's passion for cooking and food, which was the central theme in their YouTube video series called "Money on the Table." Their content is prominent on just about every digital platform and is great for anyone interested in pursuing F.I.R.E., especially those thinking about entrepreneurship as their post-financial independence endeavor.

White Coat Investor

Let's talk about a group that stereotypically makes the big bucks: doctors. The White Coat Investor (www.whitecoatinvestor.com) is probably one of the biggest platforms that serves physicians and other high-income earners. This just goes to show you that money doesn't solve all problems.

White Coat Investor has grown significantly since it started in 2011. Besides its digital platforms, the group hosts a Physician Wellness & Financial Literacy Conference called *WINCON*. This group demonstrates that there's a community for all kinds of like-minded people to have access to great content for anyone on the path to F.I.R.E.

Financially Intentional

Naseema McElroy, the mind behind Financially Intentional (www.financially intentional.com), is probably the most well-known nurse in the F.I.R.E. community. Although her primary platform is the Financially Intentional website, she brings the magic when it comes to social media (mostly Instagram and TikTok), and she has a massive following.

Besides her dance moves (which I can't seem to keep up with), she is incredibly transparent in how she achieved her goals. She shares that she paid off almost $1 million in debt while living in a high cost of living area in California. She also represents many facets of diversity in the F.I.R.E. community, including single moms and African Americans.

Glossary

4% rule: A guideline that says 4% is the amount you can withdraw from your investments each year (adjusted for inflation) with little chance of it running out in retirement.

401(k) retirement plan: A tax-advantaged retirement account sponsored by private employers.

403(b) retirement plan: A tax-advantaged retirement account sponsored by state or local government or nonprofit employers.

457(b) retirement plan: A tax-advantaged retirement account sponsored by state or local government or nonprofit employers. A unique IRS provision allows you to take penalty-free distributions from this account once you separate from service, regardless of age. This plan can exist in addition to a 403(b) plan.

backdoor Roth: Workaround strategy used by those who make too much to contribute directly to a Roth IRA. Instead, they make contributions to a nondeductible traditional IRA and then convert it to a Roth IRA.

brokerage account: Also called a *taxable brokerage* or *regular brokerage* account. Only the growth portion of the investments you sell is subject to tax at favorable rates called capital gains. There are no age requirements or early withdrawal penalties to make distributions.

capital gain: When an investment increases in value, and you sell it for more than you paid for it.

cost basis: The original amount you paid for an investment.

dollar cost averaging: Making contributions on a regular schedule (weekly, monthly, per pay period, and so on) to your investments over time.

F.I.R.E. (Financial Independence, Retire Early): Getting to a point where you no longer have to depend on income from a job and have the ability to retire much earlier than the standard retirement age (60 to 70). F.I.R.E. is also a movement and community of people who optimize personal finances to achieve greater freedom with their time.

F.I.R.E. number: The target amount to have met your F.I.R.E. goal. Usually 25 times your expected expenses in retirement.

FICA (Federal Insurance Contributions Act): Funds the U.S. Social Security and Medicare programs.

FINRA (Financial Industry Regulatory Authority): The agency that helps regulate U.S. financial firms and professionals. They provide a tool called BrokerCheck (https://brokercheck.finra.org) to help research the background and experience of financial professionals.

FSA (flexible spending account): A savings account that allows employees to set aside a portion of their pre-tax earnings. It is owned and managed by the employer on your behalf, and you must spend down the funds each year (with a few exceptions) — what's referred to as a "use it or lose it" situation.

golden handcuffs: When employers offer financial incentives like matching 401(k) contributions, stock options, or other benefits to retain employees.

The Great Reshuffle: Leaving a job for something that is a better and more fulfilling fit for your life and career.

The Great Resignation: The elevated rate at which U.S. workers resigned from their jobs starting in the spring of 2021, amid strong labor demand and low unemployment.

hedonic treadmill: The tendency for people to quickly return to a base level of happiness despite experiencing major positive or negative events.

HSA (health savings account): An account for medical expenses that is tax-free going in, out, and while it grows. If contributions are made via payroll deduction, you also don't pay FICA tax. Funds in the account roll over year after year and can be saved and invested. To make contributions to an HSA, you must also have a qualified High Deductible Health Plan (HDHP).

index fund: A basket of stocks or other investments that follow a benchmark index, typically with very low fees. An example is an S&P 500 index fund that follows the 500 largest U.S. companies. Typical fees run about .04%.

Medicare: A health insurance program that provides coverage for eligible individuals, primarily those age 65 and older but also certain individuals with disabilities.

passive investing: Investments that simply follow an index rather than being actively handpicked in the hope that they will outperform the market.

net worth: What you own (assets) minus what you owe (liabilities).

quiet quitting: Doing the minimum requirements of one's job and putting in no more time, effort, or enthusiasm than absolutely necessary.

Roth conversion: Converting funds from a pre-tax account (traditional IRA) to a Roth IRA.

Roth conversion ladder: Converting funds from a traditional IRA to a Roth IRA year after year so that you can access those funds after a five-year holding period. This is a strategy that will allow you to get access to retirement funds before you turn 59.5.

Roth IRA: A tax-advantaged personal savings plan where contributions are not deductible but qualified distributions may be tax free.

Rule of 55: IRS rule that allows for penalty-free withdrawals from certain workplace retirement plans (not IRAs) if you are 55 or older in the year you separated from your employer. Qualified public safety employees can use this rule five years earlier at age 50.

Rule 72(t) periodic payments: A rule that enables you to avoid the 10% early withdrawal penalty by setting up regular distributions from your IRA using substantially equal periodic payments (SEPP). Payments must continue the longer of five years or until you reach age 59.5.

savings rate: The percentage of your income that you save and invest. You simply divide your savings amount by your income to come up with the percentage.

Social Security: A social insurance program that offers income support to eligible retirees, survivors, and people with disabilities.

Tax-advantaged accounts: Accounts that grow tax-deferred and usually come with age or other requirements to make withdrawals. No tax is incurred when you buy or sell investments within these accounts. Types of accounts include IRAs, HSAs, and most workplace retirement plans.

Tax Cuts and Jobs Act (TCJA): Major tax legislation that was passed at the end of 2017 for business and personal taxes. The changes with business taxes were made permanent, but the personal tax changes are scheduled to expire at the end of 2025.

Traditional IRA: A tax-advantaged personal savings plan where contributions may be tax deductible.

TSP (thrift savings plan): A tax-advantaged retirement account sponsored by federal government employers.

vesting: When employers require you to be with the organization for a certain period of time before the matching funds (usually in a retirement account or stock options) belong to you if you leave.

Index

K

L

M

trusts
  cost of, 129
  defined, 128–129
TSP (Thrift Savings Plan)
  contribution limits (2024), 230
  contributions to, 21
  defined, 333
  as government employee plan, 116
  as typical workplace investment account, 187
Tyson, Erik
  Investing For Dummies, 195
  Mutual Funds For Dummies, 193
  Reducing Your Taxes For Dummies, 223

U

Unclaimed Funds, 111
unemployment benefits, 166–167
United Kingdom (UK), normal retirement ages as of 2020, 54
United States (US), normal retirement ages as of 2020, 54
U.S. Bureau of Labor Statistics, on loans from employer-sponsored retirement account, 212
U.S. Census Bureau, on median household income (2022), 176
U.S. Department of the Treasury, "Treasury Hunt" search tool, 97

V

values, aligning your F.I.R.E. plans with your values, 321
Vanguard
  as big player in brokerage accounts, 119
  as low-fee broker, 199
  Total Stock Market ETF (VTI), 192
variable income, 162–166
variable/flexible expenses, 62–63
Vasquez, Frank (financial professional), 138

vehicles
  inheritance treatment of, 121–122
  titling of, 125
vesting, 333
visual learning style, 30
VTSAX (Vanguard Total Stock Market Index Fund), 21, 51–52, 315

W

W-2 job, beauty and beast of, 156–159
wealth, building of
  mechanics of, 42
  versions for, 18
Wealth Twins (website), 14
White Coat Investor, 328–329
Wild, Russell
  Exchange-Traded Funds For Dummies, 193
Williams, Hannah (creator of Salary Transparent Street), 157
wills
  cost of, 129
  defined, 127–128
  last will, 126
  living will (advance directive), 126
WINCON (conference), 328–329
wins, celebrating yours, 323

Y

You Need a Budget (YNAB) app, 76, 225
Your Journey to Financial Freedom (Souffrant), 14
Your Money or Your Life (Robin and Dominguez), 11, 325

Z

zero-based budgeting, 224

About the Author

Jackie Cummings Koski, CFP® reached F.I.R.E. (Financial Independence, Retired Early) in her 40s, after overcoming poverty, divorce, and single motherhood. She is now following her big dream of creating a financially literate society.

Jackie is a cohost of *Catching Up to FI*, a podcast focused on helping people on their journey to financial independence, no matter where they are starting. She is author of the book *Money Letters 2 My Daughter*, which was awarded the Excellence in Financial Literacy Education (EIFLE) Award in 2013. In 2015, her commitment to educating and empowering others about personal finance earned the attention of our nation's policymakers, and Jackie was officially recognized with a Congressional Commendation from the U.S. House of Representatives for her accomplishments in the field of financial literacy.

Jackie has been featured on the Emmy award–winning *Rachael Ray Show*, where she shared her best tips on retiring early. At the 2020 EconoMe Conference, Jackie gave a provocative main stage talk entitled "Unveiling My Real Numbers Behind FIREing" (www.youtube.com/watch?v=J7xm4RCV4i0), in which she openly rejected the taboo of talking about money by transparently sharing her own numbers. Her fascinating F.I.R.E. journey was chronicled on both CNBC's *Make It* (www.youtube.com/watch?app=desktop&v=uhXY-sNDeGM) and *MarketWatch* (www.youtube.com/watch?v=G_I5oRum7Co&t=4s), two of America's top money media platforms. Her inspiring story and personal finance tips have also been profiled in many other well-known media outlets, including *Forbes*, *Business Insider*, *People*, and *Real Simple*.

Since retiring early, Jackie has earned a master's degree in Personal Financial Planning and Financial Therapy from Kansas State University. She also earned the AFC (Accredited Financial Counselor) and CFP (Certified Financial Planner) credentials.

You can visit her online at www.finomenalwoman.com.

Author's Acknowledgment

I'd like to acknowledge the first-class team at Wiley that showed me how the pros do it. I was honored to have the guidance and expertise of the team in bringing this book to life.

I'm forever grateful to my dear friend and mentor, Sarah Catherine Gutierrez, who opened my eyes to this book project in the first place. It seemed impossible, but your vote of confidence made all the difference.

Thank you to one of my favorite F.I.R.E. friends and technical reviewer for this book, Cody Garrett. Your fresh approach and ideas inspire me, and you are making a difference in the world of financial planning.

Finally, I am immensely thankful to the F.I.R.E. community for all the knowledge and support you've given me over the years. I'm a student of the F.I.R.E. movement, and there are so many brilliant teachers who have shaped my journey.

Dedication

This book is dedicated to my daughter, Amber Koski. Thank you for being my biggest cheerleader on my F.I.R.E. journey and during this book writing process. It's thrilling to watch you grow and become a member of the second generation of F.I.R.E.

Publisher's Acknowledgments

Acquisitions Editor: Tracy Boggier
Project Editor: Charlotte Kughen
Copy Editor: Jennifer Connolly
Technical Editor: Cody Garrett, CFP
Managing Editor: Sofia Malik

Sr. Editorial Assistant: Cheri Case
Production Editor: Tamilmani Varadharaj
Project Manager: Charlotte Kughen
Cover Image: © liveslow/Getty Images